This is the first book to chronicle fully the history of London's Old Vic Theatre. After Drury Lane, Covent Garden and the Theatre Royal, Haymarket, the Old Vic is London's oldest theatre, with a continuous history since 1818. Drawing on important archives both here (notably the Royal Victoria Hall's) and in the United States, George Rowell sheds new light on the management, audience, productions and players. In particular he offers fresh information on its early years, when such famous figures as Edmund Kean and William Charles Macready appeared there, and Paganini gave his farewell concert.

Over 175 years the Old Vic has served many purposes and many publics. It welcomed the young Princess Victoria on one of her first visits to the theatre. It has been the home of spectacle, 'blood-and-thunder' melodrama and Variety. Subsequently it was used as a temperance hall and housed a working-men's college. The Theatre was the first permanent home of opera in English, as well as British Ballet. Above all it was the birthplace of the world-famous Old Vic Company and saw the first appearances of Britain's National Theatre Company, directed by Laurence Olivier. Among the actors to perform at the Old Vic were Ralph Richardson, Charles Laughton, Laurence Olivier and Vivien Leigh.

The book contains numerous illustrations from the early years of the Theatre and of important productions. It includes a chronology of plays produced at the Theatre by the Old Vic, National and other companies. It will be of interest to students and scholars of theatre and social history as well as to theatregoers.

The Old Vic Theatre

The Old Vic Theatre:
A History

GEORGE ROWELL

formerly Reader in Theatre History
University of Bristol

Published by the Press Syndicate of the University of Cambridge
The Pitt Building, Trumpington Street, Cambridge CB2 1RP
40 West 20th Street, New York NY 10011-4211, USA
10 Stamford Road, Oakleigh, Victoria 3166, Australia

© Cambridge University Press 1993

First published 1993

Printed in Great Britain at the University Press, Cambridge

A catalogue record for this book is available from the British Library

Library of Congress cataloguing in publication data
Rowell, George.
The Old Vic Theatre: a history / George Rowell.
p.   cm.
Includes bibliographical references and index.
ISBN 0-521-34625-8 (hardback)
1. Old Vic Theatre (London, England) – History.   2. Theater –
England – London – History – 19th century.   3. Theater – England –
London – History – 20th century.   I. Title.
PN2596.L70766   1992
792'.09421 – dc20   92-1379   CIP

ISBN 0 521 34625 8 hardback

Contents

Illustrations

Acknowledgements

My first responsibility is to thank the Trustees of the Royal Victoria Hall Foundation, in particular their Chairman, Tom Vaughan, and Clerk, Carol Cooper, for their encouragement throughout the (unforeseeably protracted) period during which this book was in preparation, and for allowing me unlimited access to their Archives.

I am most grateful for financial assistance from the Trustees of both the Royal Victoria Hall Foundation and the Old Vic Trust Limited.

I am greatly in the debt of Christopher Robinson, Keeper of the University of Bristol Theatre Collection, where those Archives are now housed, for his patience and assistance in unravelling the various strands of which they are made up.

The Libraries and other Collections to whose staff I am indebted include: the Theatre Museum, London; the British Library; the Garrick Club; the Library of Morley College, London; the Minet Library, London Borough of Lambeth; the City Parochial Foundation, London; the Raymond Mander and Joe Mitchenson Theatre Collection.

I am deeply grateful to the Curators of the Harvard University Theatre Collection and of the Folger Shakespeare Library for opening the wealth of their holdings on the Old Vic Theatre to me.

Amongst many individuals who have helped me I must mention: Janet Birkett; Richard Foulkes; James Fowler; Lyn Haill; Hugh Hunt; Andrew Leigh; Angus Mackay; Jack Reading; Denis Richards; Molly Sole; Pieter Van Der Merwe; Roy Waters; Sarah Woodcock.

Perhaps the individual to whom I owe most is someone I never met. His name was George Evans and he was on the stage-staff of the Old Vic when it housed the National Theatre Company. His main duties then became the maintenance of the Company's scenic store in Grange Road SE1, and it was here that (in the words of Molly Sole, for many years Clerk to the Trustees) 'he reserved the best and driest part of the store for the Old Vic Archives, and personally guarded them from weather and souvenir-hunters. I have no doubt their preservation was entirely due to him.'

George Evans died on 26 July 1979, trying to save a stack of scenery from falling. I am sad that I cannot thank him in person.

I

The search

In the spring of 1991 the Old Vic staged the London premiere of *Carmen Jones*, adapted by Oscar Hammerstein from Bizet's opera. It was the first time in its history that the Theatre had housed an 'open-ended run', as opposed to a limited season, short runs by a resident company, or even a number of productions alternating 'in repertoire'. It was also the most expensive undertaking, both actually and relatively, ever to have been mounted on that stage. Although *Faust* and *Carmen* were standbys of the Theatre when it began a hundred years earlier to put on 'opera in English', it is doubtful if Emma Cons, the moving force behind that enterprise, or her niece Lilian Baylis, on whom Miss Cons's mantle descended, would recognise Bizet's work in Hammerstein's adaptation. *Carmen Jones* transplants the scene from Seville to Carolina and Chicago, replaces bullfighting by heavyweight boxing, uses a cast of negro characters and supplies appropriate dialogue and lyrics, so that part of the Habanera becomes

> You go for me and I'm taboo;
> But if you're hard to get, I go for you.

The Old Vic Theatre, in fact, as it approached the last quarter of its second century, was continuing that search for a new function, a new public, fresh fields to conquer, which has been its goal and its glory throughout its history.

Tracing that history also involves a search. In its various chapters and under its various names (the Coburg; the Victoria; the Royal Victoria Coffee-Tavern and Temperance Music Hall) the Old Vic has attracted the notice of many famous figures: it appears in the 'journals' of William Charles Macready, 'the Eminent Tragedian', and of Queen Victoria herself; in the fiction of Charles Kingsley and the journalism of Charles Dickens; in the dramatic criticism of William Hazlitt and the music criticism of George Bernard Shaw. Some of these phases have been well documented, notably the career of the unique Lilian Baylis and the stirring years under Tyrone Guthrie's direction, when Charles Laughton, Edith Evans, Laurence Olivier and Ralph Richardson in turn led the Company. But other chapters are tantalisingly obscure, for example the ambition of the stage-struck tallow-chandler's son, Joseph Glossop, to make the Theatre a Bankside Drury Lane or even a La Scala, London. We know next to nothing of the entertainment which pioneering Emma Cons offered at her Temperance Music Hall. We can only guess how 'opera in English' was mounted in her day. We do not know what plays Lilian Baylis first staged when she finally obtained a full dramatic licence, as opposed to a music hall permit. We know the titles but next to nothing of the casts of the first Shakespeare plays staged at the Old Vic under her management. The search for answers to these and other questions has inspired the following account.

It has also influenced the proportions of that account. The three histories of the Old Vic published in the last fifty years are Edward Dent's *A Theatre for Everybody*; Harcourt Williams's *Old Vic Saga*; and Peter Roberts's *The Old Vic Story*. Of these writers, both Dent and Harcourt Williams contributed materially to the success of the Old Vic and were eyewitnesses of that marvellous transformation from obscure community centre to leading opera house and classical theatre which took place in the first quarter of the present century. Not surprisingly all three books concentrate on the Theatre's last hundred years. Its earlier history, crammed with variety and vicissitude, remained something of a mystery to their writers, and to their readers. It is therefore to the unravelling of that mystery that this account chiefly addresses itself, and while endeavouring to pay tribute to the achievements of the Theatre over the last half-century, does not examine them in the same detail as earlier historians have done.

There remains the relationship of the Old Vic Theatre and the Old Vic Company. While the worldwide renown of the Old Vic undoubtedly springs from the reputation of its Company, it operated only for fifty years, from 1914 to 1963, while the Theatre will celebrate its 175th birthday in 1993. Proportion alone suggests that a history of the Old Vic Theatre should not give more than a third of its space to the Old Vic Company which already has its historians in Harcourt Williams (*Four Years at the Old Vic*); Audrey Williamson (*Old Vic Drama 1934–1947*); and others. Moreover the years in which the National Theatre Company resided at the Old Vic (1963–76) have been amply documented in John

Elsom's and Nicholas Tomalin's *History of the National Theatre* and elsewhere. It may also be pertinent to record that for ten crucial years (1940–50) the Old Vic Company did not operate at the Old Vic Theatre, and that these years included the seasons at the New Theatre under the leadership of Laurence Olivier and Ralph Richardson. The brilliant success of those seasons and the prestige they won for the Company may be seen as complicating the function and compromising the future of the Old Vic Theatre by opening to question its suitability as the permanent home of the National Theatre.

The sources for an authoritative record of the Old Vic Company's most successful years and of the Old Vic Theatre's pre-eminence in London stage annals are not difficult to find. The search for the truth about the Theatre's fortunes outside this period is hazardous and exacting, but for that reason greatly rewarding. To seek the unknown is the challenge all searchers look for; to find an answer is the reward only given to some. To find all the answers is not within human capacity, but it is human nature's redeeming grace to persevere.

2

Seeking a public

1816–1834

The site

For at least half of its history London's Old Vic Theatre served its own local public, the working-class community of Lambeth and Southwark. Indeed the name 'Old Vic', an affectionate version of the Royal Victoria, suggests a long-standing, intimate acquaintance. In the twenty-five years she ran the Theatre like a family, Lilian Baylis was given to calling her audience 'my people', thereby differentiating them from the wide theatre public. When towards the end of that time the new ideas and soaring standards of Tyrone Guthrie and others began to attract a wider section of support and interest, she viewed the development with suspicion. 'My people', she felt, could not be at ease sitting alongside strangers. So, in retrospect, historians have categorised the nineteenth-century Old Vic, in its various phases and under its various names, with the other Surreyside theatres, notably Astley's and the Surrey itself, as 'transpontine' – across the bridge – and classified their strengths and weaknesses as shared, if not identical.

Certainly its beginnings point to such a common purpose. When in 1816 James Jones, lessee of the Surrey Theatre, and his creditor, James Dunn, were faced with an impossible rise in rent (from £220 to £4,200) by their ground landlord, Templeton West,[1] it was natural to retaliate by planning a rival theatre nearby, and to implement this challenge by taking much of the furnishings and fittings with them. Thomas Dibdin, their successor, confirms their plunder of the scenery, costumes and more solid fixtures.[2] But by seeking a third partner with more genteel, even Royal, associates, they opened up greater potential. Thomas Serres was Marine Painter to His Majesty, and it was presumably his standing that obtained the patronage of the Princess Charlotte, only child of the Prince of Wales (soon to succeed as George IV), and of her husband,

4

Prince Leopold of Saxe-Coburg. This gesture was almost unprecedented: not since the days of the King's (Charles II) and Duke's (James
II, then Duke of York) Men had Royalty conferred its name and
protection on a theatrical enterprise. Even the select Theatre Royal,
Haymarket, began life as an an 'anti-establishment' house, repeatedly
prosecuted and closed down. It owed its Royal patent not to artistic
standing but as an act of redress to the actor-manager, Samuel Foote,
crippled in a riding accident after a courtier's practical joke. The favour
of the Prince and Princess of Saxe-Coburg therefore transformed Messrs
Jones's and Dunn's riposte into an enterprise several classes above that
of Astley's and the Surrey, or even of other unpatented house recently
opened in Westminster, such as the Olympic and the Adelphi.

This distinction poses a large question as to the intentions of the
Theatre's builders. At first glance their site must have looked unpromis-
ing for a 'quality' house: the sparsely populated Lambeth marshes,
mostly worked as nursery-gardens. But seven years before 1816 when
the Surrey magistrates granted these speculators a licence, the far
grander speculation of a fourth bridge across the Thames had begun,
ultimately named Waterloo Bridge in tribute to the victors over
Napoleon. The new Theatre's location was therefore more accessible to
central London than either of the existing Surreyside houses, and in fact
the Waterloo Bridge Company duly took a modest financial stake in this
theatrical enterprise. Clearly they foresaw the new Coburg drawing
much of its support from north of the river, and given that the site
though soggy was undeveloped, may have envisaged further developments for pleasure-seekers. The southern approach to the bridge was
built on land once known as Cupar's (or more happily Cupid's) Gardens,
which offered concerts, fireworks and other summer diversions until
closed in 1760. Several popular pleasure-gardens, like Vauxhall and
Marylebone, provided entertainment, and one at least, Sadler's Wells, a
playhouse.

If this was the vision of the Theatre's planners, it was not shared by
the public, particularly by investors. An appeal for £12,000 drew little
response; the appointment of an architect, Rudoph Cabanel, who had
shared in the design of Drury Lane after its destruction by fire in 1809,
was offset by difficulty in laying the foundations, ultimately solved with
stone stripped from the site of the Savoy Palace in the Strand.[3] At a more
exalted level the death in childbirth of Princess Charlotte in November
1817 robbed the project of its patroness. The Prince of Saxe-Coburg
remained the justification for its name and prestige, but he was now a

Prince without a Consort, and his prospects blighted. Even before this set-back work on the building had been suspended for lack of funds, and the whole enterprise was only rescued by the intervention of a family far less distinguished than their Royal and Serene Highnesses, but ultimately much more influential in the early years of the theatre: the wealthy tallow-chandler Francis Glossop, and his stage-struck son, Joseph.

Their interest in the theatre world had found practical expression long before the building of the Coburg. Francis Glossop, so his son asserted, came to Sheridan's aid when Drury Lane was burnt down in 1809, and found him £13,600 to pay the company's expenses when they took refuge at the Haymarket.[4] Joseph Glossop owned a share in the East London Theatre at the time he rescued the Coburg, and transferred some of its staff, notably the young scenic artist Clarkson Stanfield, to his new house. More importantly he made repeated attempts to acquire authority in the patent theatres during the early 1820s, offering to buy a share of the Haymarket and entering into protracted negotiations with Elliston to become joint lessee of Drury Lane.[5] Clearly his ambitions stretched beyond a transpontine house. At the end of 1822 he left the country under mysterious circumstances and for the next ten years was active in several Continental opera houses, his name being associated with both La Scala, Milan, and the San Carlos, Naples. He was married to the singer, Elizabeth Feron, and he undoubtedly helped to launch Michael Balfe as a theatrical composer at Milan.[6] Could he have dreamt of the Coburg flowering into an English Versailles or Schönbrunn? He certainly saw it as a step towards a more exalted sphere.

The building

The laying of the foundation stone on 14 September 1816 'by His Serene Highness the Prince of Saxe-Coburg and Her Royal Highness the Princess Charlotte of Wales' (but in fact by a proxy, Alderman Goodbehere) was to be the ill-fated Princess's only association with the Theatre that bore her husband's name for its first fifteen years. Happily the stone, though moved to the Webber Street side, survived when its patroness did not. The building proceeded less than smoothly, with the workmen striking for their wages and the Glossops obliged to inject further funds on two occasions. When it did open, on Whit Monday, 11 May 1818, it was still only equipped as a 'summer theatre', though this would not necessarily conflict with the notion of the Coburg as the focus of some newly laid-out pleasure-gardens. In the event it was decided that autumn to install heating and more comfortable seats, providing theatrical entertainment all the year round.[7]

The nineteenth-century reputation of the Old Vic suggests a huge barracks of a house, packed to suffocation with the simplest of spectators, but this was certainly not the architect's original concept. Cabanel had worked on alterations to the Surrey and Drury Lane, but his lasting legacy to the Coburg seems to have been solidity rather than size. Some of his roof trusses survive, and of the three London theatres built between 1810 and 1820 (Drury Lane, the Old Vic and the Haymarket) which still stand, the exterior of the Old Vic is the least changed. Serres, the Royal link in the enterprise, seems to have concentrated on its internal decoration, his *chef d'œuvre* being the Marine Saloon. Most contemporary accounts stress the intimacy and refinement of the theatre and its fittings. A first night reporter claimed:

> It is not too large, and yet will hold more company, we should think, than could get into the Little Theatre, Haymarket:[8]

– a significant comparison since the Haymarket in question was the eighteenth-century house, replaced in 1820 by the building which survives today. When the future Queen Victoria paid her only visit to the Theatre then bearing her name, on 27 November 1833, she noted: 'It is a very clean and pretty little theatre, and the box we were in was very comfortable.'[9] Even unfriendly witnesses testified to its attractions. Henry Crabb Robinson, a diarist of the period who mostly lived up to his second given name, found it 'a very pretty suburban playhouse, not so large, but a fit match for the Paris suburban theatres'.[10]

The size and capacity have been the subject of greatly varying estimates. When George Davidge, at that time lessee, gave evidence before the House of Commons Select Committee on Dramatic Literature in 1832 he claimed the Theatre held 'near 4,000',[11] a figure that startled the Chairman, Bulwer-Lytton, into asking for particulars. Davidge's answers, though detailed, were devious. He quoted the maximum figures for different parts of the house, but recorded at widely separated dates e.g.

Boxes	1,230	[1 August 1828]
Pit	1,090	[17 December 1824]
Gallery	1,512	[27 December 1830]

Given the opening night prices (Boxes 3/- and 4/-; Pit 2/-; Gallery 1/-) Davidge's figures indicate a full house earning £435. On the other hand

Thomas Allen in his *History of Surrey* (1829) claimed: 'The house holds three hundred and twenty five pounds.'[12] The truth was probably that the capacity was limited only by the public's willingness to be squeezed into the space available. All accounts agree, however, on the size and equipment of the stage. Allen's dimensions: width 32 feet, depth 94 feet, give an area of 3,008 square feet (compared with Drury Lane's present 6,400), and Davidge pointed out to the Committee that the horseshoe design of the theatre brought all parts of the house close to the stage, providing an intimacy not attainable in the amphitheatres of Drury Lane and Covent Garden. The first night reporter already quoted adds: 'The audience are not here contained in an illuminated Wilderness of a Theatre, where Pantomimes, Melodramas and Shrieking Tragedies alone succeed', and pinpoints the management's dilemma by commenting: 'We could not help lamenting that on such a stage the regular drama cannot be displayed.' The Coburg, which could have offered Shakespeare and Sheridan, was to be barred as a 'minor' theatre from doing so.

The patrons

In seeking and obtaining the patronage of Prince Leopold and Princess Charlotte, the promoters of the theatre clearly hoped for Royal and courtly attendance at their performances. In its early years these hopes were regularly fulfilled, although Prince Leopold himself, in his lonely exile at Claremont House, seems to have shown little interest in 'his' Theatre. More than a year after its opening he attended a performance of the topical and spectacular *North Pole* (to which Clarkson Stanfield's designs contributed greatly), and a subsequent bill speaks of 'the Royal Visitor's most flattering appearance'.[13] He made a second – and apparently final – appearance on 15 May 1820 to see Booth in *The Horatii and the Curatii*, and there may be a touch of irony in the announcement that the performance will be given 'under the patronage of His Royal Highness Prince Leopold of Saxe-Coburg, who will on this Occasion Honour the Theatre with his Rare Presence'. Certainly the proud boast of the opening night: 'Under the immediate patronage of His Royal Highness' had been modified to 'Under the patronage' by the start of the winter season, in November 1818, and presently disappeared altogether.

But if Leopold stayed away, other members of the Royal family proved more attentive. Prominent among these were the Duke and Duchess of Kent, whose daughter Victoria was only six weeks old when they first graced the Coburg on 14 August 1819. Two months later they returned for a performance in aid of 'the Royal Coburg Theatrical

Fund', a bold but short-lived attempt to rival the patent theatres in providing pensions for members of the company. Within three months of that visit the Duke had died, leaving his daughter, still less than a year old, a likely heir to the throne. Nevertheless the Duchess came alone during the week of 18 September 1820, precipitating a change of bill 'from motives of delicacy', *Mary Queen of Scots* (not the most tactful of Royal offerings) being replaced by *The Vampire*, apparently a thoroughly safe choice.

There were also diplomatic embassies: Prince Esterhazy, the Austrian ambassador, and his Princess, graced the Theatre in November 1820 and again in March 1823; the Spanish Ambassador was 'expected' on 3 March 1823 to see *The Spanish Patriots*, and the 'Greek Committee' were positively present on 24 November 1823 (at the height of the struggle for Greek independence) for *Lazarana; or the Archon's Daughter*. Another mark of distinction the Coburg enjoyed in these years was its use for charitable benefits under Royal patronage: George IV was the patron of the Royal General Dispensary and the Dispensary for Children, both of which profited by performances in 1822, and the Duke of Sussex presided over the Philanthropic Institution, which benefited by the proceeds on 4 June 1821, and the Distressed Letter and Press Printers Fund, to which a performance as late as September 1826 was devoted. Members of the aristocracy were regular patrons: an early offering, *Wallace, the Hero of Scotland*, was given on 10 June 1818 'by desire of the Duchess of Wellington', and the last night of the winter 1819–20 season was 'under the Patronage of Lady Caroline Lamb' (wife of the future Lord Melbourne but then more intimately associated with the present Lord Byron) 'and several Other Persons of Distinction'.

The most sensational Royal visit was that of the reckless and ill-fated Queen Caroline on 26 June 1821. George IV's efforts to divorce her by Act of Parliament having failed, she determined to attend his Coronation, fixed for 19 July 1821. Her visit to the Coburg (where she saw *Marguerite; or The Distressed Mother*) was evidently part of her campaign to achieve popular support before presenting herself at Westminster Abbey three weeks later. It happened to follow a bitter dispute between Joseph Glossop, proprietor of the Coburg, and James Winston, the Drury Lane acting manager, which came to a head during a Command Performance there on 9 May. Winston ejected a servant of Glossop's who, he believed, was sent to create a disturbance, and abused Glossop, as 'the lamplighter's boy', referring to his father's trade as a tallow-chandler.[14] The editors of Winston's *Diaries* believe Glossop to have been 'a noted Queen's man', but this seems unlikely in view of his position as Clerk of the Cheque in the King's Household. Next day Glossop waited for Winston outside Drury Lane and horsewhipped him, resulting in his prosecution and payment to Winston of £150 damages (which he donated to the Drury Lane fund). In fact public life during the summer of 1821 proved more melodramatic than anything the Coburg could offer on stage: the Queen's foray to Westminster Abbey on Coronation Day was repulsed, and within a month she died suddenly (poisoned, so her friends alleged, during a visit to Drury Lane).

Royal visits and aristocratic patronage do not necessarily indicate regular support of the Coburg by the well-to-do, but some evidence does survive of attendance in these early years by a fashionable public. The playbills regularly mention booking agencies at such smart addresses as '182 Piccadilly, opposite Burlington House' and 'Mr Samm's Library, St James's Street, Corner of Pall Mall'. There are also indications that the fashionable used them. When the journalist E. L. Blanchard contributed an article on 'The Victoria Theatre' to *The Era Almanack* for 1873, he was able to cite receipts for the summer 1821 season, which included:

week ending 5 May	£312 19s. 0d.
12 May	£404 3s. 0d.
19 May	£354 8s. 6d.
26 May	£402 4s. 0d
16 June	£523 4s. 6d.

On the night of Monday 21 May alone the theatre took £152 2s. 6d. Blanchard found these 'very large sums',[15] and the figures certainly indicate consistent support.

One of the most damaging (because widely quoted) accounts of the Coburg audience in this period is contained in Hazlitt's essay 'The Minor Theatres', contributed to *The London Magazine* in March 1820. He evidently visited the theatre in the last week of January and saw J. B. Booth in *Lucius Junius Brutus*, but did not like what he saw, either on the stage or in the audience:

> The play was indifferent, but that was nothing. The acting was bad, but that was nothing. The audience was low, but that was nothing. It was the heartless indifference and contempt shown by the performers for their parts and by the audience for the players and the play, that disgusted us with all of them . . .
>
> The genius of St George's Fields prevailed, and you felt yourself in a

bridewell or a brothel, amidst Jew-boys, pickpockets, prostitutes and mountebanks, instead of being in the precincts of Mount Parnassus, or in the company of the Muses. The audience did not hiss the actors (that would have implied a serious feeling of disapprobation, and something like a serious wish to please), but they laughed, hooted at, nick-named, pelted them with oranges and witticisms, to show their unruly contempt for them and their art . . .[16]

Somewhat perversely Hazlitt attributed this contempt to the intimacy of the buildings:

> We cannot help thinking that some part of this indecency and licentiousness is to be traced to the diminutive size of these theatres, and to the close contact with which these unmannerly censors come with the objects of their ignorant and unfeeling scorn.
>
> You here see Mr Booth as Brutus, with every motion of his face *articulated*, and with his underjaws grinding out sentences and his upper lip twitching with words and syllables – as if a needle and thread had been passed through each corner of it.

This does not sound like the performance or the playhouse which four months later the Duke of Saxe-Coburg would honour with his 'Rare Presence', and the whole tone of the essay seems designed to contrast the familiarity and close quarters of the Minors with the grandeur and remoteness of the two major houses. The Adelphi is only a little less harshly dismissed, save for the three Misses Dennett, whose dancing anywhere delighted Hazlitt. The 'quality' element in the Coburg's audience seems to have been maintained at least until Joseph Glossop's departure for the Continent at the end of 1822, leaving the day-to-day management in other hands. His father's statement to Thomas Dibdin that 'he was thirty thousand pounds *minus* at the Coburg' is more likely to have been made after March 1823, when Dibdin himself was forced to quit the Surrey with losses of 'nearly eighteen thousand pounds'.[17]

The management

It is clear that the original founders of the Coburg ceded authority to the Glossop family from its earliest days. The deeds indicate that in July 1818 Francis Glossop paid £9,346 to acquire the interests of Serres and Dunn, and that on 24 February 1819 Joseph Glossop paid James Jones £1,465 0s. 6d. for his share in the enterprise.[18] By July 1820 James Winston noted in his diary: 'Russell [his stage-manager] told me Glossop had given Dunn and Serres each £3,000 for their shares in the

Coburg Theatre. NB He has now seven-eighths',[19] suggesting the remaining eighth was held by the Waterloo Bridge Company. In fact both Serres and Jones were facing financial disaster, Serres as a result of the extravagance of his wife which resulted in his imprisonment and death in prison in 1825.[20] A benefit in July 1823 'for Mr Jones the Founder of this theatre' hints at financial pressure, and in 1834 and 1835 there were benefits for Miss Jones and Mrs Cross, 'daughter of the late Mr Jones, Founder of the Theatre'.

Glossop had brought with him from the East London Theatre a useful adjutant, William Barrymore, whose relationship to the actor Barrymore prominent at Drury Lane twenty years earlier has yet to be clearly established. Since both apparently were born 'Bluet' they seem likely to have been father and son. This Barrymore had no ambitions as an actor, but besides stage-managing he contrived numerous spectacular pieces, including *Trial by Battle*, staged on the opening night, and two later Coburg favourites: *El Hyder, The Chief of the Ghaut Mountains* and *Gilderoy, the Bonnie Boy*. Glossop's confidence in him was such that he also placed Astley's under his supervision during the years 1819–21, when he took over that house as well.

That Glossop was no mere theatrical dilettante but closely involved in the running of his theatres is apparent from a recently discovered letter from Robert Fairbrother, treasurer at the Coburg, to Glossop 'at Messrs Lafitte, Bankers, Paris' (where he was staying to study the working of looking-glass curtains), and written on 13 November 1821. Much of it details payments made, received, or withheld, but there are some revealing insights:

> Hill is so extremely ill that he can hardly walk – and Fillingham could not be spared from the Royalty – performing in both pieces – therefore we got our lad Asbury to clown the rope which he did without a murmur – and it passed of [*sic*] quietly – only some boy call'd out where is the other clown . . .

and referring to an actor named Ebbsworth,

> Mr Dunn would not pay him on Saturday – and said you had inform'd him that you knew nothing about him – this Sir must have been a mistake – and escaped your memory as you were pleased to engage him at two pounds a week – his old salary – and you particularly said you [and] Ebbsworth differed with Mr Dunn about the 10/-, Mr Dunn having offered him 30/- – and Sir, 'tis but justice about the 10/- – as he would have gone out of Town with Mr Terry to Scotland – but thankfully received *your* commands.

The troubled treasurer adds: 'his salary until your pleasure is known or you shall I hope safe return will be paid by me from my private acct.'[21]

Nevertheless Glossop needed an acting manager on the spot. During the period 1820–2 when he leased Astley's and Barrymore was involved in running that house, the Coburg was mostly under the command of Thomas Potter Cooke, the ex-sailor whose name became increasingly identified with Jolly Jack Tar roles in nautical melodrama, although at this date his greatest success, William in *Black-Ey'd Susan*, was still eight years away. 'Mr Cooke being busily employed in getting up the new piece of *Greeks and Turks*' writes Robert Fairbrother, justifying to Glossop his paying the ill-used Ebbsworth his £2. Indeed Cooke continued to receive billing as manager of the Coburg during these years, even when carrying out engagements elsewhere. Many of his parts were in his nautical line: Jack Gallant in *The Shipwreck of the Medusa* (first played there on 20 May 1820) and Ben Billows in *The Faithless Friend; or A British Seaman's Fidelity* (Coburg, 17 May 1821) are two examples from these years. But his range was extensive: he could play 'noble savages' like *Christophe, King of Haiti* (Coburg, 29 January 1821), comic relief – Darby O'Kelly in *Glenarvon; or The Mysterious Heir* (Coburg, 13 July 1819), and heroic roles: Prince Azor in *Beauty and the Beast* (Coburg, 29 November 1819). At the opening of *Greeks and Turks* (the play Fairbrother refers to his 'getting up') he played Mich Rattline in the new piece, and the villainous smuggler *Dirck Hatteraick* in an adaptation from Scott's *Guy Mannering*.

If Glossop's hopes of establishing the Coburg's image hung from the looking-glass curtain he had planned in Paris, they were frustrated. Its first showing on Boxing Night 1821 proved an anti-climax. The account given by J. R. Planché may be prejudiced – he was then engaged as resident dramatist at the Adelphi – but it tells the tale:

> After the overture the promised novelty was duly displayed . . . within an elaborately gilt frame. The effect was anything but agreeable. The glass was all over finger or other marks, and dimly reflected the two tiers of boxes and their occupants. It was no imposition however . . . and in those days must have cost a great deal of money. There was consequently considerable applause at its appearance. The moment it ceased someone in the gallery . . . called out 'That's all werry well! now show us summut else!'[22]

No doubt Glossop had counted on pleasing the smart section of the audience with a reflection of themselves, just as forty years later the Bancrofts wooed Society to their refurbished Prince of Wales's by transforming the stage into one of their own drawing-rooms. The Coburg gallerygoers, however, looked to the theatre to transport them to the realms of the exciting and exotic, not to reflect their shabby and deprived selves. In fact the costly curtain was subsequently used as a background for such performers as Ramoo Samee the juggler and 'Il Diabolo Antonio', an acrobat. More seriously its five-ton weight proved a structural hazard, and it very soon had to be dismantled and displayed piecemeal throughout the building. The bill for 5 April 1822 announces 'A New Looking-Glass Ceiling', which sounds suspiciously like the old looking-glass curtain, and fragments were still in use in the dressing-rooms well into the twentieth century.

There may be a connection between this disappointment and Glossop's sustained efforts in the early summer of 1822 to obtain a share of the Drury Lane lease. Winston's *Diaries* report him negotiating with Elliston in April for joint control at a reputed price of £10,000. A successful outcome was unlikely in view of Glossop's bad relations with both Elliston and Winston, and the negotiations came to nothing. On 6 November Winston reports: 'Sir Richard Birnie [a City magistrate] told me application had been made for warrant to take up Glossop for forgery this evening, he being about to leave England tomorrow', and on 18 November: 'Mr Burke [his solicitor] called today to say Glossop had run away.'[23]

Whatever the circumstances, it seems clear that Joseph Glossop did go abroad towards the end of 1822, though he was resilient and resourceful enough to acquire a share in the running of both La Scala, Milan, and the San Carlo, Naples, in the next two or three years. Meanwhile he left the Coburg under the stewardship of his long-standing coadjutor, William Barrymore, who had taken over from T. P. Cooke; 'under the management of Mr Barrymore' appears on the bill for 22 July. It was in this month too that the great Grimaldi made his only appearances, opening on 1 July with *Salmagundi; or The Clown's Dish of All Sorts*, and achieving scenic success two weeks later with *Disputes in China; or Harlequin and the Hong Kong Merchant*, to which Stanfield's designs, based on his Far Eastern experience as a Merchant Seaman, contributed greatly. The engagement was, however, fraught with difficulty. Although only forty-four, Grimaldi's powers were failing. The bill of 22 July refers to 'the continued and dangerous indisposition of Mr Grimaldi', but by 29 July 'Mr Grimaldi is recovered', and he played out his contract on 14 August.

In the spring of 1823 Barrymore transferred his centre of action to

Drury Lane, where he devised a number of spectacular entertainments. The next three years saw a succession of acting managers at the Coburg, responsibility being assumed by several members of the company. Huntley, a popular performer, took over in April 1823, to be succeeded in November by Leclercq, the dancer who had supervised all the Theatre's ballets since opening night. A year later in October 1824 Huntley took a Farewell Benefit, having been 'long borne down by a Severe Indisposition'. Leclercq seems to have shared authority with another actor, Watkins Burroughs, but on 26 December 1826 a significant announcement placed the Theatre 'under the sole management of Mr Davidge'. George Bolwell Davidge's name had in fact featured on the first night bill, when (at the age of twenty-five) he played Old Walter, the heroine's good-hearted father, in *Trial by Battle*, and it had never been long absent. He was to control the theatre for the next six years, a period of steady decline not wholly attributable to his management.

For the district as a whole was deteriorating. Any hopes Serres and Glossop might have entertained of a theatre set amongst pleasure-gardens or elegant mansions were dashed by the development of the New Cut (linking the two thoroughfares, Waterloo Road and Blackfriars Road), with what, according to the *Survey of London*, was stipulated as 'third-class housing' in the builders' leases.[24] The Coburg management seems to have reacted to the increasing squalor of its setting by desperate attempts to make the interior more attractive. The Saloon, used by those awaiting admission, was adorned in April 1821 by a PHUSEOZELOMATA exhibiting 'a highly finished view of Venice, introducing upwards of 500 Figures', and in June by 'a most Beautiful View of Moscow previous to its Conflagration'. For the winter season of 1822–3 'A new and Magnificent Saloon calculated to hold 600 Persons' was opened to Box and Pit Patrons at 5.30 p.m. and to half-price Patrons at 8 p.m. There were also numerous additions and adornments to the auditorium itself, including in 1824 'the Entire Reconstruction and Reembellishment of the Interior', and in March 1826 'An Entirely New Proscenium' and 'A Spacious and Magnificent Portico'.

Nevertheless the audience was evidently drawn from a progressively smaller locality and limited mentality, as the playbills demonstrate. In the early years successful pieces could command a public for appreciable runs: *The North Pole* for six weeks in 1818; *El Hyder* from 16 November 1818 to 8 February 1819; *Edward the Black Prince* for two months in 1822. But following Glossop's withdrawal to Italy and Barrymore's departure the bills reflect increasing dependence on a local public, demanding constant change, so that by July 1825 there were nightly alterations. The management attempted to retain its 'quality' patrons by announcing that special attractions and favoured performers would be offered them. Their version of Goethe's *Faust*, for example, was billed on 7 June 1824 as a 'First Piece' (with *The Battle of Trafalgar* and *Harlequin and the King of the Ruby Mine* thrown in for the locals), but by 17 June

> in consequence of the repeated and earnest Enquiries of Many Families, the Remoteness of Whose Residence renders it impossible for them to attend at the Theatre at any early Hour, the favourite Drama of FAUSTUS, which Nightly increases in Popularity will be performed at HALF PRICE!

Even then it only survived until 26 June.

There was also an increasingly damaging competition with the Surrey, to which Elliston had returned after his eventful but financially disastrous reign at Drury Lane. On 1 October 1828 the bill announced:

> In consequence of numerous Ladies and Gentlemen having, through some error, inadvertently visited the Surrey Theatre when it was their intention to adorn the Boxes of the Royal Coburg Theatre, the Proprietors find it necessary to state in order to prevent future Mistakes, that no 'Shilling Box Orders' are admitted at the Surrey, but received from respectable Bearers at the Coburg.

Evidently the Coburg management was being driven to undercutting its competitor's prices. By November 1831 the situation was serious enough to warrant a general reduction of charges. 'The changes in the Situation, Sentiments and Prospects of Society . . . and the General Convention that Exists of the Necessity of *Retrenchment and Economy in all Branches* . . . has [*sic*] determined MR DAVIDGE to yield to the Current of Opinion . . .' so that by 1833 he had reduced admission to: Boxes 2/-; Pit 1/-; Gallery 6d.

It was against this background of poor houses and price cuts that Edmund Kean made his only appearances at a Surreyside theatre. His engagement at the Coburg (for a reputed fee of £50 a night) seems to have been linked to earlier performances at an East End house, the City Theatre, in which Davidge may have had an interest. Kean's six appearances, starting with Richard III on 27 June 1831, have become encrusted with legend. The most sensational of these is usually assigned to 29 June, when he played Othello, and attributed to the partiality shown to the Iago, a local favourite named Cobham. According to Charles Kean's biographer:

> The great tragedian felt disconcerted, and by the time the curtain fell, he overflowed with indignation, a little heightened by copious libations of brandy and water.
>
> He was then loudly called for, and after a considerable delay came forward, enveloped in his cloak, his face still smirched, not more than half cleansed from the dingy complexion of the Moor, and his eyes emitting flashes as bright and deadly as forked lightning. He planted himself in the centre of the stage, near the footlights, and demanded with laconic abruptness, 'What do you want?' There was a moment's interval of surprise, when 'You! you!' was reiterated from many voices. 'Well, then, I am here.' Another short pause, and he proceeded: 'I have acted in every theatre of the United Kingdom of Great Britain and Ireland, I have acted throughout the United States of America, but in my life I have never acted to such a set of ignorant, unmitigated brutes as I see before me.'[25]

The *Theatrical Observer*, however, suggests that the reproof occurred after *King Lear* on 4 July:

> On Monday night Kean was playing *Lear* at this Theatre, when the gods conducted themselves very uproariously, and one man threw a piece of orange at his feet. He came forward, evidently in great anger, and said that whatever talent he possessed, he considered himself degraded on being obliged to appear before such *things* as those, (pointing to the gallery). Cheers issued from the pit, which the gallery, not knowing what had been said, re-echoed.[26]

Whatever the facts, Kean was able to complete his engagement with Othello on 8 July.

That his appearances in a 'legitimate' repertory provoked no opposition from the patent theatres seems a comment on his declining status – he was to die less than two years later at the age of forty-three. Nevertheless the fortunes of the Coburg were clouded from the start by the legal restrictions on a minor theatre aiming to attract a discriminating audience, and its programme consistently reflects this hazard.

The playwrights

Attempting a meaningful distinction between 'patent' and 'minor', and 'legitimate' and 'illegitimate' drama was a source of concern and confusion to the early nineteenth-century mind, and it has concerned and confused historians ever since. When Robert Walpole imposed his Licensing Act on the theatre in retaliation for satiric attack from the stage, he sought to place the London theatre wholly under the control of the Lord Chamberlain and restrict the spoken drama to the patent houses, Drury Lane and Covent Garden. Such powers as were subsequently granted to magistrates in outlying areas extended only to music and dancing. At least until the turn of the century this distinction worked well enough; the two early Surreyside theatres originated as circuses and did not conspicuously transgress the statutory provisions. But as the new century advanced, resistance to the patents' monopoly stiffened: a London Theatres Bill, aimed at ending their privileges, was introduced in 1811, and brought up again unsuccessfully in 1812 and 1813. Both Astley's and the Surrey acquired stages to supplement their rings and began to offer narrative to show off their horsemanship. Essential dialogue was conveyed by banners, pointing forward to the captions of the silent screen. In particular the Surrey under Elliston's management flouted the spirit of the law with 'musical' versions of *Macbeth*, *The Beaux' Stratagem*, and other favourites, the provision of an increasingly selective musical accompaniment being claimed as characterising the 'burletta' permissible under a minor theatre's licence. It was therefore under legal restrictions more breached than honoured that the opening bill at the Coburg consisted of 'a new melodramatic spectacle', *Trial by Battle;* a ballet, *Alzora and Nerine; or The Fairy Gift;* and the pantomime *Midnight Revelry; or Harlequin and Comus.*

The make-up of this bill should not be dismissed as a sop to transpontine taste. Melodramatic spectacle and pantomime were as staple a diet at the patent theatres in the Regency period as in minor houses. On the night of 11 May 1818 when the Coburg opened Drury Lane offered *The Jew of Malta*, with Kean as Barabas; and *Obi; or Three Finger'd Jack*, a sensational piece with a West Indian background, in which T. P. Cooke played Jack. That night Covent Garden housed a new drama, *Bellamira; or The Fall of Tunis*, in which Macready had to 'black up' as the villain Amurat, an African renegade, followed by the burlesque *Bombastes Furioso*, and its own pantomime, *Harlequin Gulliver; or The Flying Island*, with Grimaldi as the Lord Chamberlain of Laputa (afterwards Clown). The taste, North and South of the Thames, did not vary greatly.

Nevertheless the managers of the patent theatres, faced by heavier expenses than their rivals, were determined to preserve such rights as their increasingly challenged privileges allowed. On several occasions the lessees of minor theatres had been successfully prosecuted for exceeding their functions, notably John Palmer at his newly opened Royalty Theatre in East London in 1789 and again in 1790. The patentees' wrath was directed against the Coburg nearly two years after its opening. In the winter of 1820–1 the management succeeded in engaging Junius Brutus Booth, a 'classical' actor who, having achieved success at Covent Garden, rashly accepted an invitation to play Iago to Kean's Othello and was totally eclipsed. To Glossop the first appearance on his stage of a tragedian with a 'legitimate' reputation was irresistible. Booth was announced for 29 December 1820 as Richard III, though pain was taken to minimise the play's Shakespearean origin by billing it as *Richard III; or The Battle of Bosworth Field*, "a Melodrama founded on Cibber's compiled tragedy from Shakespeare'. The managers of the two patent theatres were not conciliated. On 19 January 1821 information was laid against Joseph Glossop for infringement of the Licensing Act, and the Act of 25 George II c36 which empowered magistrates to license music and dancing only.

The Coburg playbills decried the 'Persecution' of the Theatre for 'rationalising their performances', and affirmed that the Proprietors 'would take every means in their power to resist this attempt at abridging their sources of Amusement and instituting a Monopoly'. After various delays the hearing took place on 9 February. An assistant in Covent Garden box office gave evidence that he attended the Theatre on 29 December; that the performance had been 'a play with scenery'; that the lines 'Now is the winter of our discontent/Made glorious summer by this sun of York' had indeed been spoken; that the only deviation from convention was 'a musical instrument not audible beyond the orchestra, now and then slightly touched', and the murder of the two Princes onstage as opposed to Covent Garden's tactful killing 'off'. Booth himself was called and replied haughtily to the magistrates' questioning: 'No, sir, I am not engaged as a dancer, but to recite speeches, to personate dramatic characters in a stage-dress.' Glossop's counsel vainly cited plays such as *Macbeth* and even *Richard III* performed at the Surrey under Elliston himself. The court ruled that the Coburg had infringed the conditions of their licence and fined Glossop £50. An appeal was heard at Guildford on 13 April, but rejected 'on technical grounds'.[27]

The Coburg management reacted to the summons with further circumlocution on the playbills. Booth appeared on 26 January 1821 in *The Judgment of Brutus*, described as 'A new Historical Drama . . .

compiled from Lee's *Lucius Junius Brutus*, Duncombe's *Junius Brutus*, Voltaire's *Brutus*, Downman's *Lucius Junius Brutus* and Cumberland's *Sybil; or The Elder Brother*'. The bill also sought to allay the 'considerable degree of apprehension' which the impending prosecution might have aroused in the public. Booth's engagement finished at the end of January, but he was signed to return in April. Following the rejection of the Theatre's appeal against a fine Glossop announced cheekily:

> The Proprietors of this Theatre having given this Gentleman permission to Perform a limited Number of Nights at the Theatre Royal, Covent Garden, he will not have the honour of appearing before the public here until Monday April 24th.

When he did appear, it was in *The Lear of Private Life* by Moncrieff, not a 'compilation' but a dramatisation of Mrs Opie's novel *Father and Daughter*, which owed something to Shakespeare's example and also contained a premonition of *East Lynne*. The bill pontificated: 'At a moment when modern Tragedy seems to have forsaken the Stage for ever, this endeavour to yield a faint reflection of her charms, as far as the powers of a Minor Theatre will allow, may not be totally unacceptable.' In fact the play established itself not only at the Coburg but in Booth's and many others' repertory.

Of course the grounds on which the patent theatres had obtained their verdict – that the performance of *Richard III* had included speech, scenery and costume, with only a minimum of music, not that it was by Shakespeare or any other 'legitimate' writer – were applicable to most of the plays presented at the minor theatres, and demonstrates the extent to which the authorities turned a blind eye unless prompted by offended privilege. In fact Elliston at Drury Lane was encouraged to press the authorities further. On 2 February 1821 he staged an adaptation by John Howard Payne of Ducange's melodrama: *Thérèse: or The Orphan of Geneva*. According to Winston, Glossop attended the performance, stayed up all night with the professional 'copyist' Meddox reconstructing the text, and at eight o'clock next morning woke Moncrieff with instructions to complete his own version, presented at the Coburg a week later. The next day Elliston obtained an injunction against the Theatre for performing the piece, but at the hearing on 11 February this was rejected on the grounds that Moncrieff's version derived directly from the French. If Winston's account is to be trusted he 'had no French book' and relied on the pirated Drury Lane text.[28] When *Thérèse* was repeated at the Coburg, the bills proclaimed:

> The Information obtained on Saturday last by the Lessee of the
> Theatre Royal, Drury Lane and Others against the Proprietor of this
> Theatre in the Court of Chancery for the Performance of the
> Melodrama of *Thérèse: or the Maid of Geneva* is DISSOLVED by Order of
> the Lord Chancellor.

Piracy and plagiarism were a regular feature of theatrical practice in this
period. The copyist Meddox who colluded with Glossop over *Thérèse*
seems to have acted against him on another manager's behalf (pres-
sumably Elliston) over an unidentified piece mentioned in some detail
by Robert Fairbrother in his letter to Glossop on 13 November 1821.
The passage refers to 'Deboos' (possibly Dubois, presumably another
copyist), 'Mary' (evidently also on the Theatre's staff), as well as
Clarkson Stanfield, the resident designer, and H. M. Milner, the resident
playwright.

> *New Piece*: I mean that one Mary gave you last and which you gave to
> Mr Stanfield – here I feel there is some foul play going on – for Deboos
> told me this afternoon about three o'clock that Mr Medox [*sic*] had
> importun'd him, and in your absence he understood by your order, to
> copy a piece, and has copied the first act theref[ore] – on being asked
> by me what was the subject he replied – *Canute the Dane* – write no
> more, Deboos, said I, for the *Judas* has betrayed my master, for that is
> the piece I want you to copy into parts and is ordered to be played on
> Monday the 26th instant. I sent a note to Mr Stanfield for the piece for
> him [Deboos] to copy parts and he [Stanfield] brought me only the
> second act – saying you had given the first and third acts to Mr Milner
> – I have sent him of[f] to Mr Milner for them, and your orders shall be
> obeyed thereon, and if they purloin the manuscript Mary will rewrite it
> of hand. They must not have the start of us. Depend on it, there is foul
> play. What you are pleased to do, we bow to, but they must not trick
> us.

There is no indication that a piece on King Canute was performed either
at the Coburg or elsewhere at this time, but in the absence of any
effective copyright legislation, theatres could and did steal each others'
material with impunity.

In the early years Glossop could call on experienced writers like
Moncrieff and Barrymore whose work was recognised and performed
widely. The increasingly hectic pace and demand for 'novelties',
however, made a resident dramatist necessary; the younger Charles
Dibdin served in this capacity at Sadler's Wells and elsewhere, Planché at
the Adelphi, and Fitzball at the Surrey. The Coburg's needs were mostly

met by the writer mentioned in Fairbrother's letter, H. M. Milner, who between 1821 and 1829 contributed at least fifty-six new pieces to their programme. Since he had already acquired some reputation, his name usually figured on the bills, and his work can be identified with some accuracy. The indispensable 'Handlists' appended to Allardyce Nicoll's *History of English Drama* attribute only thirty-two of these titles to Milner; thirteen are assigned to 'Unknown Authors' and a further eleven are not noted. Since only nine were published, and the Theatre, lying outside the Lord Chamberlain's jurisdiction, did not submit its scripts for licensing, little more than the titles have survived. Sometimes Milner was called on to adapt established works of literature: Goethe's *Faust* as *Faustus; or The Demon's Victim* in 1824; *Romeo and Juliet* as *The Lovers of Verona* in 1826; and numerous Scott novels. But more often he was required to set a sequence of melodramatic moments against an exotic background, as some of his titles indicate: *The Indian Father; or The Bride of Mexico* (1821); *The Massacre of Cyprus* (1823); *The Siege of Acre* (1824); *The Assassin of Smolensk* (1824); *The Heart of the Red Mountains* (1827); *The Fugitive of Molwitz* (1829). The extent of his work goes some way towards outlining the mass of early nineteenth-century drama lying largely undetected beneath the surface.

It also throws doubt on Douglas Jerrold's claim to have been resident dramatist at the Coburg for much of the same period. His son reported his serving Davidge in this capacity between 1825 and 1828, when, overworked and underpaid, he removed to the Surrey, where *Black-Ey'd Susan* soon scored an enormous success. Since Jerrold was unknown in 1825, his name never figured on the playbills. By his own account he contributed two pieces in 1825 and two in 1826, including an abridgement of Poole's comedy, *Paul Pry*, in which Davidge played Liston's popular role. Compared with Milner's known output of fifty-six titles over nine years, this suggests an occasional hearing rather than the load of a resident dramatist. Davidge did not become sole lessee until December 1826, and Jerrold's account suggests nothing for 1827.

Undoubtedly he was employed by the Theatre – at a salary of 'four or five pounds a week' – between September and December 1828, when he supplied six plays, and on at least one evening (13 October) the entire bill (*Ambrose Gwinett*; *Two Eyes between Two*; *Wives By Advertisement*; and *The Tower of Lochlain*) without acknowledgement of any kind. It is from this period that Jerrold's jaundiced memories of Davidge must date. When he died, early in the evening of 3 January 1842, Jerrold commented: 'Humph! I didn't think he'd die before the half price had come in!'

Ironically Jerrold was even more ruthlessly exploited by Elliston at the Surrey: *Black-Ey'd Susan* ran for 150 nights and was taken up by numerous other theatres, including the Coburg, which actually opened its version, where it only lasted a fortnight, the week before the Surrey's. Jerrold's play gave T. P. Cooke a certain winner for the rest of his career and earned Elliston £5,000 in a year. Jerrold was paid £60, together with £10 for publication, although of course it led to other openings.[29] When Davidge staged his *Mutiny at Spithead* (1830) and *Martha Willis the Servant Girl* (1831), they were billed as 'by the author of *Black-Ey'd Susan*'.

The plays

The Coburg set a high standard of presentation from its opening. The American actor-manager Edward Simpson, visiting in its first weeks, found the 'Stage very good indeed and very convenient' (compared with the English Opera House which he condemned as 'dirty – scenery vilely painted – and the whole Stage department horrible').[30] 'The scenery was imposing and that was all of course' is the grudging tribute of Henry Crabb Robinson to *The North Pole*.[31] That there was some concern for style and taste in the texts themselves may also be illustrated from the same play. Its main attraction was the 'Ship of Immense Size', manned by a 'Crew of Sixty Persons', but Serres had also to supply a 'Vision' of Eddystone Rock, Elsinore and Labrador; amongst the allegorical characters introduced were Britannia, Neptune and Amphitrite, and dancers represented the four elements, the four winds and the four seasons. Such features point back to Inigo Jones and the Stuart Masque, as well as forward to the photographic realism of later melodrama.

Increasingly, however, the audience's taste ran to spectacle and sensation. In November 1825 the management announced: 'This theatre has from the period of its first Opening maintained a Character for the Production of Historical and Local Dramas with which no Similar Establishment can venture to compare.' This can hardly mean 'local' in the sense of 'parochial', popular as such pieces were to prove twenty years later. Perhaps 'depicting a locality' is intended. The Coburg certainly reflected some contemporary scenes, but they tended to reach beyond Lambeth and Southwark. *Scenes in London* was staged to coincide with George IV's Coronation, and *Life in Paris* (1822) gave Stanfield a chance to depict the Park of St Cloud; A View of the Seine; The Louvre; The Square de Chatelet; The Boulevard des Italiens; and The Interior of a French Theatre. Such successes as *Magna Charta* (1823); *Edward the*

Black Prince (1822); and *Mary Queen of Scots* (1825) testify to the appeal of the pseudo-historical, but the most extraordinary episode staged in the Coburg's first decade was undoubtedly *George III: or The Father of His People* on 30 August 1824, and described as 'A Catalogue of Portraits Sketched Principally from Life'. The dramatis personae included not merely the late lamented monarch but the present King (played by the manager, Burroughes), the future William IV (by Mrs Leclercq, wife of the ballet master), and other notables either living (Wilberforce) or recently dead (Sheridan, Charles James Fox). It seems to infringe all the hallowed rules against impersonating the sacred and eminent, but was received with tolerance if not actual contempt. The press wondered how George IV as Burroughes presented him had ever acquired the character of the First Gentleman of the Age, and commented frankly on Fox's 'imposing pair of black eyebrows, made with burnt cork'.[32] In fact the piece seems to have been more panorama than history, the scenes including Windsor Forest, the Terrace of Windsor Castle, Westminster Abbey, the House of Lords and Hyde Park.

Notwithstanding the 'invidious and almost criminal opposition', *George III: or The Father of His People* ran until 9 October. The sole official notice taken seems to have been by the local magistrates who at their next licensing deemed this choice of play 'injudicious'. The only occasion on which the Coburg risked suppression appears to be in May 1832, when the agitation provoked by the Third Reform Bill tempted Davidge to stage Fielding's *Tom Thumb* (somewhat sophisticated fare for his audience at that date) and to illustrate on the playbill a scene of the Populace crying 'Reform! Reform!', with the King replying:

> Petition me no Petition, Sir, today!
> Her Majesty the Queen is in a Passion.

In his evidence to the House of Commons Committee the following month Davidge disingenuously defended his choice of play by arguing that *Tom Thumb* does not introduce 'sacred characters' and concerned King Arthur and Queen Dollololla, not King William and Queen Adelaide, but agreed that he had withdrawn the playbill 'after receiving a polite communication from Mr Roe, the magistrate of Bow Street'.

Like Glossop and other early managers Davidge sometimes risked the patent theatres' wrath by presenting Shakespeare under other names: his accession to sole control was marked by a number of such transparent stratagems: *The Three Caskets; or The Jew of Venice* 'founded on a most popular drama'; *Hotspur; or Percy and Plantagenet*; *The Moor of Venice*; and

Florizel and Perdita followed in steady succession between February and July 1827. Encouraged by the apparent disinterest of Drury Lane and Covent Garden, he embarked on a further sequence during the winter of 1827–8. 'A Favourite Melodramatic Burletta, founded on a play of Shakespeare's, *The Jew of Venice*' was staged on 17 December, and the 'Serious Melodrama called *The Life and Death of King Richard III; or The Battle of Bosworth Field*' two weeks later. The New Year opened with 'A Grand Historical Serious Drama, founded on one of Shakespeare's most admired Tragedies, *Queen Catherine and Cardinal Wolsey; or The Life of King Henry VIII*'. H. M. Milner was required to supply

> an entirely new Tragic, Comic, Historical Drama to be called *Hamlet, Prince of Denmark*. This piece is not an alteration or adaptation of Shakespeare's admirable tragedy of the same name, the language, incidents and in many respects the plot being wholly different. It is partly founded on the celebrated French Tragedy by Ducis, partly on a French Serio-Pantomime from the same Story, and is principally constructed from various striking Incidents and painful Situations by the Historical Facts, and which appeared capable of being Melo-dramatically treated . . .

This was duly staged on 4 February and a 'Melodramatic Burletta called *Macbeth, King of Scotland; or The Weird Sisters*' announced for a fortnight later. By now the patents had decided that this systematic nose-thumbing must cease, and Davidge had to concede the postponement of *Macbeth* 'in consequence of the following circumstances':

> Mr Davidge has been served with a Legal Process, for some cause to him unknown, at the suit of Mr William Dunn, Treasurer of the Theatre Royal, Drury Lane . . . The Lessee of the Coburg Theatre has hitherto studiously endeavoured to conform himself to the Laws, and it his anxious wish to continue to do so. Until, therefore, he shall know wherein he has offended, and until the Surrey Part of the Metropolis shall have time to appeal to the Legislature and the Nation against so inordinate a claim to Intellectual Monopoly and Domination, he respectfully withdraws the advertised Melo-Drama of THE WEIRD SISTERS.

The Appeal to the Legislature and the Nation seems to have stopped short with the Magistrates who, according to Davidge's evidence to the Commons Committee in 1832 fined him 'two sums of £50'.[33]

Following its success with *Black-Ey'd Susan*, the Surrey under Elliston and his deputy, the actor David Webster Osbaldiston (a name later to be displayed prominently in the Waterloo Road), presented a growing threat to the Coburg. Davidge's progressive reductions in admission charges and his complaint against the Surrey's sharp practice in letting boxes at a cut rate of 2/6 for parties of five illustrate this rivalry. Such desperate measures as engaging a fallen idol like Edmund Kean at £50 a night also suggest increasing difficulty in recruiting a resident company. He may not have resisted an approach early in 1833 from two members of the Covent Garden company to take over the lease. The last performance under Davidge's management (and under the name Coburg) took place on 11 March 1833, the final offering being appropriately *The Spectre Wreck*. In the event his supplanters did him an unintended service. The following year he took over the lease of the rival establishment, the Surrey, and in his first season there made a profit of £4,000. When he died early in 1842 he left the substantial estate of £27,000.[34] The fortunes of his successors in the Waterloo Road were to be very different.

Revival and relapse

The bid by two prominent members of the Covent Garden company, Daniel Egerton and William Abbott, to restore the artistic standards and recall the discriminating audience at which the Coburg's founders had aimed was evidently inspired by the wind of change blowing in the theatrical world in 1833. Electoral reform had been achieved the previous year; theatrical reform seemed a logical progression. The Commons Committee of 1832 had encouraged its chairman, Edward Bulwer, to introduce a Dramatic Performances Bill early in 1833, allowing any licensed theatre to stage legitimate drama, and extending the Lord Chamberlain's authority to all such houses. The example of Madame Vestris at the Olympic, which even under the restrictions of a minor theatre she had made the home of witty and tasteful entertainment patronised by a fashionable public, no doubt suggested to Egerton and Abbott that they might achieve something more in a larger and more viable house. Both had managerial experience: Egerton had previously helped to run the Olympic and Sadler's Wells, while Abbott earlier leased the Theatre Royal, Dublin, and managed the English company at the Paris Odéon which brought together the composer Hector Berlioz and the Irish actress Harriet Smithson. Their decision must also have been influenced by the retirement in 1832 of Charles Kemble, breaking the Kemble family's thirty-year rule of Covent Garden, and the prospect of both patent theatres coming under the control of the upstart Alfred Bunn.

A new beginning called for a new name. Leopold of Saxe-Coburg was no longer resident in England, having accepted the crown of the Belgians in 1830 (after refusing that of the Hellenes the previous year), and in any case his interest in the Theatre had always been tenuous. The change to the 'Royal Victoria' has invariably been regarded as a tactful gesture to the Heir Presumptive (still only a girl of fourteen), and no doubt that thought did cross the new managers' minds. But it should not be forgotten that her mother's name was also Victoria; at the reopening on 1 July 1834 they announced that 'Her Royal Highness the Duchess of Kent has been graciously pleased to take this Theatre under Her Royal Highness's immediate protection', and it continued to be 'under the patronage of HRH the Duchess of Kent' during the Egerton–Abbott management. All reference to patronage then disappeared, so that the establishment can never be said to have enjoyed that sovereign's favour, though its reputation as 'Queen Victoria's Own Theayter' was later the source of much caustic comment.

Its nearest approach was the visit paid by the patron and her daughter on 28 November. Bearing in mind that the Princess had already visited the King's (Italian) Opera House in the Haymarket regularly, and made the occasional outing to Drury Lane and Covent Garden, her account carries some authority:

> At 10 minutes past 6 we went with dear Lehzen and Sir John [Conroy] to the play to the Victoria Theatre. It is a very clean and pretty little theatre, and the box we were in was very comfortable. The 1st performance was the Opera of Guy Mannering in 3 acts, which is very pretty. The principal characters were, Col: Mannering, Mr Forrester; Henry Bertram, Mr Hunt; Dominie Sampson, Mr Chippendale; Dandie Dinmont, Mr Latham; Gabriel, Mr Morely, etc., etc. Lucy Bertram, Miss E. Romer; Julia Mannering, Miss P. Horton, a pretty little person; and Meg Merrilies, Mrs Egerton, who acted and looked very well. Mdlle Rosier danced a Highland Fling in the second act. Gustavus the Third was the next piece, a drama in two acts. The principal characters were, Gustavus the 3rd, Mr Abbott; Count Ankarstroem, Mr Butler; Count Warthing, Mr Hunt; Count Sbiigel, Mr Forrester; Oscar, Miss P. Horton, etc., etc. Amelia, Countess Ankarstroem, Miss Mason; Ardweska, a sorceress, Mrs Egerton. In the last scene, the Masqued Ball, Mdlle Rosier danced La Dance de Folie. She is a very plain person but dances very well. We came home at a $\frac{1}{4}$ to 12. I was soon in bed and asleep.[35]

The 'pretty little theatre' is especially significant, bearing in mind Davidge's assertion to the Commons Committee that the house held 'near 4,000'. The Coburg had always impressed observers as being small and intimate, for better or (in Hazlitt's case) worse.

The company assembled by Egerton and Abbott drew on Covent Garden for its nucleus, and included James Warde, who played 'heavies', Robert and Mary Keeley, outstanding comic performers, and Priscilla Horton (the Princess's 'pretty little person'), who was to serve Macready's management at Covent Garden with distinction, not least as the first Fool in *King Lear* for more than 150 years. Neither Egerton nor Abbott, however, had established themselves as leading Shakespearean actors. Egerton was by now in his sixties and mostly contented himself with 'comic old men'. Abbott had lived too long in the shadow of leading actors like Charles Kemble and Charles Mayne Young, and years of playing secondary parts: Laertes, Buckingham (in *Henry VIII*), Cassio, had undermined his confidence. Hazlitt's comment on his Romeo at Fanny Kemble's debut was 'Must we speak of Abbott's Romeo? We hear he is a pleasant person everywhere but upon the stage', and when Abbott came to mount the play in July 1834 he cast Priscilla Horton as Romeo.

Yet leading Shakespearean actors were essential if the new image of the Theatre was to be established and the return to the original prices of admission justified. 'It was near this spot that Shakespeare wrote and Shakespeare acted, and has left us the vivifying sense of his immortal and unapproachable glory. Here too the potent Author and Actor, Ben Jonson, triumphed, and here was witnessed first the friendly and ever-lasting union of Beaumont and Fletcher' proclaimed a bill of 25 October 1833. There was little sign of immortal and unapproachable Shakespeare on the opening night: T. P. Cooke in *Black-Ey'd Susan* and *The Forest of the Ardennes; or The Minstrel* sounded suspiciously like the mixture as before, and when Abbott made his first appearance on 17 July it was as Francis I in *The King's Fool; or The Old Man's Curse*, an adaptation of Hugo's *Le Roi s'amuse*. When Shakespeare did get a hearing with *Othello* on 26 September (oddly described as 'the Author's Night'), Abbott was still playing Cassio, with Warde as Othello and Iago taken by 'A Gentleman'. Rumour seems to have circulated early that the management was in some difficulty. On 20 November the bill proclaimed: 'Statements having appeared that our interest in the theatre expires in June next, we beg leave to say that we have the lease for seven years.' The visit of the Duchess of Kent and daughter the following week may have been sought to restore public confidence in the new venture.

Lacking a local Shakespeare, the new management put a good deal of its faith in Sheridan Knowles, the Irish playwright whose *Virginius* had provided Macready with one of his early and enduring successes. Between October 1833 and July 1834 Knowles made regular appearances in his own plays: *The Wife: A Tale of Mantua*; *The Hunchback*; *William Tell* and a specially rewritten version of *The Blind Beggar of Bethnal Green*. Knowles's strong Irish accent did not deter him from attempting Swiss archers or Italian husbands, nor from playing Macbeth (with Mrs Egerton as his Lady), but he left Virginius to its creator. On 28 July Macready was induced to make his only appearance at the Victoria for Knowles's Benefit:

> My dressing-room was more inconvenient and ill-appointed than many provincial ones, and when I went on the stage I found the wings literally choked up with people. I was rather inclined to be out of temper with this, but soon recollected myself and acted as well as I could – much of the character, Virginius, very well – really and with heart. My reception was *most enthusiastic* – certainly the most of any that appeared. At the end I was called for, but declined going on and went to undress. In consequence of the continued clamour Abbott promised that I should appear at the end of the farce . . . Went on the stage, or rather was pulled on by Knowles – the applause was tumultuous – I bowed and retired.

By this time the management was in deep financial trouble. Egerton's resources were exhausted; he was declared bankrupt, imprisoned for debt and died there a year later. From 9 June the playbills announced the theatre as 'under the sole management of Mr Abbott', and Macready records that at Knowles's Benefit

> Abbott *distressed* me with importunities, on personal grounds particularly, to engage for a few nights. I good-naturedly but firmly resisted, and *I was right in doing so*. How satisfactory it is to be able to say that to oneself on any occasion![36]

One famous name Abbott did succeed in attracting was that of the violinist Paganini, who gave what proved to be his farewell concert in England at the Victoria on 17 June, with considerably increased prices: Orchestra and First Class Boxes 7/-; Dress Circle and Upper Boxes 4/-; Pit 2/-; Gallery 1/-. The concert was for the benefit of the young singer Charlotte Watson, daughter of a Covent Garden violinist with whose family Paganini had lodged in Gray's Inn Road. Evidently his interest in her was more than charitable; four days after the performance he crossed to France where he was joined by the young lady (whose age was variously given as sixteen and eighteen). A furious father chased after and confronted them. Eventually the Watson family emigrated to America, while Paganini retreated to Nice, where he died six years later.[37]

Abbott's approach to Macready was clearly a last desperate recourse. Within a month he had to admit defeat, and though his name was included in the list of artistes engaged when the theatre reopened in September, he never appeared, and his career did not recover before his death in 1843 in America. The contrast between his and Egerton's fates, and the resuscitation of Davidge's fortunes at the Surrey is poignant. The promising circumstances under which they had set out to rescue the Coburg also proved illusory. Bulwer's bill for the freeing of theatrical restrictions, having passed the Commons, was defeated in the Lords, and the next ten years, until the passing of the Theatre Regulation Act in 1843, were marked by a final resurgence of the patent theatres. Macready moved into management for the first time at Covent Garden in 1837 (to be succeeded by Vestris and Charles James Mathews, transferring their base from the Olympic), and at Drury Lane in 1841. When emancipation finally arrived, the Waterloo Road house was set on a course of transpontine excess. There was no such renaissance as Samuel Phelps achieved at Sadler's Wells, or William Creswick attempted at the Surrey. But for a year the hopes entertained by Glossop and his coadjutors of a quality house south of the river had been rekindled. It would take eighty years of labour, always hard and often unrewarded, before the Waterloo Road house regained its standing and the Old Vic became a term of respect in the theatre.

3

Seeking survival

1834–1880

Egerton's bankruptcy and Abbott's hasty departure encouraged the irrepressible Joseph Glossop to return to his proving-ground of fifteen years earlier. How long he had been back in England is unclear, but his experience on the Continent had evidently fed his ambition. *Figaro in London* (a false friend, as it proved) announced in ringing tones:

> The Victoria is about to pass into the hands of Mr Glossop, the original proprietor, whose extraordinary spirit in conducting it some years ago excited the admiration of the whole metropolis. He has since been the lessee of the two largest theatres in the world, the *San Carlo* at Naples and *La Scala* at Milan, so that his intentions of splendour must have been magnified rather than diminished since he last had possession of the Victoria . . .[1]

adding, three weeks later: 'The house . . . is being considerably improved under the direction of M. Carbonel, the original architect.'[2]

Another feature now restored was the looking-glass curtain, presumably reconstructed from the fragments sited all over the building. There was also a deliberate continuation of the earlier managerial policy: the opening attraction was *Othello*, with two reputable performers, Elton and Wallack, alternating Othello and Iago, and Priscilla Horton as Desdemona. For the correspondent of *Figaro in London*, however, the splendour of the auditorium eclipsed the spectacle on the stage:

> Immediately on the opening of the doors, the house was crammed in every part by persons who testified in phraseology as various as the prices, their respective feelings at viewing the magnificence of the interior. The occupant of the dress circle, who had paid his *four* shillings, was struck with blank and perfectly silent astonishment . . . while the *sixpenny* tenant of the gallery vented his *connoisseurship* in loud exclamations of 'Crikey, Bill, an't this here magnefficient!'[3]

During the next six months there was a promising blend of classical and romantic on the bills. Elton played Richard III and William Tell; contemporary taste was met by *Jonathan Bradford* and *The Rent Day*. The longest run was achieved by an adaptation of *The Last Days of Pompeii* (the adapter, Fitzball, was named on the bill, but not the author, Bulwer-Lytton) from 5 January to 16 February, and the most intriguing item was an 'Operatic Romance', *Zameo*, billed as 'by Lord Byron's daughter, Medora', but most probably by the actor and play-carpenter, C. Pelham Thompson.[4] It opened on 27 October 1834 and disappeared for ever two weeks later.

Equally sensational was the first appearance on the Victoria stage of David Webster Osbaldiston. This experienced actor had proved useful to Elliston (whose taste for unconventional behaviour he shared) at the Surrey, and after Elliston's death in 1831 took on the lease of that theatre. In this capacity he had proved a serious threat to Davidge at the Coburg, not least by promoting the career of a local girl, Eliza Vincent, daughter of a Lambeth newsvendor, who had made several child appearances at the Coburg. In 1823 at the age of eight she had held that stage in her solo performance, *The Seven Ages of Woman*, and before long she achieved success as both actress and singer at Drury Lane. It was as much her personal as her professional attractions that interested Osbaldiston, and in 1834 he quitted the Surrey and his wife and family for his leading lady. His appearance at the Coburg on 17 November as Rolla in *Pizarro* was therefore a challenge to the moral standards of Lambeth playgoers, and the audience responded by howling him off the stage.[5] Osbaldiston was resilient: by 22 November *Figaro in London* noted: 'Mr Osbaldiston has likewise played Rolla thrice, the anticipated opposition having been unsuccessful',[6] and he remained with the company, taking a benefit (as Coriolanus) on 17 February 1835. He had established a foothold which would become secure in the following decade.

The management, however, was far from secure. It seems clear that Joseph Glossop had reinstated himself and refurbished the Theatre on credit; more particularly his father's credit. In January 1835 that much tried parent died, and his once well-filled pockets proved to be empty, no doubt turned out for the theatrical enterprises of his ambitious son. Creditors began to outnumber spectators at the Victoria. *Figaro in London* joined the importunate throng, reporting on 21 March:

> The Victoria presents the phenomenon of a crowded stage, and an empty house. We saw a bill stuck up outside the theatre, offering a

reward for a bag of sovereigns stolen from the box-office; it would be better to offer a reward for any one that could find a bag of sovereigns in such a place.

Within a week the Theatre closed, and Glossop's enemies fell upon him:

> Glossop's failure has caused a wide scattering of the pomp and pageantry of the Victoria Theatre. The singular villainy of this man deserved exposure. The various petty frauds, the mean unnecessary trickery – the shuffling – the base ingratitude to all who served and befriended him . . . the downright robbery of poor people committed by this double bankrupt are unparalleled.[7]

Even this debacle could not suppress him altogether. In 1842 the actor Walter Donaldson came across him keeping a boarding-house in Brussels, where 'he appeared as happy as when manager of the Coburg and San Carlo',[8] and though he never returned to the theatre, his family were to make a considerable impression there. His son Augustus took the surname Harris, and managed the Princess's during Charles Fechter's brief but brilliant appearances. His grandson, also Augustus, became manager of Drury Lane, and with his melodramas and pantomimes lifted that house to forgotten splendour at the end of the century, being chosen Sheriff of London, earning a knighthood and acquiring the nickname 'Druriolanus' in the process.[9]

Dark days

Over the next six years the Victoria Theatre drifted downwards. The lease passed into the hands of a Mr Lawrence Levy, apparently not a theatre man, and the first of several lessees who may have seen the sale of liquor as more profitable than the provision of entertainment. The year of Queen Victoria's accesion, 1837, was marked by a return to the cut prices obtaining at the end of Davidge's regime (Boxes 2/-; Pit 1/-; Gallery 6d.). The actual management changed with ominous rapidity, and the theatre was 'dark' for several extended periods, e.g. March to June 1837 and between May and November 1838. A familiar name is glimpsed briefly when Moncrieff returned in the early part of 1836, but more often those responsible were unproven and unproved. Established actors were also scarce. For the reopening in June 1835 Denvil, the actor who had created Byron's Manfred at Drury Lane the previous year, played Richard III, but his popularity was short-lived. More often the Victoria had to create its own idols. Newton Treen Hicks (somewhat ironically known as 'Bravo' Hicks) made an early appearance on 5 March

1838 as Rolla, and was to prove a more lasting favourite, but his fame never spread North of the Thames.

The various managers were also wary of prosecution for trespassing on the patent theatres' territory. A bill for November 1838 announced *Othello* 'by Act of Parliament', indicating a 'burletta'. More often the chief interest of the bill was anthropomorphic. *The Black Legend of Rotherhithe* on 5 February 1838 featured 'the celebrated Mare "Patty"'; 'the Human Fly' and 'the Grouse Fly' were the main attractions in January of that year. In April a pantomime was specially devised 'in the course of which the monkeys danced upon the tight and slack ropes, and went through a variety of evolutions which were not only amusing but astonishing, and the dogs were equally effective in the "trial of the deserter". An act of horsemanship by Monsieur Piebutto [one of the monkeys] produced considerable laughter.'[10] Boxers vied with actors for top billing: 29 September 1837 was 'Young Dutch Sam's Night'.

Not surprisingly the tone adopted by the press (when it noticed the Theatre at all) was mostly contemptuous. *Actors by Daylight* commented on 15 September 1838:

> A miserable production, entitled *The Smuggler's Gibbet*, has been the last new novelty, from the pen of Mr John Parry!!!! as displayed in alarming type in the bills . . . We merely dropped in to avoid a shower, and were heartily glad to escape from its walls; when we paid our two shillings, the check-taker seized them with an avidity astonishing to behold!

At the nadir of the Theatre's fortunes, early in 1841, an unlikely champion appeared in the person of David Osbaldiston. His own career since the collapse of Glossop's management had been eventful. Immediately on quitting the Waterloo Road he had made a successful bid for the lease of Covent Garden, where Bunn's attempt to run both patent theatres had foundered. After two years even Osbaldiston found the responsibility taxing, and he removed to the humbler City of London, where he was able to introduce Eliza Vincent as his leading lady. His transfer south of the river may have struck his contemporaries as another short-term assignment, but if so, they were mistaken. He was to run the Victoria until his death ten years later, and Eliza Vincent continued their regime another five years. Between them they maintained the longest continuous management of the Theatre *as* a theatre until Lilian Baylis took over in 1912 and ventured to restore drama to its stage.

Conditions of play

The years 1841–56 when Osbaldiston and Eliza Vincent controlled the
Victoria have been singled out in modern accounts of the Theatre for
particular scorn. This is due less to the standards they maintained or
failed to maintain than to the glimpses of an otherwise obscure
playhouse traceable in the works of at least three well-known Victorian
writer: Charles Kingsley, Charles Dickens and Henry Mayhew. Evidence from a recognisable name carries weight, and it is for this reason
that the Victoria's critics have cited the famous and left the unsung
unquoted. Of these three witnesses Kingsley's testimony in *Alton Locke*
(1849) seems the most suspect. The novel is strongly Chartist in
sympathy, and the author looks for support wherever he can find it. In
particular Kingsley attributed the degradation of the Victoria's audience
to the conditions under which they lived. One passage, not especially
remarked on publication but much quoted forty years later, runs:

> We were passing by the door of the Victoria Theatre; it was just
> half-price time – and the beggary and rascality of London were
> pouring in to hear their low amusement, from the neighbouring gin
> palaces and thieves' cellars. A herd of ragged boys, vomiting forth
> slang, filth and blasphemy, pushed past us, compelling us to take good
> care of our pockets.

This is followed by a lecture to Alton Locke from his workmate,
Crossthwaite:

> 'Look there! look at the amusements, the training, the civilization,
> which the government permits to the children of the people! These
> licensed pits of darkness, traps of temptation, profligacy and ruin,
> triumphantly yawning night after night – and then tell me that the
> people who see their children thus kidnapped into hell are represented
> by a government who licenses such things!'[11]

Kingsley does not describe a performance at the Victoria, and seems to
have picked on it to represent transpontine theatre in general. There is
no reason why Crossthwaite and Locke, who work for a tailor 'in a street
off Piccadilly' and lodge in St Giles, should be attending a meeting in
Lambeth, and Kingsley keeps its location deliberately vague:

> 'We'll strike while the iron's hot and go down to the Chartist meeting
> at —'

Elsewhere in the book he uses 'the Victory' as a symbolic sink of iniquity. Locke's fellow-workmen poke fun at his innocence by quoting:

'Don't his mother know he's out? . . . and won't she know it
Ven he's sitting in his glory
Half-price at the Victory?'[12]

and a kindly policeman, who finds him wandering the streets after running away from home, asks: 'Forgot the latch-key, you sucking Don Juan, that's it, is it? Late home from the Victory?'[13] All of this provided grist to the Temperance Movement's mill when 'the Victory' became 'the Royal Victoria Music Hall and Coffee Tavern'.

Henry Mayhew's account of 'the Vic Gallery' in *London Labour and the London Poor* (1851) is more exact. He describes the 'rush of costers to the 3rd Gallery' as 'peculiar and almost awful', and refers to an accident which evidently preceded the more famous disaster there of 1858. 'A crowd of lads' he found 'collects as early as 3 o'clock in the afternoon' and 'stand upon the broad wooden bannisters about 50 feet from the ground to get a good place . . . The girls shriek, men start, and a nervous fear is felt less the massive staircase should fall in with the weight of the throng, as it lately did with the most terrible results.'[14]

Elsewhere, however, Mayhew presents a humorous picture of the Victoria's public, and of the playbill-sellers who ministered to their need:

The Victoria is considered one of the most profitable stations for the playbill-seller, the box-keeper there seldom selling any bill in the theatre.

Evidently the Victoria public thought a night at the theatre a cultural experience: 'Many go to the Victoria who cannot read, or who can read but imperfectly, and they love to parade the consulting of a playbill!' It was important to these humble salesmen that all entrances to a theatre should be adjacent, or they lost part of their custom. 'The Lyceum's built shocking orkered. Vy, the boxes is in one street and the pit in another . . . Astley's and the Wick is both spoilt that way, Astley's perticler – as the gallery's a good step from the pit and boxes; at the Wick it's round the corner . . . I never seen a play but one at the Wick. I'd rather be at a Free and Heasy. I don't know as I knows the actors and actresses, either hes or shes.' Selling playbills seems to have been dangerous as well as ill-rewarded:

The youths who have been in the trade from childhood are generally those who run recklessly by the side of cabs and carriages. One of these youths said to me: 'The cabman knows how to do it, sir, when I runs and patters; and so does his hoss.'

But presumably there were not many cabs and carriages to threaten the safety of the 'Wick' bill-sellers.

Charles Dickens's account in *Household Words* of visits to his local theatre by 'Joe Whelks, of the New Cut, Lambeth' has been used as evidence of the low quality and character of early Victorian drama. A recent study, *Dickens and Popular Entertainment* by Paul Schlicke, quotes him as finding the plays 'an incongruous heap of nonsense', and writes of 'the derisory quality of the plays in the theatres he had visited'.[15] Less emphasis is placed by scholars of Dickens on the pleasure Joe Whelks derives from these outings. Yet Dickens himself insists that Whelks

> is not much of a reader, has no great store of books, no very commodious room to read in, no very decided inclination to read, and no power at all of presenting vividly before his mind's eye what he reads about. But put Joe in the gallery of the Victoria Theatre; show him doors and windows in the scene that will open and shut, and that people can get in and out of; tell him with these aids, and by the help of living men and women dressed up, confiding to him their innermost secrets, in voices audible half a mile off; and Joe will unravel a story through all its entanglements, and sit there as long after midnight as you have anything left to show him. Accordingly the Theatres to which Mr Whelks resorts are always full; and whatever changes of fashion the drama knows elsewhere, it is always fashionable in the New Cut.[16]

Dickens saw a piece entitled *May Morning; or The Mystery of 1715*, and evidently visited the Victoria between 26 January 1850, when *May Morning* was first staged, and the end of February, when it was withdrawn after a respectable run. To his (but not to the audience's) disappointment the title turned out to be the heroine's name, not an indication of spring's awakening. The lady was played by Eliza Vincent, now fully restored to the favour of her fellow-residents of Lambeth. Henry Mayhew had seen her three months earlier in an unspecified 'Dummestic Drama', set in Poland with a Cossack General as the villain. When threatened by this monster she 'turned up her swans-down cuffs, and seizing four Russian soldiers shook them successively by the collar', much to the satisfaction of the gallery who shouted: 'Bray-vo, Vincent! Go it, my tulip!'[17]

Throughout 1840s and right up to her death in 1856 Eliza Vincent was a mainstay of the Victoria. In 1847 the *Theatrical Times* painted an ingenuous – perhaps disingenuous – portrait of her:

> In private life Miss Vincent's habits are of the most retiring nature – she is devotedly attached to the study of botany, possesses a collection of plants, and has gained several prizes from the Surrey Horticultural Society.[18]

Nevertheless, it was she rather than Osbaldiston who shaped the repertoire, and her appeal that made the heroine the centre of so many of the plays presented during these years. Dickens's regret that May Morning was a woman, not a time of year, went unnoticed by the regular Victoria playgoer. The list of pieces presented tells its own story: *Susan Hopley, the Servant Girl* (1841); *Grace Huntley* (1843); *Alice Aukland* (1843); *Isabel Bertrand* (1846); *Katy O'Sheil* (1846); *Alice Duane* (1849); *Marion Hazelton* (1849) are some of the title-roles she played. It is noticeable not only that the heroine gives her name to the play, but that she is of native and often humble stock. The Victoria moved increasingly away from the exotic locations of the Coburg stage in its early and most scenic years, relying on the audience's identification with the struggle and survival of one of their own kind to compensate for the spectacle it could no longer afford. Osbaldiston was clearly making a virtue of necessity when his playbills boasted of 'Those Beautiful Domestic Dramas for which this Theatre has already under the present Management become so universally and extensively celebrated'.

His audience also seems to have found comfort and assurance in seeing the familiar reproduced onstage. The Coburg public of twenty years earlier enjoyed extending its horizons, either geographical (*The North Pole*; *Life in Paris*) or historical (*The Black Prince*; *Mary Queen of Scots*). But in 1850, as Dickens had noted, 'Put Joe in the gallery of the Victoria Theatre; show him doors and windows in the scene that will open and shut, and that people can get in and out of . . . and Joe will unravel a story through all its entanglements, and sit there as long after midnight as you have anything left to show him.' Henry Mayhew also drew attention to the Victoria audience's habit of equating theatrical practice with daily routine:

> Delay between pieces results in cries of 'Pull up that there winder blind'. . . If the view is impeded, they shout: 'Higher the blue' and 'Light up the moon' when the transparency is rather dim.[19]

Of course such detail underlines the change in the composition of the audience over a quarter of a century. The Victoria public was not merely illiterate but simple and undiscriminating. On the other hand Kingsley's picture of 'the beggary and rascality of London . . . pouring in to hear their low amusements', and 'a herd of ragged boys, vomiting forth slang, filth and blasphemy' seems obviously partial when set against Mayhew's account of the identical audience joining in a song:

> A deep silence prevails all through the stanzas. Should any burst in before his time, a shout of 'Orda-a-a-r' is raised, and the intruder put down by a thousand indignant cries.

and 'An "ang-core" on such occasions is always demanded.' The amusements, if low, were heard with attention.

Two years after Osbaldiston took over the lease of the Victoria, the Theatre Regulation Act abolished the privileges of the patent theatres, and minor theatres were transferred from the jurisdiction of local magistrates to that of the Lord Chamberlain. On 16 October 1843 the playbill announced: 'Licensed by the Lord High Chamberlain under Act 6 and 7 Victoria Cap 68 to D. W. Osbaldiston.' The following year, when the Theatre reopened after the summer recess, the licensee proclaimed:

> Parliament having placed all Theatres on the same responsible footing, and being no longer under fear of the Law for performing the Legitimate Drama of England, the Manager, with Pride, announces his intention of producing at the Victoria Theatre the Sterling Tragedies and Comedies of the British Stage on a Scale of Splendour and Effect hitherto unattempted . . .
> One of our National Theatres being closed and the Other chiefly devoted to different purposes than that of the Regular Drama, it is only in the Minor Theatres these Plays can now be performed.

The latter reference was to Covent Garden, once his responsibility, now permanently an opera house. As it proved, the Theatre Regulation Act altered very little, apart from removing the threat hanging over the heads of 'minor' managers. Drury Lane pursued an uneasy alternation of spectacular drama and opera. The anticipated outbreak of rash speculation in theatre-building did not occur. The demand had been met in the previous fifty years, and not until the 1870s, when vastly improved transport provided a much larger potential public, was there another upsurge, both in London and the provinces. The 1840s were in fact a time of theatrical and dramatic stagnation, with theatre managers struggling to hold their existing audiences. The only West End theatre to benefit immediately by the new freedom, the St James's, achieved pre-eminence through importing French companies, including stars like Lémaître and Rachel, and calling itself 'La Comédie Française à Londres'.

At the Victoria Osbaldiston made efforts to practise what his playbill had preached. There were performances of *Hamlet* and *Othello* on successive nights (26 and 27 September 1844) with Eliza Vincent as Ophelia and Desdemona. But Osbaldiston himself, although a leading actor, played the Ghost and Cassio. No doubt the demands of management discouraged his attempting the leads, but why not Claudius and Iago? There was little prospect of other leading actors being enticed to the Victoria; Hamlet was played on this occasion by a Mr Otway, and in subsequent performances 'Bravo' Hicks took in Hamlet along with his highwaymen and pirates, and played Romeo to Eliza Vincent's Juliet. The contrast between the Victoria and Sadler's Wells after the Theatre Regulation Act is marked. In Islington Samuel Phelps took over a theatre chiefly famous for its aquatic drama, and for the next eighteen years made it the home of Shakespeare and other classical dramatists, in a programme built round his own modest though undoubted talent. But Islington had many advantages over the New Cut: it was adjacent to Lincoln's Inn and the other Inns of Court, and many of its inhabitants were employed in humble but respectable service to the legal profession. The river proved an effective barrier as far as serious theatregoers were concerned, and even William Creswick's valiant attempt to rival Phelps at the Surrey in the 1850s achieved little recognition.

Of course the Victoria audience found much of Shakespeare beyond them. Even the opening *Othello*, immediately after Osbaldiston had announced his intention of producing 'the Sterling Tragedies and Comedies of the British Stage on a Scale of Spectacle and Effect hitherto unattempted' had to be offset by the 'American Southern Minstrels'. That audience was itself changing, as well as the legal situation. In particular the district was transformed by the building of Waterloo Station, which opened in 1848 as the terminus of the London and South Western Railway, previously finishing at Nine Elms. Demolition, importing the necessary labour, and diversified employment in an area until then largely made up of costermongers destroyed that camaraderie to which Dickens and Mayhew had paid tribute.

Osbaldiston tried to take advantage of the development. As early as

1847, before the opening of Waterloo, the playbill refers to the facilities at hand:

> RAILWAYS: Amongst the manifold **advantages** of Railways, with all their facilities, their cheapness, and their speed, none can be greater than the opportunity they present at the present time of enabling Parties to come and witness the superior performances of the VICTORIA THEATRE. This has indeed been the fact for weeks past, as has been proved by persons continually enquiring the time, that they may not be late for the train to take them back on their return home.

The following January the programme included a farce, *The Railway Station*, which introduced amongst other characters Mr Sampson Jones (in search of his Father); Mr William Smith (in search of his Son); and Sleeper (in search of his Baggage). But the opening of a Railway Station on the theatre's doorstep proved of little help to the Victoria; for Waterloo was even nearer to Waterloo Bridge, and so to the Strand, where theatres like the Adelphi, the Lyceum and the Strand itself could offer passengers on the London and South Western a wide choice of entertainment.

Since the Victoria was rarely noticed in the national newspapers, such glimpses as they afforded of Osbaldiston at work chiefly record his conflict with the authorities. In 1846 one of the company, Fredericks, took him to court for demanding £3 in return for the privilege of two 'orders' nightly. The court found for the manager.[20] The following year the Lord Chamberlain prosecuted him for selling spirits in the Victoria saloon, although this was a regular practice at all theatres.[21] Both incidents have been cited to suggest the low standards of management prevalent at the Victoria in Osbaldiston's time. The fact remains that for ten years he kept the Theatre open and solvent. No subsequent manager was to achieve this until Emma Cons changed its function and found wealthy friends to assist her.

Death and decline

Although he was only in his early fifties, Osbaldiston's appearances became increasingly scarce as his management proceeded. For his benefit nights he would revive one of his 'standard' roles (notably Rolla and William Tell), and occasionally appear with Eliza Vincent in such standbys as Mrs Centlivre's *The Wonder* and a Kotzebue adaptation, *The*

Stranger (of which the only trace remaining in today's repertoire is the 'touch' detectable in Gilbert and Sullivan's Heavy Dragoon from *Patience*). It is notable that such appearances, together with the token Shakespearean tragedy, were rare departures from the regular fare of 'Dummestic Drama'. On the other hand his one recorded achievement as a dramatist conformed strictly to that category. This was *The Drunkard's Children*, based on George Cruickshank's drawings, which inspired a whole crop of adaptations in the summer of 1848. Cruickshank himself supervised another version at the Surrey, and a week after the first night of Osbaldiston's arrangement, the playbill for 10 July printed the text of a letter from Cruickshank's solicitors prohibiting the use of the original title, and announcing:

> This Gloriously Successful Drama so flatteringly alluded to . . . will not be called THE DRUNKARD'S CHILDREN, but will be represented under the title of *Life! or Thrilling Scenes of Early Vice*.

A fortnight later, when the fuss had died down, the original title was quietly restored.

In December 1850 Osbaldiston and Eliza Vincent appeared in a round of popular parts: on 8 December *The Stranger* ('135th time at this Theatre'); on 9 December *Our Lady of the Willows*; on 10 December *The Honeymoon*. Boxing Day saw the opening of the pantomime *Harlequin George Barnwell* 'as originally staged by Mr Osbaldiston at Covent Garden in 1836'. But two days later he was dead at the age of fifty-seven. 'His malady was the yellow jaundice, which subsequently turned to the black jaundice',[22] and his funeral on 3 January 1851 initiated a sequence of events which might well have been found in a Wilkie Collins novel of the period.

First indications suggested that he had died a man of substance: 'He has departed this world much and deservedly respected, and the way he has disposed of his wealth is a bright and honourable trait in his character . . . He is reported to have died immensely rich and to have left his fortune to his wife, his two daughters and his son.' Both predictions were to prove false, and as if to herald the thunderbolt the day of his funeral at Norwood Cemetry proved threatening: 'Notwithstanding that the weather was most unpropitious, the rain falling in torrents, not only most members of the *corps dramatique* of the Victoria were present, but a large number of the "profession" in general.' A further ominous sign appeared when 'he was buried in a common grave fifteen or twenty

yards off the mausoleum of a contemporary manager, the late George
Bolwell Davidge'.

But the real shock was felt at the reading of his will, made only two
days before he died. The bulk of his modest £4,000 estate, including the
furniture, plate, carriage and horses at his house, were left to Eliza
Vincent, who was to be sole executor, and 'with whom resides his
daughter Miss Beatrice Osbaldiston, a young lady of about 16 years of
age'.[23] Contemporaries did not need reminding that it was a little over
sixteen years since the manager and his young protégée had eloped from
the Surrey. More importantly she was left the residue (four years) of the
lease of the Victoria, with the fittings of the Theatre. To Mrs
Osbaldiston and her daughters he left a legacy of £1,000, and his son was
to continue as treasurer of the Victoria (a post he quitted soon
afterwards). The account finished somewhat unnecessarily: 'The de-
ceased lived in good style, and to this, coupled with the fact of his
maintaining two establishments and his losses may be attributed the fact
of his not leaving such an amount of property as was generally
considered he had accumulated.'

His death constituted a double blow to the Victoria. Eliza Vincent, no
doubt seeking to avoid adverse publicity and perhaps also genuinely
broken by her partner's death, withdrew from acting, although the
Theatre was duly licensed to her by the Lord Chamberlain. On 14
February 1852 she married 'a Mr Crowley of Astley's', but misfortune
continued to dog her, for 'he was soon after seized with a mental
disorder, from which he still suffers at an asylum'.[24] Not until 14
November 1853 did she return (billed somewhat inaccurately as making
'her Reappearance upon the Stage after an absence of nearly 4 years') as
Susan Hopley, the Servant Girl, followed by other favourite parts.
Before long she distanced herself from regular participation by
becoming 'Directress', with a licensee, James Johnson Towers, under
her. Nevertheless she continued to appear occasionally until only two
days before her death on 10 November 1856. She was just forty-two.

Eliza Vincent's death, even more than Osbaldiston's, marked a break
in the continuity of command at the Victoria. For the next twenty-five
years managements would come and go, few lasting more than two or
three years, none making the Theatre pay. Towers, who now took sole
charge, had acted earlier but does not seem to have performed at the
Victoria, and began a line of managers apparently more concerned to
exploit the money-making resources of its bars. The quality and

character of the entertainment offered deteriorated in consequence. Even before Eliza Vincent's death there was increasing reliance on what might be termed 'side shows'. A typical bill for 25 April 1853 offered 'Mr Hammond and his beautiful performing Mare, Black Bess' in *Gentleman Jack*, after which 'the entire Company in the highly popular English Dance of "Pop Goes the Weasel"'. It was in this period that E. F. Saville (a transpontine actor, improbably the brother of Helen Faucit, Macready's leading lady and later married to Sir Theodore Martin, biographer of the Prince Consort) became a favourite at the Victoria. John Hollingshead, founder of the Gaiety Theatre and briefly associated with the move to tranform the Victoria in the 1880s, has left a picture of Saville as Bill Sykes in a performance there of *Oliver Twist* which has been widely reprinted:

> The gallery of the Victoria was a huge amphitheatre, probably containing about fifteen hundred perspiring creatures; most of the men in shirt-sleeves, and most of the women bare-headed, with coloured handkerchiefs round their shoulders, called 'bandanna wipes' in the slang of the district, and probably stolen from the pockets of old gentlemen who were given to snuff-taking. This 'chickaleary' audience was always thirsty – and not ashamed. It tied handkerchiefs together – of which it always seemed to have plenty – until they formed a rope, which was used to haul up large stone bottles of beer from the pit, and occasionally hats that had been dropped below . . .
>
> It was this body – the unregenerate playgoer – who always has existed and always will exist, in spite of theatrical reformers – the 'groundlings' of Shakespeare's time, the swinish multitude of ours – who were maliciously tortured by Mr E. F. Saville and half a dozen other representatives of Dickens' criminal animal. The murder of Nancy was the great scene. Nancy was always dragged round the stage by her hair, and after this effort Sykes always looked up defiantly at the gallery, as he was doubtless told to do in the marked prompt copy. He was always answered by one loud and fearful curse, yelled by the whole mass like a Handel Festival chorus. The curse was answered by Sykes dragging Nancy twice round the stage, and then, like Ajax, defying the lightning. The simultaneous yell became louder and more blasphemous. Finally when Sykes, working up to a well rehearsed climax, smeared Nancy with red-ochre, and taking her by the hair (a most powerful wig) seemed to dash her brains out on the stage, no explosion of dynamite invented by the modern anarchist, no language ever dreamt of in Bedlam, could equal the outburst. A thousand enraged voices, which sounded like ten thousand, with the roar of a dozen escaped menageries, filled the theatre and deafened the

audience, and when the smiling ruffian came forward and bowed, their
voices in thorough plain English, expressed a fierce determination to
tear his sanguinary entrails from his sanguinary body.[25]

Whenever cited, this passage has been held to expose the crudity of both
acting and audience, and certainly the standards obtaining even ten years
earlier had obviously deteriorated. What has not been pointed out is that
the Victoria public could still be totally absorbed and aroused by a
performance. That drunken contempt attributed to it by the reformers
had yet to take hold.

The episode in Towers's management most frequently mentioned is
the disaster occuring on Boxing Day 1858 during a matinee of the
pantomime. This was nearing its conclusion at about five in the
afternoon, and a crowd had already gathered on the gallery steps,
waiting for the evening performance. According to the *Era*, a young
man in a box struck a 'fusee' or match, and some of the furnishings were
set alight, although the fire did not spread. The incident was seen by
'two females in the eighteen-penny boxes, who screeched "Fire"'.[26] A
panic ensued; the fleeing gallery audience tore down the barriers
separating their outlet from the gallery steps and ran headlong into the
waiting crowds. In all there were sixteen fatalities – although a news-
paper account that 'Every chymist's and doctor's shop was crowded
with the dead and dying'[27] seems exaggerated – and significantly at least
twelve of the dead were under the age of eighteen. There were no female
casualties, a fact variously interpreted as indicating chivalry in the New
Cut or simply an avoidance of the gallery by the gentle sex.

Although he defrayed the funeral expenses of the victims and claimed
to have spent £300 on strengthening and improving the gallery stairs,
Towers's position was clearly damaged. When he surrendered his lease
in 1863 he was succeeded by the scenic artist, Fredrick Fenton, in
partnership with Frederick Frampton who served as stage-manager.
Fenton was something of an outsider after a series of local lessees. The
Theatre Regulation Act obliged leaseholders to put their addresses at the
top of the bills. Osbaldiston's was 'The Lawns, Balham Hill', and later
'Rushbrooke House, West Brixton'. Eliza Vincent's 'Barkham Terrace,
St George's Road', Towers's 'Clapham Road' and 'Kennington Green'.
Fenton, however, lived at Ampton Street, Gray's Inn Road. He had
earned a considerable reputation as scenic artist for Samual Phelps at
Sadler's Wells, and it seems likely that the end of Phelps's management
there prompted him to look for a stage of his own on which to display
his artistry. 'New and Splendid Scenery'; 'New and Startling Effects',

both overworked commonplaces of the playbill, were regularly and probably rightly employed at this period.

But another assertion, claiming the Victoria as a 'Rescued Temple of the Drama', was less easy to swallow. The nearest approach to such resuscitation the managers seem to have achieved was the appearance at Easter 1864 of Madame Celeste, the colourful directress of the Adelphi, in (appropriately) *The Woman in Red*. The most suitable outlet for Fenton's skill were the pantomimes, played not only at Christmas and Easter but also in the summer. Increasingly, however, the audience's taste turned to local themes and settings: *Life in Lambeth* (1864) and *The London Arab* (1866, with scenes of Lambeth, Clapham and Wandsworth) reflect this taste. Perhaps it was to study these locales at first hand that in 1866 Fenton moved to 9 Southampton Street, Camberwell.

In that year Charles Dickens as Editor of *All The Year Round* decided to commission from the playwright and journalist Andrew Halliday another series of 'Mr Whelks at the Play'. His contribution on 30 June 1866 is headed: 'Mr Whelks over the Water', and though the Victoria is not specifically identified, the theatre in question is 'a large commodious building, duly licensed by the Lord Chamberlain', and is 'in the main street of the New Cut'. The play he saw was *Woman's Trials*, but he found himself more tried than the woman of the title. In particular he commented on the public's disinterest and disrespect:

> It strikes at once as being very odd that Mr Whelks, who pays his money to enjoy a play should be so constantly disposed to make a disturbance and interrupt the proceedings of that play. But when we have witnessed *Woman's Trials* and reflected upon the trial which the play must have been to Mr Whelks's patience, we no longer think it odd that he should whistle.

The contrast with Dickens's Joe Whelks, fifteen years earlier, happy to sit in the gallery till the small hours is striking.

By 1867 Fenton had obviously had enough, and the lease passed to Joseph Cave, an experienced performer with a successful management of the Marylebone to his credit. He was evidently brought in to restore order, and his early playbills suggest the sergeant major as much as the stage-manager:

> Any Person Whistling or Making Other Disturbance will be expelled by the POLICE, it being the Determination of the Manager to enforce perfect order, and trust the Patrons of this Establishment will assist him in abolishing so absurd a custom.

He was also determined to cut out the indiscriminate provision of encores, even in pantomime. Thus when *Charles II; or Pretty Nell Gwynn; or Harlequin Oliver Cromwell and the Little Fairies of the Enchanted Oak* was staged in March 1868:

> The determination to prevent ENCORES, a system which entails extra exertion upon the Artistes and causes unnecessary disturbance in the front of the House, has given universal satisfaction in those Theatres Mr Cave has hitherto managed.

His aim was to revive 'what is termed the sterling drama', and the examples he cited make an odd collection: *Macbeth*; *The Hunchback*; *Rob Roy*; *Guy Mannering*; *Little Emily*; *The Willow Copse*.[28] Certainly he assembled a more solid company than the Victoria had seen since the mid-1830s. It included two 'heavies', one of whom, John Ryder, had served Charles Kean well, and the other, Tom Mead, was to serve Henry Irving similarly, in addition to two former managers of 'smart' theatres, Ben Webster (Haymarket) and Horace Wigan (Olympic).

But though Cave might tame the Victoria public, he could not refine it. During his regime the journalist Arthur Sketchley wrote *Mrs Brown Goes to the Play*, published in 1870. There were many *Mrs Brown* outings: she figured as an early cartoon character in words, a verbal predecessor of Ally Sloper, and Sketchley's account of her trip to the Victoria should not be taken too literally. But it has been much quoted – notably the reference to 'Queen Victoria's Own Theayter', which H. Chance Newton introduced into the title of his history (1923) – to illustrate the decline of a once respected establishment.

It would seem that Mrs Brown's only previous visit to any theatre had been to the Coburg:

> I 'adn't been at a play since a mere gal as an aunt of mine took, and werry lovely it certingly were, for a dark-coloured forriner set cross-legged like a tailor, with a turbot on 'is 'ead, a-shyin' cheyney oranges round it afore a lookin'-glass, as were called Rammer Sammy . . .[29]

Mrs Brown comes from the East End, and her reluctance to visit the New Cut is only assuaged when her husband assures her his 'orders' are for 'Queen Wictoria's werry own theayter':

> I says, 'Whyever didn't you tell me that afore, as makes all the difference, for in course for it's good enuf for 'er, it's good enuf for me, as am not a-goin' to look down upon anythink as belongs to Queen Wictoria.'[30]

But even the outside disappoints her:

> So on we went, me a-'obblin' thro' a lot of brokers' shops, and pickled
> eels, and all other sorts of wegetables, as was opposed for sale, as the
> sayin' is, along with whelks, as is things I don't 'old with; till Brown
> says: 'There you are, old gal, that's Queen Wictoria's werry own
> theayter oppersite.' I says: 'Oh! indeed. Well, then,' I says, 'if I was
> Queen Wictoria, give me a better, for I considers it rather a ramshackle
> place for a Queen to go to constant.'[31]

The interior proves even less promising. 'There were forms all over the
place, and disgraceful forms too, with nails a-stickin' out, as 'ave made
the back breadth of my Norwich crape for all the world as if it had been
cut with a knife', and after inspecting her surroundings Mrs Brown
concludes: 'If this is your theayter as were so grand inside, I don't think
much on it, as is wot I calls a dingy 'ole.'[32] Her reaction to the piece (not
apparently one of Cave's 'sterling dramas', since the heroine – 'a deer
creetur; but in my opinion 'er things is full short' – is pulled out of bed
by the villain and his accomplice) is to shout for the police, who eject
Mrs Brown instead, and she concludes: ''Owever Queen Wictoria can
allow sich shameful goin's on at 'er theayter puzzles me.'[33]

The 'dingy hole' was more than fifty years old when Mrs Brown
visited it, and no doubt showing its age. In 1871 major renovation was
decided on, and for the last performance (9 September) Cave chose to
round off the Theatre's first span by reviving the opening attraction:
Trial by Battle. It was a miscalculation. Though ingenuous by Regency
standards, the play seemed archaic to this audience, and in his words
'produced sniggers'. He went on stage and pointed out that when it had
been presented in 1818 the audience had paid three times as much for
admission, 'so all was well that ended well'. He could silence the public's
sniggers, but not, as it proved, command the tide of their taste to turn.[34]

A false start

It has been repeatedly asserted that in the 1870s the Victoria operated as
a music hall, but the evidence of the playbills scarcely sustains this claim.
Only for a very brief period (November 1876–January 1877) did it style
itself 'the Royal Victoria Palace Theatre of Varieties', and offer a
recognisable variety bill. On the other hand there is some indication that
the rebuilding of September–December 1871 was undertaken with the
intention of opening it as a music hall. The name under which it did open

– the Royal Victoria Palace Theatre – though equivocal, does suggest a music hall rather than a theatre. Grand titles like 'Palace' and 'Alhambra' were coming into fashion to dignify the new 'family' music hall, attracting a family audience, rather than the earlier working man's 'Free and Easy' or rakes' 'Coal Hole'. The Alhambra in Leicester Square (earlier a 'Panoptikon' and then a circus) had reopened as the Alhambra Palace Music Hall in 1860, and then renamed itself the Royal Alhambra Palace of Varieties in 1871, eight months before the opening of the Royal Victoria Palace Theatre. The choice by the new lessee, Romaine Delatorre, of Joseph Cave as his 'director of entertainment' also lends some weight to the conjecture. Cave had begun his career in the tough world of the 'Free and Easy', and continued to perform in musical entertainment.

Further significant, if tantalising, evidence can be found in the plans and correspondence surviving in both the Lord Chamberlain's and Greater London Council's archives. The architect, J. L. Robinson, fell foul of the Lord Chamberlain's Office by introducing a 'promenade' behind both Dress Circle and Pit, and was firmly instructed that 'the Lord Chamberlain would not sanction a promenade in a theatre where women and smoking take place'.[35] He did not specify how a woman 'takes place'. In the end it appears that a definite partition rather than promenades behind the Stalls and Circle was introduced. A further modification insisted on seems to have been an architectural proscenium-arch, instead of open-stage with access to the auditorium, as Robinson proposed. This rejected feature very definitely suggests the purpose of the rebuilding had been to convert the Victoria to a music hall, with a chairman and constant interplay between artistes and audience.

Difficulty in interpreting these plans arises from their marked disparity with the sketches included in the bill of sale when the building was unhappily auctioned only three years later. The extremely short period elapsing between the last night of the old Victoria (9 September) and the first night of the new (24 December) also suggests a modified scale of alteration. Robinson's original plans would seem to demand many months of closure. Presumably Delatorre was discouraged partly by opposition from official quarters, and perhaps also by realisation of the competition from other music halls on Surreyside, including the Canterbury, the Winchester, the Union, the South London and the Rotunda.

Even in its modified form the Royal Victoria Palace Theatre ('a foolish name' according to the *Builder*'s decidedly captious critic) was substantially altered. 'The whole of the interior has been re-arranged, so that of the old building the external walls and roof only remain', noted the same critic. 'The first tier or dress circle is reached by a centre stone staircase, leading from a spacious entrance-hall, laid with tiles. The gallery is gained by a stone staircase on the left of the building. Over the entrance-hall is the Saloon, 40ft. by 22 ft., with an ornamental ceiling, very badly painted.' This dress circle was presumably carved out of the former central boxes, and the remaining boxes ('there are three tiers of private boxes on both sides of the proscenium') equipped with their own staircase. The *Builder* insisted that 'an inner lobby must be found at the box entrance, to prevent the draughts which at present make the theatre in parts unbearable'.[36]

There are other indications that Delatorre had planned to refine the taste of his public as well as refurbish the Theatre. Some of his prices Stalls 2/-; 'Lounge' (presumably the new Circle) 1/-; were appreciably higher than before the closure. He also replaced the old playbills, wet with printer's ink which worked off on the playgoer's fingers, by elegantly printed programmes, at this date a rarity even in select theatres like the Haymarket. These programmes carried advertisements (themselves a novelty) for products such as Rimmels' Choice Perfumery, clearly not aimed at the traditional New Cut audience. It is tempting to believe that Delatorre had noted the transformation of another run-down theatre in a dubious quarter of London and sought to rival its renaissance. The former Queen's Theatre in Soho dated back to 1810, even earlier than the Coburg. It has passed under several other names (most commonly 'the Dusthole') and its rechristening in 1865 as the Prince of Wales's offers an interesting parallel with the rechristening of the Coburg as the Victoria. The Queen in question had withdrawn from all public appearances, including theatregoing, on the death of the Prince Consort in 1861, leaving her eldest son the most active playgoer in the family. But the Prince of Wales's had been restored by a performer, Marie Wilton, with a considerable following, who rapidly assembled a semi-permanent company, a permanent leading man, Squire Bancroft (whom she married), and a resident dramatist, T. W. Robertson, whose miniature cup-and-saucer comedies perfectly suited the modest dimensions of the Prince of Wales's and the refinement of its new clientele.

Delatorre never found a permanent company, a particular style, or a house dramatist. The opening attraction: *The Bronze Horse; or Harlequin the Sly Sultan, the Pert Princess, and the Fascinating Fays of Fairyland* (with Cave as the Sly Sultan) was clearly a traditional pantomime. The programmes then reverted to the 'stirring drama' rather than the 'sterling drama' he favoured. *Across the Continent: Scenes from New York Life and the Pacific Railway* on 2 March suggests the kind of panorama-play the Coburg had offered fifty years earlier, with the horizon suitably extended. Cave himself felt misled. 'After a quarter of a year, I began to think that I did not care for the yoke of servitude, so I gave it up and became once more my own master.'[37] Within six months Delatorre had allowed the name to revert to the Victoria Theatre, and before long advertisements in the programme for Choice Perfumery gave way to Ready-Made Men's Wear, and then significantly to the prices charged at the theatre's various bars. His stage-manager, Charles Burleigh, took over responsibility and many leading parts, with his wife. By July a return had been made to one or more changes of the main attraction during the week. Some of the devices employed to draw the public suggest desperate measures. *Othello* was followed by *The Twin Brothers; or The Butcher's Dog of Ghent*, with 'Dog Hector' featured, and on 5 November 1873 *Romeo and Juliet* was offered as a prelude to the spectacular historical drama *Guy Fawkes*. But it was Delatorre whose hopes and plans had been blown up. On 25 March 1874 the auctioneers Green and Son of St Swithin's Lane London EC offered the Theatre ('adapted for representation of High Class Entertainments or the More Stirring Drama') for sale, and it is from their Particulars and Conditions of Sale that knowledge of the actual alterations in 1871 derives.

Running down

From 1874 until the Theatre's closure in 1880 'High Class Entertainments' deferred to the 'Stirring Drama'. The next licensee, W. J. Frewer, petitioned for bankruptcy within months of taking over, one of his largest creditors being a gas engineer, Mr R. Vincent, which suggests complete insolvency. His successor, W. H. Swanborough, was an experienced manager whose family had run the Strand Theatre successfully for many years. But even he could not withstand the competition, not merely from neighbouring music halls but also from rival theatres. The Victoria's traditional competitors, Astley's and the Surrey, were themselves in difficulties, and the Surrey, which had been burnt down in 1866, was now struggling to reassert itself. The major threat to all three was from the new Elephant and Castle Theatre, opened in 1872 and even closer to the Victoria than its two older competitors.

In this situation successive managers opted for quantity rather than quality. Under Swanborough, for example, the Victoria was advertised as 'the People's Theatre' and 'the only theatre on Surreyside playing two Sensation Dramas at Christmas Nightly' (the plays in question being *The Angel of Midnight* and *The Ostler's Vision*, with 'A Troupe of Bedouin Arabs, 14 in No.' as a bonus). This was 'the More Stirring Drama' in excess. The only concession to 'High Class Entertainments' seems to have been on benefit nights, when the Victoria playgoer caught a glimpse of Shakespeare. On 2 May 1874, for example, with Tom Mead amongst the beneficiaries, the programme included:

> Act V of *Richard III*
> Act II of *Hamlet*
> Act I of *King Lear*
> Act V of *Macbeth*

with Act IV of *Richelieu* (not admittedly by Shakespeare but qualifying as a 'Sterling Drama'). Some of these items were evidently merely extracts: the programme names only Richard and Richmond, and later on Macbeth and Macduff. But the *Hamlet* scene involved six characters, *Richelieu* seven, and *Lear* ten, and however rudely staged, the scenes must have meant extra preparation. What did the Victoria audience make of such roughly amputated limbs? One explanation could be that actors of proven Shakespearean reputation were expected to give some taste of their wares, just as opera singers on the concert platform are still called on to perform arias from their repertoire. At any rate the New Cut clientele were sent home satisfied (or rather satiated) with *Black-Ey'd Susan* on top of all the Shakespeare.

With managers following and failing in quick succession, the Victoria might have closed its doors by the mid-1870s but for the ambitions of John Aubrey, licensee of the Elephant and Castle. His success there encouraged him to take over the Waterloo Road house as well, apparently as a show-case for the talents of his wife, Marie Henderson, who had been a supporting actress under Delatorre and had delusions of Shakespearean grandeur. Aubrey became lessee of the Victoria in March 1876, and at once mounted *Richard III* (with Miss Henderson as Queen Elizabeth) and *Macbeth* (with his lady as The Lady). The audience response seems to have been predictably muted. In the autumn he decided to try another tack and another member of the family: Lizzie Aubrey, 'la Petite Serio-Comic'. A 'Grand Opening Night' was announced for 13 November, with the house actually styled 'The Royal Victoria Palace Theatre of Varieties'. There were gymnasts, a comedian, a soubrette ('Susie Vaughan, the Surrey favourite'), and even a 'Grand Ballet, *Nero*', to support 'la Petite Serio-Comic'.

As the weekly bills were announced, an ominous note of regression crept in. For the week of 17 December the Elephant and Castle company were called on to fill in with *Black-Ey'd Susan*, and Variety offered only on the Saturday night. Christmas presented further problems: a full-scale pantomime would compete with Aubrey's other theatre, so the Victoria offered 'a Grand Shadow Pantomime by the Vernon Ballet Troupe' as well as 'Stead the Original Cure' and Ted Traynor, 'the Great Delineator of Negro Character'. The following week the Original Cure and the Great Delineator of Negro Character were combined with a version of *A Christmas Carol*. All to no avail: on 14 January 1877 the name 'Royal Victoria Theatre' was restored, and by 20 January 'three dramas nightly' were offered, the three on this occasion being *Obi; or Three-Finger'd Jack*; *Pauvrette*; and *The Surgeon of Paris*, making a panorama of nineteenth-century melodrama.

Even more significant was an announcement in the *Era* for 14 January 1877: 'This elegant theatre open for Travelling Companies. Share of certainty.' This brief statement indicated a major development in the theatrical pattern of the times. Improved railway transport was making possible the touring of complete productions, with full company, settings and costumes, instead of one or two well-known performers moving from one provincial theatre to another in a round of parts. Before long theatres were being built specifically for tours, some of those in the provinces being called Lyceum after London's leading playhouse. In the 1880s and 1890s the suburbs followed this example, though not of course the name. In Lambeth, for instance, the Princess of Wales's, Kennington, had its foundation stone laid by Henry Irving.

Run-down theatres like the Victoria in unsavoury streets like the New Cut were ill-equipped to compete. By 27 May Aubrey was forced to show his hand:

> Mr Aubrey begs to announce that he has engaged the following companies to appear up to Christmas:
>
> | June 11th | Mr J. H. Clynds and Company | 4 weeks |
> | July | Vacant | 5 weeks |
> | August 13th | Don Edgardo Colona and Company | 2 weeks |

August 27th	Mr Taylor's *Sirion* Company	2 weeks
September 10th	Harry Simms's *Nicholas Nickleby* Company	2 weeks
September 24th	Vacant	1 week
October 1st	Auguste Creamer's Company	2 weeks
October 15th	J. Jacobs and Company	4 weeks
November 12th to December 22nd	Vacant	5 weeks

Kate Raymond and O. B. Collins's *Waifs of New York* Company to follow

Managers of Good Companies are requested to send in dates 6 weeks after Christmas till 22nd December 1878.

To his fellow-professionals the salient points of Aubrey's announcement must have been the number of weeks still vacant, and the motley character of the companies he had engaged. It was out of the question for the Victoria to attract top-class tours, but the striking feature of those he had signed was their reluctance to disclose their repertoire. Only Mr Taylor and Harry Simms had actually committed themselves, and although the Bancrofts ten years earlier had established the precedent of touring a single play, most of Aubrey's visitors needed to change the bill constantly to draw an audience.

Worse was to come. Kate Raymond and her *Waifs of New York* did not follow, and for Christmas Miss Henderson found herself playing Waitanoe, the Indian Queen, in a 'Sensational Drama written specifically for this Theatre'. The New Year brought no new cheer. On 3 March 1878 'Mr Aubrey begs to inform Managers of good Travelling Companies that the Season commenced on February 4th', but the earliest date he had been able to fix was 22 April, when the *Stolen Fortunes* Company would be playing. Three weeks later, on 26 March, the Elephant and Castle Theatre was totally destroyed by fire. The Aubreys' future was threatened, and after providing house-room for the homeless Elephant and Castle company for a few weeks, the Victoria closed, nominally 'for renovation and decoration', in fact because John Aubrey was surrendering the lease.

In this situation Joseph Cave, who had been back at his old haunt, the Marylebone, since parting company with Delatorre six years earlier, decided to renew his association with the Victoria. He had recently taken a partner, Albert West, and there was evidently a suggestion that they run the two theatres in tandem. In July 1879, for example, Cave (born in Kent in 1823) played Boucicault's 'broth of a boy' Conn the Shaughraun at the Victoria for four weeks, and then took the production north of the River to the Marylebone. But generally he maintained a separate if extraordinarily diverse programme at the Victoria: an early attraction, Miss Sophie Miles, 'the great English tragedienne', played Hamlet, Leah the Forsaken, Lucrezia Borgia and Jane Shore on successive evenings, to be followed the very next night by *Uncle Tom's Cabin*. This offered 'Nigger Hymns, Banjo Soloists, and Plantation Dances', and proved very much more to the New Cut's taste, running for eight weeks and being revived the following year. Cave seems to have preferred old favourites to new fare: in April 1879 he offered *Don Giovanni in London*, 'revived with the same care as when originally produced at Drury Lane over fifty years ago', but what suited Regency rakes when Madame Vestris played Don Giovanni must have left the coarser appetites of the Vic audience unsatisfied.

By the summer of that year Cave was growing reckless. For his benefit on 3 July he chose *The Corsican Brothers* with guest artistes, including 'the Great Macdermott', the music hall *lion comique* who in the previous year had proclaimed:

> We don't want to fight, but by Jingo! if we do,
> We've got the ships, we've got the men, we've got the money too!

playing Chateau-Renaud, the villain. At Christmas 1879 the pantomime was *Bluff King Hal; or Harlequin Herne the Hunter and the Miller of Dee*, with Cave more suitably cast as Bluff King Hal than Conn the Shaughraun. But he was evidently finding the whole enterprise unrewarding. In his Memoirs he covers in some detail his earlier management from 1867 to 1871, but makes no mention whatsoever of this second term of office. He must have welcomed a bid to take over the lease, however unexpected the quarter. For early in 1880 he received an approach from 'a Committee of Gentlemen, interested' according to the *Era*, in using the Theatre 'for other purposes'.[38]

As one door closes

In 1879, when Joseph Cave was struggling to reimpose his authority on the Royal Victoria, a very different personality was imposing her authority a quarter of a mile away. Surrey Lodge, at the junction of the Lambeth and Kennington Roads, was one of the few large houses with a garden in the area. Its owner, a local JP, had just put it up for sale. An indomitable worker for improving the housing of the poor found the backing to set up the South London Dwellings Company, bought the house and grounds, and proceeded to build a quadrangle of three-storey flats on the site and let them at a modest rental to approved tenants. Shortly afterwards she and two of her sisters moved to part of the development, 5 and 6 Morton Place. She was Emma Cons, and the South London Dwellings Company provided the momentum for the 'Committee of Gentlemen' who were negotiating in the spring of 1880 for the lease of the Royal Victoria.

Emma Cons, then aged forty-three, came from a family of German immigrants (originally Konss) who had established themselves in London at the end of the eighteenth century as cabinet-makers, more particularly piano-manufacturers.[39] They were not wealthy, and Emma had, against considerable opposition from male workers, established herself as a craftsman in stained glass. But she had the gift of making friends with equally high principles and considerably higher incomes: notably the Martineau family (Caroline was an intimate and loyal supporter) and the Hills (Octavia was one of her oldest friends). With their help she was able in the 1870s to buy, refurbish and let to working-class families tenements in North London, particularly the Paddington, Marylebone and Drury Lane districts. It was this task that reinforced her lifelong commitment to temperance. Liquor, she believed, was the dominant cause of much working-class misery and degradation, and the liquor-sellers, including those in music halls and other places of entertainment, amongst the worst perpetrators of this scourge.

Her sentiments concurred with those of other reformers who sought to provide the working man with an alternative source of refreshment and relaxation: the temperance tavern. Emma persuaded two highly connected associates, the Duke of Westminster and Lord Mount Temple, to form with her the Coffee Tavern Company, which helped to swell a total of fifty-six such companies by 1880, and which stimulated such commercial enterprises as the Lockhart and Aereated Bread Company chains. These competed effectively with the public houses and bars, but had nothing to offer as a counter-attraction to the music hall. It was for this reason that she set up in 1879 the Coffee Music Hall Company 'to provide for the working and lower middle classes recreation such as the music hall offers, without the existing attendant moral and social disadvantages'.[40]

Whether the original idea was hers is open to doubt. There seems to have been little or no theatrical interest in her life before 1880 (although of course she had considerable artistic gifts). Credit for suggesting the

Victoria as the base for the enterprise was claimed by a very different kind of impresario: John Hollingshead, builder of the Gaiety Theatre and torchbearer for the sacred lamp of burlesque. At first glance he seems an improbable begetter of a Coffee Music Hall, but his interests were wider than his reputation for gaiety and glitter might suggest. His theatre was also the home of Shakespearean and 'old comedy' productions, he was particularly proud of the rehabilitation he had effected at the Alhambra during his management there in the 1860s, and as a journalist before becoming theatre manager he had seen at first hand the degrading conditions obtaining in the New Cut area, to which he had devoted a section of his book *Ragged London in 1861*.

Unfortunately his association with the Coffee Music Hall project became more liability than asset. In his own words: 'Eventually I found that my connection with the Gaiety Theatre was not a good and safe qualification for me to have a leading part in carrying out my idea.'[41] The initiative therefore passed to the certainly inexperienced and perhaps apprehensive Emma Cons. At least the location of the project would meet with her approval. Since she was converting the Surrey Lodge estate to working-class tenements at the same time, she had ample first-hand evidence of the wretched conditions prevailing in the New Cut. She knew that the Victoria was struggling to survive, and that the lease might be available. She persuaded her supporters to enter into negotiations for it. The various stages of her campaign are not without significance: first housing, then refreshment, then recreation. Entertainment was to remain the last (and therefore least) of her passions. The Victoria was to be acquired as a building, not as a theatre.

The original lease of ninety years dated from 1808 and had been acquired by Francis Glossop on his son's behalf in 1817. Though subject to various annuities which the improvident Joseph had contracted to pay during his period of management, it still remained in the hands of the Glossops, who had presumably approved if not helped to fund the interior reconstruction of 1871. In 1880 the family were represented by Francis Henry Newland Glossop, Squire of Silver Hall, Isleworth. By an agreement finalised on 6 January 1881 Glossop sublet the Theatre to the Coffee Music Halls Company at a rent of £950 p.a., renewable annually, for a maximum term of seventeen years.[42] Meanwhile some £3,000 of the Company's modest resources were committed to making alterations.[43] The architect responsible was Elijah Hooley, not a theatre man but a 'specialist in non-conformist ecclestiastic and scholastic architecture',[44] and his main task was to transform the foyer into a coffee tavern.

Joseph Cave's reaction to this development seems to have been one of relief. His interest in the Victoria had clearly waned, since he passed over the whole episode when writing his memoirs. The last night was fixed for 12 June 1880, and though he advertised a 'great Victoria Festival' for the occasion (with a programme made up of *The Mountain Devil*; *The Iron Clasp*; and *Sweeney Todd*, all strong rather than 'sterling' dramas), the *Era* sadly notes: 'Mr Cave did not address the house', and refers to 'a demonstrative rather than appreciative audience; the noise causing the performance to be one of dumb-show'. What had become of the stern authority Cave had earlier exercised?

In fact the *Era* account ends: '"Queen Victoria's Own Theayter" closed without even "God Save the Queen" being sung. It is to be reopened as what a Gentleman present called "A Temperance Sing-Song".'[45] But another playgoer present – no Gentleman, but conscious of the momentous occasion – did contribute a valediction. Sitting in the Gallery, he turned to his companion and said: 'The poor old Wick! Pass us the 'arf and 'arf, 'Arry.'[46]

His 'arf and 'arf was the last drink to be served officially at the Old Wick for more than half a century.

4

Seeking improvement

1880–1914

In expanding their activities from the provision of cheap, decent accommodation and refreshment to the provision of cheap, decent entertainment Emma Cons and her helpers in the Coffee Music Hall Association were entering uncharted and, for them, hazardous waters. While they could cite the success of several Temperance Music Halls in the North of England as a precedent, they were themselves wholly inexperienced in the provision of entertainment of any kind. Indeed one may question whether the provision of any sort of stage entertainment was really the prime motive behind the Association, rather than a sweetener to the temperance pill which, for sincere and substantial reasons, they sought to administer to the working classes of Lambeth and Southwark. The fact that the Coffee Music Hall Association was dissolved within four years of its foundation without attempting to open any further Halls suggests a lack of drive, or at least unity of purpose, amongst its generous but unqualified sponsors. The miracle is, not that it foundered so soon but that during its brief existence it succeeded in establishing one unique and priceless institution: the new Old Vic.

What was actually presented on the stage of the Old Vic during the first twenty-five years of Emma Cons's regime is often difficult and sometimes impossible to establish. Few printed programmes still exist, and may not have been regularly provided, while the surviving records of the Theatre itself are sadly depleted. Curiously enough the earliest years are better documented than the decades which followed. A decision was evidently taken to advertise the Vic's programme at regular (though not weekly) intervals in the *Era*, and from these advertisements a skeleton schedule can be established. It is clear that the Association originally intended the Theatre to be a full-time music hall, open six nights a week, with a resident company, varied by the occasional special engagement. Also, although the terms of a music hall licence (as opposed to a theatre licence) imposed major restrictions on the permitted bill of fare, every effort was made to offer a wide range of turns. Besides the predictable ballad-vocalists, acrobats and 'serio-comic effusions', could be found a 'lightning cartoonist', the 'Berisor Troupe of Roman Gladiators', and even 'Miss Mattie Mitchell's Living Statuary'. The only fundamental difference between the Royal Victoria Coffee Music Hall and the many other music halls competing for the South London audience was the Vic's refusal to permit alcoholic refreshment being served or consumed on the premises.

No amount of programming, however, could conceal the unpalatable truth that the undertaking, as originally planned, was doomed to failure. In particular the choice of a transpontine theatre with a reputation for disorderly conduct of various kinds in which to stage temperance music hall was rash to the point of recklessness. How the theatrical profession viewed the attempt can best be illustrated from its own organ, the *Era*, which adopted a sceptical attitude to the project from the very start.

> The adoption of the term [Temperance Music Hall] seems to suggest that in the opinion of the adopters other Music Halls are intemperate . . .

wrote their first night critic, and continuing in the same vein;

> We heard it whispered that the stage-management is entrusted to a clergyman, and that propriety is always at hand to regulate the length of the skirts of the serio-comic ladies.[1]

Another periodical with a theatrical and sporting bias, the *Age*, viewed the Association's teething troubles with ill-concealed glee. On 21 April their columnist, 'The Boy Next Door', confided:

> At the Victoria Palace Temperance Music Hall, coffee and comic singing don't seem to work well together. Whether it is the fault of the singing (which is none of the best) or the coffee (which is worse), I can't pretend to say, at any rate, I hear that the establishment is soon to close down.

Clearly the theatrical profession watched the undertaking with a smile which could easily turn to a sneer.

Of course there were cross-currents flowing behind all this. The *Era* was the trade paper not only of the theatrical profession but also of the licensed victualling trade, which did not take kindly to the closing down of a profitable outlet in the Waterloo Road. The critic already quoted went on to report:

Refreshment is to be had in the shape of tea, coffee, aerated waters, bread and butter, jam, ham, beef and chops, steaks etc. etc., and there is no prohibition against tobacco. The bill of fare announced the supply of cold ham and of beef at the rates of 2d., 4d., and 6d. We made bold to ask for a supply at 2d., but the caterer evidently though we were joking, and answered our demand by informing us that he had never been asked for such a quantity, and that he though 2 pennyworth would have to take the form of a sandwich.

It was not merely the brewers and distillers who lost by this insistence on strict teetotalism at the new Old Vic. Many if not most music halls depended for their survival on the management's share of the bar takings, above all the sale of liquor, and this lucrative form of subsidy was renounced by Emma Cons and her successors for well over fifty years. It was not until the 1930s that alcohol was available to Old Vic patrons within the Theatre itself.

Teething troubles

Thus the Coffee Music Hall, launched with pride at a matinee on Boxing Day 1880 (in fact December 27, since December 26 was a Sunday), to an audience which included the six-year-old Lilian Baylis, with her mother Elizabeth, née Cons, amongst the volunteer attendants, soon ran into difficulties. Except on Saturday nights audiences were decidedly sparse. By February 26 the *Era* was reporting with ill-concealed glee:

The good people who think that nothing stronger than ginger beer or coffee should go with music and other entertainment and that lemonade or tea is quite sufficient for the 'wetting of the whistle' of those who consume the 'fragrant weed', do not appear to be meeting with overwhelming patronage . . .

or as Lilian Baylis was later to put it:

It must not be imagined that the movement to 'elevate the masses' met with immediate success; on the contrary, the masses showed plainly enough that they did not much want to be elevated.[2]

Changes were made. The original manager, W. J. Bullock, whose name had been put forward by his former employer, Carl Rosa, was replaced by one Alfred Young, and with the new manager there appeared new artistes, including 'Dusoni's Troupe of Performing Dogs, Monkeys and Goats' and 'Pasha Rekklan on the Invisible Wire'. But all was to no avail; even the Performing Goats failed to attract; and by May 14 the *Era* carried the advertisement:

ROYAL VICTORIA HALL AND COFFEE TAVERN: to be let.

The original enterprise, launched with such good intentions and great expectations, had lasted less than five months.

Behind the scenes there were doubtless anxious discussions and emergency meetings. The greater part of the funds raised had been used on refurbishing the theatre (£3,000) and a commitment to the lease at £950 a year for eighteen years. By the summer of 1881 the Coffee Music Hall Association was overdrawn at the bank to the tune of £2,800,[3] and several of its supporters were ready to admit defeat. But Emma Cons was not of their number, and nor were some of her closest friends, including the Martineau family and the distinguished politician William Cowper-Temple (by now Lord Mount-Temple). Between them they found the money to reopen the Hall in October 1881 under a manager more suited to their needs: William Poel. This twenty-nine-year-old enthusiast for 'authentic' staging of Shakespeare had begun to make his mark by playing Hamlet in the First Quarto text at St George's Hall in April of that year. While such an achievement can hardly have singled him out for the post of manager at a Temperance Music Hall, his dedication to 'purified' drama and to the theatre as a means of instruction and improvement, rather than mere diversion, may have caught Emma Cons's eye. Their actual meeting, however, seems to have been pure coincidence. In what was apparently his only account of his time at the Vic, an article in the *Old Vic Magazine* for December 1930, Poel suggested that he was (mistakenly) directed to Surrey Lodge when reponding to an appeal by 'a lady who was organising a special charity performance in which I was to take part' – presumably in the summer of 1881. Shown into Miss Cons's presence, he obviously struck her as a gift from the gods in her desperate search for a manager at the Vic. He was certainly a change from the managers who had preceded him in quick succession, while for Poel in return the post of manager of a Coffee Music Hall marked a complete change from his previous job as director of the Bijou Theatre, Rosherville Gardens, Gravesend.

The new broom

Poel's biographer, Robert Speaight, claims that during his two years at the Old Vic he 'reduced the expenses of management, raised the tone of the entertainments, and attracted audiences to the Hall'.[4] Certainly the programmes took on a different aspect from the original concept. There was a marked emphasis on spectacle, offered in the form of panoramas and *tableux vivants*, such as 'The Burial of Sir John Moore' (11 March 1883) and 'The Bombardment of Alexandria' (31 March 1883). There was even a 'Grand Military Spectacle', *The Girdle Duellists*, devised by Poel himself for the Christmas attraction in 1882, 'with new Scenery, Soldiers and Chorus numbering 200 performers', which was billed as 'the most successful spectacle ever produced in South London'.[5] Equally notable was the introduction of 'pantomimes' and 'musical entertainments' such as *The Country Fair* (December 1881) and *Dame Trot and Her Comical Cat* (September 1882), though how elaborate such offerings were must remain problematic. To the modern mind their presentation seems incompatible with the terms of a music hall licence, and essentially the preserve of a theatre equipped with a full dramatic licence; but the test of what did and did not constitute drama seems to have been the continuity of the story, not the scale of the spectacle.

In any case the most important element in the programme during Poel's time as manager of the Old Vic was not its music hall evenings but its 'ballad concerts'. As early as April 1881 the *Illustrated London News* had reported that 'the hard-working enthusiastic dwellers in the New Cut crowd the place to suffocation to hear Sir Julius Benedict play and Miss de Fontblanque sing'. A less charitable account is given by the reporter for the *Age* already cited:

> I dropped in for a few minutes on Thursday evening, and found Madame Liebhart in command. The ballads were fairly well appreciated, but it was easy to detect on the part of some of the nobility of the New Cut an ill-repressed desire to shout 'Hornpipe!' at intervals.

Two years later George Bernard Shaw attended one of the Vic's concerts in his capacity as a free-lance music critic, and reported in the *Musical Review*:

> If the whole of them [the audience, estimated at 1,500] had been skilled musicians, the verdict on each item could not have been more discriminating . . .

proceeding to contrast the apathetic reception of 'a number of weak songs weakly interpreted' with the encore given to Beethoven's Violin Romance in G *op.* 40 (*Musical Review* 17 March 1883). Many years later he claimed to have participated as a pianist in a concert performance of extracts from *Faust* and *Trovatore*, and on a separate occasion to have contributed 'noises off' in the 'Miserere' of the latter work:

> I was such a failure that the *prima donna* struck at rehearsal and silenced me; but what could do I do with a length of gaspipe on a string and an old poker to hit it with?[6]

Presumably these concerts were hastily arranged when it became clear that a nightly music hall bill had no prospect of paying its way, but whatever their derivation, they soon became a fixture on Thursday nights, and were to become a foundation stone of the Old Vic's work. Although they gradually developed into operatic recitals and thence into fully staged performances, they continued to draw the Thursday night audiences until the opera company finally quitted the Old Vic for Sadler's Wells more than fifty years later. Their immediate success was due at least in part to the generosity of the performers, who either gave their services or accepted much reduced fees.

In the early days the arrangements for a concert were often handed over to an outside organisation or individual. Some of the earliest programmes, in May and June 1881, were given by 'the Cecilia Choir', and 'Dr Verinder's Choir', while titled amateur performers such as Lady Simeon added a touch of style. In fact the management was more than glad to let the Hall for a worthy cause. An *Era* advertisement (1 October 1881) at the very start of Poel's term of office announced:

> This fine hall to let (Mondays, Thursdays and Saturdays excepted) for Entertainments complete in themselves. Also use of large Stage during the day for Rehearsals, Meetings, Classes etc.

and a later entry cites the hiring rates as

> Tuesdays and Wednesdays £7 7s. od., Fridays £6 6s. od., including Gas, Attendants, Scenemen, and Full Orchestral Band (20 May 1882)

Even these modest terms do not seem to have attracted many takers, and failing outside applicants a cheap alternative use of the Hall when not required for Variety or Ballad Concerts began to take shape during Poel's time. This took the form of 'Penny Readings', lectures, and 'Temperance Nights', at first combined into a single evening but before long separated and assuming a regular pattern, Tuesdays being earmarked for the lectures and Fridays for the Temperance Nights. The lectures rapidly established their subject-matter as science and travel, popularly treated. 'Telegrams and How They Come' (22 September 1882) and 'Extinct Animals' (5 October 1882), both given by William

Lane Carpenter FCS, were two of the earliest titles in a series from which much of the educational work of Morley College was later to spring.

For Poel, however, it was the dramatic potential of the enterprise which offered its greatest attraction, and it seems plausible to detect his influence behind the unprecedented step of offering on 1 June 1882 a 'Grand Shakespeare Night', consisting of Glees and Songs selected from Shakespeare's Plays. Locke's Music from *Macbeth* was sung by a 'Select Choir, accompanied by a Full Orchestral Band', and even more to his taste, 'Scenes from the Third and Fifth Acts of *Othello* will be given in Costume. Othello: Mr Albert Alberg; Iago: Mr Charles Sennett; Desdemona: Miss Muriel Campbell; Emilia: Madame Carlotta Leclercq'. Such a departure from the Vic's 'non-theatrical' policy is certainly surprising. At least three of the performers had some standing in the legitimate theatre, Alberg being a well-known Danish actor, Charles Sennett an even better-known local performer, and Carlotta Leclercq an actress whose career extended right back to the 'archaeological' productions of Charles Kean at the Princess's in the 1850s. The *Annual Report* for 1881–2 also claims that 'single scenes from *Hamlet* and *The Hunchback* have been given'.

Again it may be due to Poel that the 'Ballad Recitals' began to pay some attention to the operatic repertoire. On 5 June 1882, for example, the programme offered 'Scenes from the Italian Opera, sung in English under the direction of Signor Garcia', and on 7 June 1883 there was a 'Grand Operatic Concert under the direction of Signor Gilardoni' which took the form of 'Selections in Costume from Beethoven's *Fidelio*'. But undoubtedly the major musical occasion during Poel's period of management was the evening of 9 February 1882 when the Prince and Princess of Wales gave their patronage to a 'special Irish night' at the Vic. A few months earlier Princess Frederica of Hanover (a cousin of the future Edward VII) had paid two visits, at the earlier of which Lilian Baylis, now seven, carried out her first 'official' duty by presenting a bouquet.[7] Since the last Royal visit to this Theatre had been undertaken in 1833, almost fifty years earlier, the new directorate could feel a real sense of achievement on these gala occasions.

Nevertheless the public as a whole stayed away. By the autumn of 1883 the financial situation looked grave, and a rift in the Committee between those who favoured more entertainment and those who wanted more education, both scientific and temperance, added to the difficulties. Perhaps it was these squabbles which induced Poel to look elsewhere; at any rate he resigned in December 1883, to become stage-manager for

Frank Benson's happy-go-lucky company of touring Shakespeareans. Miss Cons, growing impatient with this rapid turnover of managers, took up the reins herself, but even more decisive steps were needed if the Hall was not to stagger from one crisis to another. The Coffee Music Hall Association had clearly lost confidence in its cause. A smaller body, exclusively concerned with the Victoria Hall, might yet save the day, but meanwhile there were debts to be settled and overdrafts to be cleared. Miss Cons took up her pen once more, and within a few months of Poel's departure had secured a gift of £1,000 from a close associate, Ethel Everest, and another £1,000 from Samuel Morley, industrialist, MP and reformer.[8] By an agreement dated 20 June 1884 Emma Cons on behalf of the Trustees of the Hall purchased the remainder of the lease from F. H. N. Glossop for £4,000. The Coffee Music Hall Association then tactfully dissolved itself, and a new Council was formed with a small working committee under Samuel Morley which proceeded to take major decisions. The stresses and set-backs of the early years would recur, but now Emma Cons had a valuable new ally beside her and valuable experience to draw on.

On trial

Poel's departure and the financial difficulties in which the Hall found itself forced Emma Cons to take on the responsibilities of manager herself. No doubt the heavy losses sustained accounted in part for dropping advertisements from the *Era*, but there may also have been the feeling that such publicity associated the Hall too closely with the theatrical and – even more damaging – licensed victualling interests which that publication served. Certainly Samuel Morley, who figured increasingly prominently in the Vic's fortunes during the years 1884–6, was strictly opposed to the theatre, and had to be coaxed into attending (and, it should be said, enjoying) the Variety performances. His favourite turn, so Miss Cons informed his biographer, was that of a conjurer who 'cleverly pretended to cut off a boy's head and put it on again'. So delighted was Morley with this particular act that, when called away during the evening bill, he begged her 'not to have the boy's head cut off until he came back to see it'.[9]

Even if Emma Cons was tempted to repeat some of Poel's quasi-theatrical innovations, such ideas received a rude set-back at Christmas 1885, resulting in the highly respectable and respected manageress being sued for a breach of the peace. As a seasonal attraction

Miss Cons and her assistant manager Frederick Phillips had contracted with an entrepreneur David Batchelor to mount an entertainment under the title: *King He's A Bore; The Pride of His Mama*, which they described as a pantomime. It was, even by the standards of that amorphous genre, a very odd affair. Only one character, Prince Amoroso (played by an actress with the unlikely name of Ada Clarisse), spoke. There was no connected story, and though there was singing and dancing mingled with acrobatic turns and even a performing donkey, the songs introduced 'had nothing to do with what she [Ada Clarisse] spoke'. Nevertheless this gallimaufry roused the jealousy of Joseph Cave, now manager of the Elephant and Castle, who plotted with Arthur Ring, a licensed victualler, to bring a prosecution against Miss Cons for infringing her music hall licence. Two other interested parties, Bernard Isaacson, who had been Cave's Musical Director at the Vic, and an actor, John Findley, lent their weight to the attack. The case was heard at Southwark Police Court on 3 January 1886, before the magistrate Mr Slade, and though Phillips and Batchelor seem to have spared Miss Cons the humiliation of actually appearing in court, it was on her that the magistrate imposed a 'nominal penalty' of half a crown and a guinea costs.[10] The price paid may seem trivial, but as the lady pointed out, it resulted in the cancellation of the pantomime with heavy financial loss.[11]

Perhaps the most mysterious aspect of a curious episode is Cave's and his colleagues' reason for taking action against this particular entertainment. After all, several of Poel's programmes seem at first glance to have come much closer to drama than the mulish breed described in the court proceedings. There was surely a far greater theatrical content to *The Country Fair*, *Our Mary Anne*, *Dame Trot and Her Comic Cat*, and above all the 'Grand Shakespeare Night', with its lengthy extracts from *Othello*, than poor Prince Amoroso's adventures. Can the object of Cave's spleen have been, not *King He's A Bore* but increasing support for the Hall itself? Until the end of 1885 its fortunes were to say the least chequered. Managers of rival establishments, like the Elephant and Castle, could reassure themselves that Miss Cons's enterprise was doomed to fail, as it had so nearly done on at least two occasions. But with the wealth and influence of such as Samuel Morley behind it, the corner seemed to have been turned. Christmas 1885 was therefore the strategic moment to ensure that at least the Hall's resurgent fortunes would not encompass a theatrical renaissance.

In this calculation the prosecuting party was proved correct. The fine imposed may have been modest, but the humiliation of being sued was grievous to one of Miss Cons's temperament. Any chance that she might be tempted to emulate William Poel's quasi-dramatic experiments was immediately and irreversibly rejected. While impetus was undoubtedly added to the Hall's musical and nascent operatic endeavours, no hint of a real play would enter Miss Cons's mind from that bleak moment in Southwark Magistrates' Court in January 1886 until her death in July 1912. Less than six months later her niece obtained a dramatic licence for the Vic.

Principles and practices

So Miss Cons turned her back on pantomime and concentrated on temperance music hall. In this genre the tone had been firmly set during Poel's regime, and such evidence as has survived indicates that his successor stuck to the established order of things. A decision was evidently made to advertise occasionally in the local paper, the *South London Press* (filling the gap left by withdrawing all billing from the *Era*), and emphasis seems to have been placed squarely on comedy. The first bill to be so advertised included: 'Knockabout Nigger Funniosities', and 'Victor Verran, Great Character Comedian, and his Excruciating Funny Eccentricities. You MUST laugh at him.' Prices ranged from 3d. (Gallery) to 1/- (Stalls), with boxes at 6/-, 10/- and 21/-, and an interesting footnote adds: 'Her Majesty's Soldiers, Sailors, Postmen, and Firemen in uniform admitted at half price to all parts.'[12]

No doubt men in uniform could be relied on not to give trouble, but there seems to have been an occasional throwback to the rowdiness of the Good Old/Bad Old Days, and a legend survives of the diminutive Emma (in her bonnet?) marching up to the Gallery and physically expelling the offenders. Like all the best legends this defies documentation, but what can be attested is the strict control Miss Cons exercised over her stage. In December 1887, for instance, the Hall succeeded in signing up Charles Coburn ('The Man Who Broke The Bank At Monte Carlo') for six performances at a fee of £10: something of a *coup* – the Vic could not normally attract top-billing artistes. There were, however, no exceptions to the House Rules. Coburn had to subscribe to the dictate that

> No Artiste shall, by inference, direct or indirect, innuendo, or by attitudes or by-play, or by the words of any dialogue or song, introduce anything obscene, or demoralising in idea or otherwise, or

make any jocular allusion to Religious Subjects. A violation of this Rule will be deemed a sufficient reason for the cancelling of this agreement forthwith, and without any notice whatever.[13]

He duly subscribed, the contract being counter-signed by 'Lizzie Cons' (i.e. Elizabeth Baylis, Lilian's mother and Emmie's sister, using her maiden name and presumably acting as a go-between).

That the programmes on Monday and Saturday nights were clean as a whistle is self-evident. Whether they were also entertaining except at an elementary level is open to question. A hostile witness can be found, surprisingly enough, in the young Beatrice Webb, at this time beginning her studies of social conditions and economic hardship amongst London's working classes. On 8 November 1885 (a month before the production of the ill-fated *King He's A Bore*) she

> went with two fellow-workers to the Vic, managed by that grand woman, Miss Cons. To me a dreary performance, sinking to the level of the audience, while omitting the dash of coarseness, irreverence, and low humour which give the spice and the reality to such entertainments. To my mind the devil is preferable, and in every way more wholesome, than a shapeless mediocrity.

It should of course be emphasised that neither Beatrice Webb nor her two fellow-workers were remotely like the audience for which the Vic was catering. ('Sinking to the level of the audience' is a revealing phrase. Others might have written: 'Bravely exhorting the audience to improve itself'.) Indeed her whole pen portrait of Emma Cons at this period is full of contradictions: 'Not a lady by birth, with the face and manner of a distinguished woman, almost a ruler of men . . . very little culture or interest outside the sphere of her own action . . . All her energy devoted to the practical side of the work. No desire to solve the general questions of the hour.' Miss Potter (as Beatrice Webb then was) had the decency to add: 'I felt ashamed of the way I cross-questioned her.'[14]

Certainly Miss Cons herself had no doubts about the change for the better in the audience's behaviour and even appearance. As early as 1882 she noted in her *Annual Report* for that year:

> The girls known on the Surreyside as the 'Madame Blackfriars type' – girls with white aprons, mysteriously propped up hats and ridiculous fringes on their foreheads – instead of lolling on their sweethearts' shoulders and absorbing spirits and suggestions as is their wont too often at the music hall here sit quiet and attentive.

Although Mondays and Saturdays were now firmly established as 'Variety Nights', variety turns were also introduced into the Temperance Meetings on Fridays to sweeten the abstainers' pill. How these were selected is a tantalising but profitless question. Did the teetotallers respond more readily to acrobats? slapstick comedy? amusing (but impeccably sober) monologues? tuneful temperance ditties? An endless but inevitably frustrating field of speculation. Certain clear facts about these Friday night gatherings, however, can be established. For one thing admission to the Gallery was 'free to Teetotallers showing their cards' (paying participants were asked anything from 1d. to 1/-). For another the strictly crusading aspect was not restricted to prayer, preaching and hymns. There was often a brass band and sometimes what might be described as a 'Special Event' or even 'Stunt'. Thus in the first week of March 1884 a temperance campaigner, Edward Payson Weston, undertook what was billed as 'the Great Temperance Tour of 5,000 Miles' by walking fifty miles every day for 100 days ('Sundays of course excepted'). He had reached the creditable total of 4,700 miles, and completed his target during the next week (10–15 March), finishing at the Vic each night and capping his day's achievement with a temperance talk entitled 'Struggling'.[15]

Musical moments

Meanwhile the Thursday evening concerts, certainly the most successful feature of the Coffee Music Hall regime, began to develop their much loved character. That they were from the start as much 'Ballad Concerts' as orchestral performances is a pointer to this development. It was above all the songs and singers who commended themselves to the Victoria supporters, but if the Thursday audience was drawn from the same streets and the same strata of Lambeth society as the music hall public, it was from those inhabitants who craved something finer than the variety patrons and richer than the teetotallers. While ballads of the drawing-room kind figure regularly in the bills, it was increasingly the operatic repertoire that made the strongest appeal. Was there something about the lure of these 'vocal gems' that satisfied in simple Lambeth hearts the need for colour, emotion, excitement, which 'blood-and-thunder' drama had provided before 1881? After all, many of the operas from which these selections were taken began life as melodrama before becoming opera.

It is customary to date from the early 1890s the 'tableaux' which became standard Vic practice. Even Richard Findlater, wise and well read, records their first appearance as in 1889.[16] But in some (admittedly primitive) form they go back almost to the opening of the Hall. There were 'scenes from the Italian opera, sung in English' in June 1882, and a selection in costume from *Fidelio* in June 1883, which must have included posing and gesture. There would have been no point in putting on doublet and hose to stand to attention all evening like the tenor in a chapel account of *The Messiah*. Findlater also maintained that 'it was not until the spring of 1894 that a chorus was added to the opera', but this can only hold good if a professional chorus is meant. As has been seen, amateur choirs were the mainstay of the Thursday concerts from the very beginning, and it is inconceivable that they were not drawn into the operatic programmes. How could the 'Miserere' from *Trovatore* in which Shaw represented the Angelus have been performed without a chorus?

What is much more difficult to pin down is the precise nature of the 'tableaux'. Evidently both their name and nature derived from Emma Cons's and her supporters' fear of further offending the authorities over the music hall licence they had been granted. Such published programmes as survive underline the lengths to which the management would go to avoid further infringement. For *Fra Diavolo* in May 1891 a distinction is made between the principals 'who will sing the music of Lord Allcash, Zerlina' and others, and the small-part mute performers, like 'Mr Smith, who will take Matteo, the innkeeper, in the Tableaux'.[17] This seems to suggest that the singers did not appear in the tableaux, but obviously such a convention would be untenable in any meaningful performance. When Edward J. Dent wrote his *A Theatre for Everybody* in 1945 he quoted from a programme of *Il Trovatore* in 1892 which demonstrates this:

> The management requests the kind of indulgence of the audience during the unavoidable pauses which they will endeavour to make as short as possible, but the artistes require time between the songs and tableaux to get behind the scenes and group themselves. Some of the tableaux also require considerable change of dress and scenery.[18]

This clearly indicates that the singers also appeared in the tableaux. More often, however, the evidence of the programmes, scarce as they are, is inconclusive. That for *Pagliacci* in May 1899 includes such elaborate information as the following:

> TABLEAU 5: Tonio, overhearing them, in jealous rage, fetches Canio
> who arrives just in time to hear the parting words between Nedda and
> Silvio.[19]

These particulars define a situation far too complex to be presented in
one static *tableau vivant*. In this instance either the programme was using
the term tableau to mean 'scene', and describing to the audience events
they would hear about but not witness, or the tableau introduced
movement, including exits and entrances. The first explanation clearly
applies to this extract from the programme of a 'Costume Recital' of
Rigoletto in February 1900:

> TABLEAU 8: Rigoletto in anticipation of his revenge comes to the
> Bravo's house to receive the body of the Duke, but instead is given
> that of his daughter which, wrapped in a sack, he is about to throw into
> the river, when he hears the voice of the Duke singing – astounded, he
> opens the sack, and is horrified at beholding the body of his beloved
> child.[20]

Perhaps the only safe conclusion to be reached on the whole tangled
topic is that the handling of the tableaux was at once improvised and
evolving. Each opera presented its own problems and found its own
solutions – so long as the cherished licence was not put at risk.

Lecture programme

If the Thursday night concerts, alternating in the 1890s with regular
opera 'recitals', were the Hall's most prestigious and popular attractions
the Tuesday night lectures were next in importance, above all for what
would grow out of them. They fitted happily into the Hall's purpose of
improving the standards of New Cut life, and it was after a lecture on
'Electricity' by William Lant Carpenter, who had inaugurated the whole
series in 1882, two years earlier, that the three legendary working men in
the audience made their historical intervention, pointing out that

> the lectures were wonderful things but that being only weekly and on
> different subjects by different speakers they left a host of important
> points unanswered. In short, the young men felt the need not only for
> individual talks of this kind, but also for more systematic instruction.
> Could Miss Cons not supply this by starting regular scientific classes in
> the evenings?[21]

Miss Cons could and did, helped from 1885 by the Science and Art
Department at South Kensington (out of which the Education

Department was to grow). This gave some sort of official imprimatur to the lectures themselves, and the request that they should be 'science' lectures was answered. The instruction – as opposed to the information – the Hall increasingly offered was on the sciences rather than the humanities, or even on technical subjects, which were left to the neighbouring Polytechnics now beginning to emerge. The scientific character of the work appealed to Caroline Martineau, who from an early point took charge, a devolution of Miss Cons's responsibilities which was to lead to her friend's assumption of the post of Principal of the future Morley College.

Perhaps even more seminal than the lectures themselves was the use in the mid-1880s of the backstage accommodation for club activities of various kinds, including a gymnasium under the stage (earlier peopled by the clowns and acrobats of the pantomimes). It was these activities which transformed the Hall from a locale for lectures (however lofty in intention) into an institution with an identity of its own. There is a peculiarly dramatic irony about the use of the saloon at Dress Circle level (subject of so much heart-searching during the rebuilding of 1871) as a working-men's meeting-place. Undoubtedly the opening up of the Hall's ancillary space for these social purposes promoted the feelings of pride and proprietary interest expressed by the early students who added to their names the initials OVS (Old Vic Student) or, in due course, OVSMMC (Old Vic Student, Morley Memorial College).[22]

The premature death in 1886 of Samuel Morley provided the impetus to bind the teaching resources of the Hall into a coherent, integral unit. But the history of the public lectures may be conveniently followed before the emergence of Morley Memorial College itself. These lectures were open to a wider public than the classes, and embraced a wider range of subjects, though popular science, travel and topography remained their chief concern, and literary topics (other than the conventional 'Shakespeare' talk from time to time) were left uncovered. One area which was not merely neglected but actually shunned was politics. Even before the Hall acquired official funding, the principles of its management were strictly non-political. Such a decision was not always easy to implement, and in the 1890s, when the Hall (with the College) was in receipt of a grant from the City Parochial Foundation, led to a number of embarrassing situations. The most painful was undoubtedly the decision in November 1892 to refuse the offer of a lecture on 'Africa' by Henry Morton Stanley. A contribution from Dr Livingstone's rescuer would seem to be eminently desirable, but Stanley was at that time the

Conservative candidate for North Lambeth, and the New Cut denizens did not love him for it, as Caroline Martineau's letter declining his offer makes clear:

> . . . from the manner in which his name has sometimes been received by our audience when mentioned in connection with African exploration (not politically, for, as you know we rigidly exclude politics here), I fear we could not answer for his being well received by our audience, and (after consultation with some other members of the Committee) I think it will be best not to run the risk of unpleasantness to him.[23]

This rebuff Stanley had no option but to suffer. However, three years later a chance of retaliation offered itself. The Governors had granted a request from the supporters of the 'Direct Popular Veto' movement (not itself regarded as a party political issue) to hold a meeting in the Hall in March 1895. It was to be chaired by G. P. Trevelyan, the Radical candidate for North Lambeth, and this provided a heaven-sent opportunity. Mrs Stanley grasped it on her husband's behalf:

> I wanted to ask you whether such a meeting may be held at the Victoria Hall? and if political meetings *may* be held, are they only to be for the interest of the Radical Party and Radical Candidates . . .

and (harking back to the rebuff three years earlier):

> The refusal came from Miss Cons, who is a very strong partizan of the Radicals, and who works for the Radical party in Lambeth . . .[24]

Inevitably the Direct Popular Vetoists had to move elsewhere, and Miss Cons vowed to steer clear of such stormy waters in future, though her course ran into the occasional controversial issue even so. An edict from the City Parochial Foundation in 1898 listed three 'taboo' topics:

> Meetings held in support of candidates for the London School Boards.
> Meetings held in support of candidates for the London County Council.
> Meetings held in connection with Women's Suffrage.[25]

All the same, it was sometimes difficult to draw a demarcation line, as with a meeting about 'the Armenian question' (one of Emma's Pet Causes) in 1896, a 1907 Pan-Anglican Congress, or a 1908 Temperance Demonstration (did this threaten gin-bottle-smashing?).

Building foundations

While the Tuesday lectures continued as a regular and little varied feature of the Hall's activities for over thirty years, the classes developed rapidly and demanded increasing supervision and funding. The decision to found a 'College for Working Men and Women' (its availability to both sexes was a striking novelty in the 1880s) as a memorial to Samuel Morley involved reorganisation both of the Hall itself and of its funding. The latter was eased by seeking the support of the Charity Commissioners, acting through the City Parochial Foundation, though the actual transference proved a lengthy and anxious affair. The conversion of the backstage area to Collegiate use was evidently improvised (and cannot have eased the lot of the performers who after all used the building quite as much as the teachers and the taught), but gradually there emerged not merely a number of makeshift classrooms, but more spacious areas such as the gymnasium, the library and a students' common room. There was also a separate entry to the College in the Waterloo Road, cheek by jowl with the (former) stage-door, now the only entrance to the Hall, since the old foyer was devoted to its Coffee Tavern purpose.

The enthusiasm which regular classes in scientific subjects sparked off turned Emma Cons's thoughts to less hand-to-mouth methods of funding the Hall. The Trust's lease was due to expire in ten years, and if the freehold could be acquired a major problem would be solved. Her determination on this course was strengthened by the outcome of a Conference on Technical Education held at the Hall in December 1887 at which a spokesman for the Charity Commissioners made a firm offer of funding *provided* the freehold was acquired. The ground landlords were an Irish family by name Croker, whose title went back to 1773 when the then Archbishop of Canterbury, as Lord of the Manor of Lambeth, had devised the plot to a forebear, Robert Nettles. His lineal descendant in 1888 was Edward Croker of Curryglass, Tallow, County Cork. Miss Cons's lawyers ascertained that the freehold could be purchased for £16,000, though representatives of the licensed victualling trade were apparently willing to bid much higher. A public meeting at Grosvenor House presided over by the Duke of Westminster proved an auspicious launching for the appeal, and with help from the Duke, several friends and the loyal Morley family, the sum was raised. By an agreement dated 31 March 1888 between Emma Cons and Edward Croker, the freehold passed to the Trustees for £16,000 and the vendor offered the purchaser a mortgage of £8,000 at 3.1 per cent p.a.[26] There were still painfully protracted negotiations before Royal approval to the setting up of a new Trust was obtained by Order in Council on 23 February 1891.[27]

The terms of this Order give the most explicit account of what Emma Cons and her supporters conceived to be the purpose of the building, and make surprising reading in view of its later history. Unequivocally it stated:

> The Theatre shall be primarily for the holding there of public lectures and musical and other entertainments and exhibitions suitable for the recreation and instruction of the poorer classes. Admission shall not be gratuitous, but it shall be at such prices as will make them available to artisans.

So there could be no recourse to the earlier practice of 'special prices' for the appearance of a Paganini or Edmund Kean. Indeed the Governing body was empowered to hold 'without charge meetings and entertainments especially designed to promote temperance and thrift amongst the poorer classes'. The Order specifically laid down 'No intoxicating liquors shall be introduced into any part of the building', and confirmed as the caterer John Pearce, who was to occupy the front portion of the house and run a temperance restaurant which he confidently described as 'Pearce and Plenty'.

The regulations for Morley Memorial College embodied in the same Order in Council laid down that the College existed '. . . to promote the advanced study by men and women belonging to the working classes of subjects not directly concerned with or applied to any handicrafts, trade or business'[28] – a restatement of the scientific basis of the earliest classes. They were also notable for the approval from the start not only of women as students but also of women as administrators. The original Council included Miss Cons, Caroline Martineau and Lady Frederick Cavendish (a name to be increasingly honoured in Hall and College records), and it was laid down that there should always be at least three women members on the Council. A Consultative Committee, including all the teaching staff together with six students, ensured that the Council should never lose touch with the feeling of the College as a whole. One senses the hand of Emma Cons herself behind many of these provisions. It was in 1889 that she stood for and was elected Alderman of the new London County Council, although technical objections forced her to resign in the following year.

The clearly defined and authorised functions of the Hall align it with at least two institutions, one long-established, one exactly contemporary, which must have been in Miss Cons's thoughts. The existing model was the Crystal Palace, established in Sydenham since 1854 and advertised immediately next to the Hall in the *South London Press*. The other model was the People's Palace in the Mile End Road, the first stage of which (the Queen's Building) was opened – by the Queen – in 1887. The Crystal Palace was of course laid out on an altogether more lavish scale than either of the other institutions and had the enormous advantage of 200 acres of grounds for its summer programme. On the other hand the attractions of the Palace itself, which included lectures, concerts and exhibitions, offered the Royal Victoria Hall a surprisingly exact blueprint to follow. Most interestingly the theatrical programme (chiefly for a matinee audience) consisted of a largely classical selection of plays, with Shakespeare and 'Old Comedy' dominant, very closely anticipating what Old Vic drama was to offer thirty years later. The Mile End Road house was purpose-built (and largely financed from the fund left by a local man, J. T. Barber Beaumont), which placed much emphasis on 'in-house' entertainment, taking the form of amateur concerts, choirs and competitive shows of all kinds. But it too had an educational function (in the shape of the 'Technical Schools', ultimately to mature into Queen Mary College), and Emma Cons's recognition that the Mile End Road could teach the Waterloo Road something was embodied in her own description of the Hall – 'The People's Palace for South London' – adopted for much of the pre-1914 period.

The promise of subvention (later fixed at £1,000 a year and subsequently raised to £1,500) offered at the meeting of educational authorities in December 1887 encouraged the Governors of the Hall to go ahead, both with the purchase of the freehold and the conversions backstage for educational purposes, and the official opening of Morley Memorial College took place on 29 September 1889. But the procedural delays involved in obtaining the Order in Council, on the authority of which the City Parochial Foundation would fulfil the promise entered into, left Miss Cons in serious difficulties. A sequence of surviving letters to the Trustees not only highlights the Hall's problems but vividly illuminates its achievements. Thus a letter of 20 April 1892 reminds the Chairman:

> It must not be forgotten that, catering for the class we do, any serious disturbance of the labour market (by strike or otherwise) might at any

> moment send down our receipts for admission at the doors to a very
> serious extent . . .

but at the same time notes

> I enclose bills of the Entertainments, Lectures and Concerts at the
> Hall. 70,400 persons, chiefly of the very poorest and roughest class,
> attended on Saturday nights during 1891. 28,400 attended the
> Thursday Ballad Concerts and 19,000 the popular Lectures, besides
> smaller numbers on other nights of the week, about 30,000. In the
> College (of which I enclose a Prospectus) 692 persons entered (many
> of them for several classes) during the first term of this Session, and we
> had an average attendance of 113 per night.[29]

These figures are striking testimony to the popularity of the Hall by
1890. Since it was invariably closed during August, they suggest that the
average attendance on Saturday nights was at least 1,500. They also
illuminate the seating capacity which the backless benches in the cheaper
parts of the house afforded. During its later history as the home of the
National Theatre its total seating accommodation amounted to 850.

Less than a month later, on 13 May, Emma Cons was voicing an
anxiety recurring many times in her lifetime and many more times in the
life of the Old Vic:

> The new requirements of the County Council have already entailed
> considerable additional expense, and are likely to entail still more,
> both in increase of staff and in warming apparatus which may be
> rendered necessary by the removal of inner doors and draught
> excluders.

Her appeals did not fall on deaf ears. In August she wrote to
acknowledge a letter which would be put to the Vic's Governing Body,
adding

> In the meantime I beg to thank the Trustees of the City Parochial
> Foundation for their intention of increasing the annual payment by
> £500. The relief which it will bring both in the Hall and the College
> will be great, as we find more and more that our present Income is not
> sufficient to carry out the work in the thorough manner that it ought to
> be done, and my failing health makes it imperative that I should
> without loss of time train a paid manager to carry out the work of the
> Hall, which I and my Sister have long done as volunteers, but cannot
> continue to do, therefore I trust the Trustees may be so well satisfied
> with the result of their grant that they may see fit to continue it.[30]

The Trustees did indeed continue it, but the 'paid manager' – in any full sense of those words – was not to materialise for another forty years. A Miss Phillips was employed as Emma's assistant from 1892 to 1896, but the situation was only brought under full control by the arrival on the scene in the summer of 1897 of 'Auntie's Niece', the singular and memorable Lilian Baylis.

Auntie's Niece

If there is one figure in the Old Vic story who speaks for the whole it is Lilian Baylis. More than forty years after her death her name and reputation spell out the unique character of the theatre, its tragedies and its triumphs, and spell them not merely for the few survivors who knew her but for the many who were born long after her death. Because she herself was unique, both as a person and in her profession of theatre manager, she has been the subject of more stories, more jokes, but above all more affection, than anyone else who has ever been or ever will be connected with the house in the Waterloo Road, which was for forty years her life *tout court*. Because too her personality was an extraordinary and irresistible mix of contradictions: pious but bawdy; ignorant but wise; mean but golden-hearted; prim but sensual – she is also the subject of innumerable legends, none of which earns outright disbelief, because with a woman like Lilian no legend can surpass the astonishing truth. In any case her story has been admirably told by Richard Findlater, and needs no retelling.[31]

Here, therefore, the briefest of summaries will suffice. She was born in 1874, the eldest of the five surviving children of Elizabeth Cons (Emma's youngest sister) and Edward Newton Baylis. Both her parents were musical performers (her mother much the more capable) who during a large part of their lives earned a precarious existence by performing. Lilian, as has already been seen, made an early appearance in the audience of the Vic on its opening night as a Temperance Music Hall when she was six. In the 1880s her parents exercised their modest talents for the British music-lover, and Lilian studied the violin to help out (she also performed on the mandolin, guitar, piano and castanets, and would doubtless have tackled the double bass if necessary). Having achieved some little success as a musical troupe under the name of 'The Gypsy Revellers', the Baylis family accepted an engagement in South Africa in 1891, whither Lilian, now seventeen, accompanied them. Here she was rightly applauded for her 'skipping rope dance while playing the banjo', but the impresario concerned went bankrupt, leaving them stranded in the southern hemisphere for the next six years. They therefore pursued their calling under conditions which were always tough and must sometimes have seemed intolerable, but they survived; they even acquired a home of sorts in Johannesburg; and Lilian acquired a fiancé, a gold prospector whom she kept waiting for three years and then finally dismissed, whereupon he disappeared into Mashonaland and was never seen again. The loss is said to have haunted her for the rest of her life, but the years 1891–7 were marked by a modest improvement in the Baylis family fortunes, as demand grew for their services in a multiplicity of musical functions. Mark Twain always claimed to have been one of Lilian's dancing pupils (excelling in the Lancers) during a visit to Johannesburg in 1896.

Perhaps her musical activities were *too* multiple. At any rate she fell ill early in 1897, and it was as part of her convalescence that Aunt Emma, who had long been a good friend to the Baylis family as to so many others, related or unrelated, sent her the fare home. The consequences were further reaching than probably either aunt or niece had ever imagined; she did not see her parents again for sixteen years; she did not return to South Africa for thirty years (and then only on a recuperation trip in reverse); and early in 1898 she started the life-work as Aunt Emma's assistant at the Old Vic which was to provide her *raison d'être* henceforward.

Court favour

Modest in its original aims and chequered in its early history, the Royal Victoria Hall nevertheless earned its title of 'Royal' almost from the start by attracting the favour of the Royal family, if not of the Queen after whom it was named. The visit of the Prince and Princess of Wales to the special 'Irish Night' on 9 February 1882 (little more than a year after the opening) inaugurated a series of Royal visits to and courtly interest in this unorthodox and underfunded enterprise. The early recognition of its good intentions by the heir to the throne is often attributed to the fact that the ground landlord of much of the district was the Duke of Cornwall (one of the Prince of Wales's subsidiary titles); a flattering if not wholly convincing argument – he does not seem to have made any official visits to Astley's, the Surrey, or the Elephant and Castle, all of which stood on his land, though he may well have wished to patronise them unofficially.

The number of Royal and aristocratic patrons of the Hall, including such names as Princess Christian, Princess Frederica and Princess Beatrice, points to a friend in court, and there is no difficulty about filling this role. The helping hand was that of Lady Frederick Cavendish, widow of the Chief Secretary for Ireland murdered in Phoenix Park in 1882. Related to just about every figure of importance in the realm (including Gladstone) and herself Lady in Waiting to Queen Victoria and later Queen Alexandra, 'Lady Fred' took an interest in the Hall almost from the moment of her widowhood, became a Trustee immediately on the setting up of the Trust, and remained one until her death. Even more momentous for the progress of the Old Vic, there grew between her and Emma Cons an improbable but immensely valuable intimacy which the few letters that survive illuminate.[32] Referring to the second Duke of Westminster, who had succeeded his father as President of the Trust, Miss Cons could write with impunity on 30 January 1904: 'Can we do anything more to try to induce that horrid young Duke to take [the] chair? He seems so different to the dear late Duke.' Invariably it was Lady Fred's diary that decided the dates of the Governors' meetings. Here is an SOS from 17 February 1904 (a year of doubt and danger for Miss Cons and her cherished cause):

> As you know, it is *most important* to have *you* at our Gov[erning] Body meeting, so that it is you who must settle the *day, time and place*. We can meet at the Hall or the College on either day but shall we get you? As we ought to settle details of Grosvenor House meeting: *cards* (form of), names of speakers, lists of whom to invite, and other details. I regret having to bother you, but you are so important!

The meeting was evidently fixed for 26 April, and an addition to Emma's letter of confirmation shows the concern she felt for her aristocratic ally:

> PS Will your voice be well enough to read a short paper at the meeting? Or would you prefer me to ask young Mr Johnson?

Given Lady Frederick's social eminence, it is not perhaps surprising to find Emma's tone so urgent and considerate. What is surprising – and delightful – is the lightness of touch in this example of the Great Lady's side of the correspondence, dated 12 April 1897. Evidently she had persuaded Princess Christian to contribute to the Good Cause:

> There now! Don't I deserve 2/6 commission at least!! Mind you obey HRH and write *yourself* to *her* in the autumn. No doubt it's a thing you have done before; but in case you have not, I will just inform you that

one uses one's best pen, begins 'Madam', says 'Your Royal Highness' (full length!) instead of *you*; (only it's better to say 'you' once in a way rather than repeat that unwieldy business too often), and ends: 'I am, Madam, YRH's obt humble servt,' but *full-length* of course. *I* always seal a Royal letter; but I dare say this is now old-fashioned. I enclosed your appeal to HRH and see how it softened her heart!

Tact and charm can rarely have been more delicately displayed by one remarkable lady to another. Small wonder that Lady Frederick became something of a 'mascot' for the Hall and its public. The legend that working men in the Gallery would point her out in a box and remark: 'That's *our* Lady Fred' needs no further corroboration.[33]

Academic honours

From the date of its official opening in 1889 Morley College made steady progress in its backstage and below-stage accommodation. The original City Parochial Foundation grant of £1,000 had been divided with £650 going to the Hall, £350 to the College, and these proportions were observed as it increased. The appointment in 1892 of Caroline Martineau as Principal sealed the close association between Hall and College, already established not only by sharing premises but by Emma Cons's doubling as Secretary of both institutions. Miss Martineau was of course one of her oldest friends and closest associates; she had already made herself responsible for the Tuesday lectures; and her influence was strongly felt in the College long after her term of office (which only ended with her death in 1902). Her scientific bias was evident in the curriculum from the start: in 1894 she wrote in the *Morley College Magazine* that since other Polytechnics, notably the Borough, provided technical and craft instruction: 'We devote our attention mainly to Literary Classes and such branches of Science as do not need elaborate apparatus.'[34]

The account provided by the *Magazine* suggests that drama did not qualify for inclusion as literature. There was a tacit prohibition on student theatricals in the early years of the College's history. Whereas the Literary and Music Societies flourished from the start, the Dramatic Society pursued an intermittent and unrecognised path, particularly since its activities were only allowed 'if there was no dressing up'. Even the Literary Society seems to have frowned on the Stage. The invitation extended to Charles Charrington, an early sponsor of Shaw's plays, produced a nasty fright: after originally naming his subject as Ibsen (possible in an educated milieu, though itself fraught with controversy), he chose on arrival to switch to Shaw and to *Mrs Warren's Profession* in particular, which some present regarded as 'an attempt to introduce free love into the College',[35] suggesting they were far from attentive to the lecturer's theme.

On the other hand music took firm root. There was an orchestra, a choir and numerous musical occasions. Of course this discrimination in favour of music and against drama accurately reflected Miss Cons's own preference (buttressed by legal restrictions) in running the Hall. The College's musical progress, however, was enormously enhanced by the appointment in 1907 of the young Gustav Holst as Director of Music, a post he retained until the early 1920s. His initiative and inspiration raised music at Morley College to an eminence it has maintained ever since.

Family pride

Unlike the College, the Hall during the mid-1890s was inclined to falter. Perhaps Miss Cons's attention was diverted to education rather than entertainment; perhaps the Miss Phillips who assisted her during these years lacked her singleness of purpose. The *Annual Report* for 1898, while striking a note of optimism for the future, goes in for plain-speaking about the past. It compares the modest loss of £356 on the working of the Hall for 1897–8 with that in earlier years:

      1895   £1,205
      1896   £1,167
      1897   £418

and adds darkly: 'It will be remembered that in 1895–6 the management was in other hands', possibly a Parthian shot at the departed Miss Phillips. By then of course Auntie's Niece had come to her rescue; indeed it may have been the stark reality of these figures, abetted by the entreaties of Aunt Ellen Cons and Ethel Everest, that induced Lilian to throw in her lot with the Vic. At any rate the same *Annual Report* pays tribute to the able assistance (without revealing the relationship) of 'Miss Baylis, who, we hope, will be able before long to undertake the entire management'.

Not even the redoubtable Lilian could hope to do that as long as her aunt lived and thrived. But obviously her load was steadily increased and willingly shouldered, and this new blood was transfused into the circulation of the Old Vic none too soon. The turn of the century also saw a turn in the fortunes of the Hall and in the taste of its *habitués*. The Boer War had lowered the spirits and incomes of Lambeth residents. 'Since the War our neighbours are poorer' (and sit in the 2d., 3d. and 4d. seats rather than the 6d., and 1/- section) admits the 1901–2 *Report*. Another factor in the situation which Miss Cons was unwilling to admit (and of which she may have been unaware) was the major change in the function of the music hall as a part of London's entertainment scene. As far back as the 1870s the music hall had begun to attract a 'respectable' clientele (a trend the ill-fated Royal Victoria Palace of Varieties failed to swell). By 1900 this change was everywhere apparent. Most central music halls were civilised, even smart, places of entertainment. They catered for a wide range of middlebrow taste, and offered attractive bills to all who could afford their prices. This may not have diverted many of the hard-up Lambeth labourers to the Palace, the Tivoli, or a little later the Coliseum, but it certainly diverted the better-known performers, whose salaries the West End halls could meet and the Royal Victoria emphatically could not.

In any case Miss Cons was out of sympathy with 'upmarket' Variety, as she made clear in the 1902 *Report*:

> The work of the Hall is primarily Temperance work . . . The workers at this Hall have been labouring for 23 years to provide such a 'people's palace' – one that should furnish only innocent amusement, and educate its visitors to take their pleasures apart from drinking and betting.

But increasingly those visitors found her programmes lacking, and while the Thursday night concerts, and particularly the operatic recitals, were packed to the door, the Variety evenings (Mondays and Saturdays) were not. There was a lesson to be learnt here, but Miss Cons was too old, or perhaps too high-principled, to learn it. The new West End halls were under more adaptable management, men who realised that their public's taste was steadily growing, and even Miss Cons (in her 1904–5 *Report*) noted sadly:

> To a certain extent the concerts have suffered from competition, several of the leading Music Halls (e.g. the Coliseum and the Lyceum) having recently introduced operatic and high-class music into their programmes.

But there was no prospect of Miss Cons following suit, even if she could afford it. For her, Variety audiences were simple folk with simple tastes.

There is a puzzling reference in the 1902 *Report* to the Saturday night public

> joining in or whistling the Choruses of their favourite songs; cheering the Hero and hissing and groaning with all their might at the Villain in the short sketches . . .

– puzzling, because it seems to indicate the inclusion of dramatic sketches in the Variety bills (thus imperilling the music hall licence), whereas the scanty programmes themselves suggest that even the semi-dramatic items were either wordless spectacles ('The Death of General Gordon' was a typical offering, frequently repeated) or comic dance turns using knockabout comedians. The only likely explanation of Miss Cons's remark is that she applied the terms of dramatic theory to what were by every conventional definition non-dramatic pieces.

But if Auntie's head was increasingly in the sand, her Niece was keeping her eyes wide open, and those eyes saw a new phenomenon on the entertainment horizon, which was to spell a welcome relief for the Vic: the Moving Picture. Introduced to the paying public during the late 1890s, it was still mainly shown as an interpolated 'turn' in the smarter music halls, to which the inhabitants of Lambeth and Southwark rarely aspired. Lilian perceived that a modest sampling of this new and thrilling medium would revive the flagging Variety bills at the Vic, and she was proved triumphantly right. By 1904 Monday nights were devoted entirely to film shows which drew the crowds. In the season 1905–6, for example, film shows averaged an attendance of 2,000 a night, compared with Variety's 1,200, and even Thursday night concerts or recitals fluctuated between 1,600 and 2,000. Characteristically the film programmes were mostly documentary: no *Perils of Pauline* or *Escapades of Elaine* for the Vic. Instead, as Miss Cons recorded in 1906:

> These exhibitions embrace a wide variety of subjects, informative as well as amusing, and exercise without doubt a considerable educational influence.

The programme on 13 October 1904, for instance, of 'Animated Pictures by E. Holmes Fireproof Matagraph' included: 'Panorama on the Cambrian Coast'; 'A Day in the Hayfields'; and 'Hackenschmidt v Jenkins'.[36] This disdain for the more sensational products of the early cinema was shortly to cut the ground from under the management's feet, but for the time being the problem of Monday nights was solved, and moving pictures were even introduced into the concert programmes on

Thursdays. On 15 December 1904, for example, the recital of *Tannhäuser* was 'preceded by Animated Pictures'.[37]

At least this maintained the box-office takings. For behind the cheerfulness which the *Annual Reports* strove to maintain lay a nagging suspicion that all was not well. 'We are not wholly at ease as to the future', concluded Miss Cons in 1902, 'for we feel the need of new helpers who will carry on the work and bring fresh energy to it'. Not only were new workers and fresh energy needed; additional funds were essential to meet yet another financial emergency.

Cash crisis

The only regular and guaranteed financial support on which the Hall could rely was the City Parochial Foundation's contribution (shared with the College). All other sources – admission money, rents, donations, subscriptions – were variable and unpredictable. While the actual day-to-day running of the Hall could be budgeted according to the means available, this left the management wholly unprotected against any emergency which might occur. One particular concern was safety: the old Coburg/Victoria had been built in an age of lax standards of protection against fire, flood and other threats to the audience's security (and had more than once paid the penalty for such laxity). But Emma Cons and her team were working in a safety-first age. If this was true under the Surrey magistrates who granted the Hall's licence in the 1880s (the Lord Chamberlain's authority having ceased with the transfer to music hall status), it was even truer of the London County Council which was set up in 1890 and applied equal standards to all the Halls under its control. Throughout the 1890s pressure was exerted on the Vic to improve its arrangements, notably in the provision of exits and entrances. Prevarication and piecemeal improvement kept the authorities quiet until the turn of the century. There were, notwithstanding, ludicrous disputes over the 'quick-change' dressing-rooms at stage level, originally lath and plaster, which the LCC wanted rebuilt in brick, and Emma agreed to have reconstructed in corrugated iron.

But in the course of 1902–3 the LCC lost patience and insisted on improvements which resulted in the Vic running into debt to the tune of £3,052 17s. 10d., a frightening sum for that time and for a conscience as scrupulous as Emma's. She confessed her fears and her frustration to Lady Frederick in a letter of 6 January 1904:

As to our safety apparatus, I think you may take it we are safe so far as human arrangements may go. But if people take panic, nothing will prevent their being killed, crushed etc. Our Fire Curtain is let down every evening, and it is so easily worked that Miss Baylis lets it down herself, and I think it weighs '20 Ton'. Next time you come to the Vic, you must come onto the Stage and *let the Fire Curtain down yourself!* As to our exits and emergency exits, we have no bolts on at all, and have got them all to work so easily that for the last year they go so easily that wicked people pull them open from the streets, and try to come in *from the outside, without paying!* We have now to engage an attendant *for each door*, to see that people do not come in that way. It now serves also in case of panic, the men could throw the doors open very quickly! Every evening (for years) I have had one of us go round and see that each door is working *easily outwards*, before the public are admitted . . .

The emergency was met by a meeting at Grosvenor House on 26 April 1904, presided over by the 'horrid young Duke' (of Westminster), who seems notwithstanding his immaturity to have ensured the success of the appeal; the debt was thus paid off and the crisis passed.[38] But an organisation as delicately balanced as the Vic was ill-equipped for shocks of this kind, and there would be many more emergencies, meetings and appeals before, fifty years later, sufficient official funding enabled the management to ride out such storms without danger of sinking.

Change of fare

The problem of Monday nights had been solved – albeit temporarily – by Lilian's inspired introduction of film shows. But Thursdays presented increasing difficulties. The operatic recitals were perennially popular – so much so that frequency had to be increased from one a month to one a fortnight. Their preparation, no light task given the shortage of both time and money from which the Vic suffered, was in the hands of Alfred Dove, while a Gilbert King was thanked in the 1898 *Annual Report* for his help with 'the arrangement of the Selections and Tableaux'. But the following year the orchestra was handed over to a cellist already of their number. This was Charles Corri, a figure of only less moment in the annals of the Vic than those of Emma Cons and Lilian Baylis, as he was Musical Director for over thirty years. He was that rare but invaluable bird, the right man in the right job, since he had a very practical approach to the work (essential, in view of the conditions under which that work was accomplished), combined with standards to which he and his colleagues constantly aspired, however often they fell short. He also seems to have been a Character, insisting on rehearsing in a bowler hat and somehow secreting a bottle of stout into the orchestra pit, past the eagle eye of first Auntie and then her Niece.

The repertoire on which the opera recitals drew was predictably narrow. The early favourites seem to have been mostly Verdi: *Trovatore* and *Rigoletto* constantly recur, though not surprisingly *Traviata* is missing (there had been too many real-life Traviatas in the Vic's pre-history). But from the moment they were introduced, *Faust* and *Carmen* proved the perennial popular choices of the Vic audience, repeated almost every season. There was a real bond of loyalty to the 'English Ring Cycle' (*Bohemian Girl*; *Maritana*; *Lily of Killarney*) which reappeared regularly at the Old Vic long after they had disappeared from other stages, and the occasional novelty: *Nydia* (from *The Last Days of Pompeii*) – 'the very beautiful work of a very able Englishman' (George Fox), according to the *Annual Report*, was staged in 1897, to predictably thin houses.

As has been seen, a milestone was reached in December 1904 with the presentation of *Tannhäuser*, even if the moving pictures were needed to help out the occasion, and this was followed by *Lohengrin*. But non-operatic Thursday nights presented problems. The traditional 'Ballad Concert' fare (not to mention the bank balance) had hitherto ruled out large-scale orchestral works. But other, more prestigious, music halls had begun to cast envious eyes on the Vic's middle-of-the-road music, as the 1905 *Annual Report* had already noted:

> To a certain extent the Concerts have suffered from competition, several of the leading Music Halls (e.g. the Coliseum and the Lyceum) having recently introduced operatic and high-class music into their programmes . . .

and the Vic's concerts were suffering in consequence. Emma's solution was to go up market, and introduce genuine Symphonic Concerts on Thursdays, although one senses her overruling Lilian in this matter. The former Gypsy Reveller doubtless had her own view of such expensive entertainments. But Emma relished the contrast between her highbrow programmes and her lowbrow audience:

> The Philharmonic patron cannot fail to be interested by the spectacle of the audience in the Pit, smoking cutty pipes and drinking tea out of saucers while listening to Sibelius's 'Finlandia' or Haydn's Symphony (No. 2) in D . . .

according to the 1909 *Report*. Although her heart was greatly warmed by
the labourer who commented: 'But I wish you'd again 'ave given
Beethoven's Scratcher [Kreutzer] Sonata',[39] the fact remained that the
Symphony Concerts did not draw. 'Frankly they are too good' admitted
the 1907 *Report*, and there was scarcely more response to the Military
Band Concerts which Lilian pressed in their place. These became the
subject of one of Auntie's few public disagreements with her Niece, as
the Minutes of a Governors' Meeting on 7 March 1907 reveal:

> Miss Baylis felt that the loss was so great on the Symphony Concerts
> that they should be discontinued. Miss Cons did not agree, and called
> attention to the fact that our grant was given us to give good music to
> the people and raise their taste for same.[40]

Perhaps even more seriously the film shows, bacon-savers since the
beginning of the decade, were beginning to flag. Cinema performances
were increasingly an organised branch of the entertainment business:
several cinemas wholly devoted to that branch were now established in
South London, and it was unrealistic of the Vic management to believe
that their parish-hall type programmes could compete.

> When the Picture Shows at the 'Vic' were the only ones in South
> London the theatre was half-filled at the early doors, and the cheap
> seats filled to overflowing. Picture Shows have now sprung up in
> every part of the neighbourhood, the natural result being that the
> Audiences at the 'Vic', though still large, have decreased . . .

– as the *Annual Report* for 1908–9 had to acknowledge.

The operatic recitals continued to pack the house, but they were
expensive and their form severely limited by the music hall licence,
which was becoming an increasing anomaly. In fact the music hall
function of the Vic was dwindling rapidly: Monday nights had already
been surrendered to film shows, and Lilian would have liked to make
over Saturdays to a repeat performance of the operas. By 1912 the Hall
was frequently termed: 'The People's Opera House', which seems a far
cry from the 'Temperance Music Hall and Coffee-Tavern' of the 1880s.
But however it was popularly known, it was not winning increased
popularity with audiences. The high point of its pre-1914 history – a
visit by the Prince and Princess of Wales (the future George V and
Queen Mary) in March 1910 – coincided with yet another financial crisis
which, combined with the demands of the Royal visit, drove Lilian to a
nervous breakdown from which she had to be rescued by leave of
absence and a long cruise in the summer of 1910. On her return the

balance-sheets made one thing clear: opera drew the crowds; films had
done and might do so again; Variety did not. Was is possible to increase
and vary the theatrical side of the Hall's work? Such a move would need
a change in the terms of the licence. To be or not to be a theatre loomed
the largest issue on the horizon as Edward VII died and his son
succeeded only two months after he had honoured the Hall with his
presence. It was an issue the Governing body would address for the next
three years.

Dramatic interlude

The dilemma in which the Vic now found itself was by no means unique.
Over the previous decade other music halls had experienced pressure to
include a sketch or sketches in their programme. Originally these were
nothing more than comic or melodramatic anecdotes, acted visually
rather than verbally, but with the influx at the turn of the century of a
more discriminating public and the building of comfortable, even
luxurious, Variety palaces, there was a strong incentive to make the
dramatic interlude more truly a drama, and to draw on leading members
of the *corps dramatique* who would themselves draw in the playgoing
public.

For such programming there was considerable authority. A Select
Parliamentary Committee had examined the subject as early as 1892 and
given their blessing to the inclusion of sketches on the music hall bill
provided

    1 no sketch should exceed forty minutes' duration or employ more than
       six performers
    2 at least thirty minutes elapsed between sketches
    3 there was no plot connection between any two pieces.

But if a Parliamentary Committee was happy with such an arrangement,
the Theatre Managers' Association was not. For them it represented a
serious threat to their livelihood, and in the next decade they initiated
several prosecutions: of the Palace, when that house staged a shortened
version of an operetta, *La Toledad*, and of the Metropolitan, when it
offered a piece called *The Fighting Parson*, amongst other instances. Both
these cases were upheld, and the managers of the two halls fined £50 and
£150 respectively. Nevertheless the Variety houses found the appearance of major theatre stars in pieces by such reputable authors as Conan
Doyle and J. M. Barrie so attractive to their new, sophisticated public
that they brought continuous pressure to bear on Parliament to legalise a

situation they had already established in the teeth of the theatre managers' opposition. In 1908 a Committee again recommended the granting of theatre licences to music halls, if desired, and a bill was finally placed on the statute book in 1912, in which year Sarah Bernhardt appeared at the Coliseum at a reputed salary of £1,000 a week.[41]

It was against this background of Parliamentary enquiry and legislation that the possibility of the Vic acquiring a theatre licence was debated in the last years of Emma Cons's management. The Minutes of 10 January 1908, for example, record that

> Miss Baylis asked if it was possible to have our present licence changed into a Theatre Licence as she understood that the new Theatrical Law allowed smoking under the Lord Chamberlain. A Theatrical Licence would overcome many difficulties in arranging operatic recitals.

The matter dragged on until May when the Lord Chamberlain 'finally wrote regretting it was not possible to grant an occasional licence'.[42] But the issue would not go away, and on 10 January 1912 a more favourable, if cautious, response from the Lord Chamberlain, embodying numerous conditions, was discussed, and the offer declined.

The truth was surely that Emma Cons did not want a theatre licence on any terms. She had worked for over thirty years to maintain the Vic as a Temperance Music Hall, not a Temperance Theatre. Her original impulse had been to extirpate the scourge of drink as it affected working-class families in one of its chief strongholds, the music hall, which offered unbridled temptation to drink throughout the performance (unlike the theatre). Having dedicated herself to such a cause, it was understandable that she did not appreciate the changes which had come about in the habits of music hall audiences, most of whom now only drank in moderation and within the spending limits their income allowed them. Moreover, switching to a dramatic licence would mean abandoning the smoking concession in the Pit and Gallery, and Miss Cons saw the Vic as both a pro-smoking and an anti-drinking hall. Smoking was allowed not merely during the Variety programmes but (as has been seen) on Thursday nights for the concerts and operatic recitals. There were exceptions: the formidable American singer, Madame Antoinette Sterling, is widely reported as asking and obtaining a dispensation:

> On her first visit, the story goes, when told that the audience smoked, [she] urged that she could not sing in such an atmosphere – pretty strong in those days when the audience was composed entirely of what

was called 'the masses'. 'But we daren't stop them', the management pleaded, 'they are far too rough a crowd to put up with the interference.' Antoinette Sterling walked on to the stage and, with her rare smile, said: 'I want to sing to you, but if I do, all this smoke will hurt my voice. Now, if you like your pipes better than my singing, why, you go on smoking.' And every pipe was knocked out.[43]

But Madame Sterling was exceptional in more ways than this – and in any case insisting on the audience's right to smoke suited Miss Cons's purpose.

Lilian Baylis was younger and more adaptable in her view of what might suit the Vic. Over the years there had been several requests for the use of the stage for plays by respectable performers: in 1906 by William Poel,[44] no less, and in 1912 by W. Bridges-Adams[45] who was to prove an influential Director at the Shakespeare Memorial Theatre, Stratford-on-Avon. To obtain a dramatic licence must have seemed not only a solution to the intransigent problems of staging opera but to the empty benches on Monday and Saturday nights. Then just when another clash seemed to be threatening between Aunt and Niece, Emma Cons died, on 24 July 1912, aged 74. She had been in command of the Old Vic for thirty-two years, and was present at the Governors' meeting only two months before her death.

There is a moving story that towards the end Emma summoned Lilian and went over the dispositions she had made. '"What about the Vic, Emma?" I said at last, and her answer was "You are there, dear." . . . I felt humbled at her faith in me.'[46] However, her humility did not stop Lilian changing things radically and rapidly. Less than two months later, at a Governors' meeting, 'It was resolved that an application be made in due course for this [dramatic] licence to the Lord Chamberlain',[47] and on 13 November 'the Chairman reported that this was granted'. No less momentous was the dropping of Variety altogether. By the beginning of 1914 opera held the stage on both Thursday and Saturday nights. The new broom was sweeping clean.

The play opens

Reading between the innocuous tone and formal lines of the *Annual Reports* and Governors' Minutes at this time there is a sense of Lilian up to something in the months following her aunt's death. After the lengthy debates on Poel's and Bridges-Adams's requests to use the stage for dramatic purposes, this announcement at the meeting on 8 January 1913 comes with breath-taking suddenness:

> *Drama*: Miss Baylis reported that drama on Wednesdays and Saturdays had been started as at Christmas, and at present showed a loss. It was decided that the performances should be continued until the next meeting of the Governing body.

(There had been no reference to such a development at the meeting on 13 November 1912, and no meeting at all in December.) Moreover, until very recently it was far from clear what this 'Drama' comprised. Richard Findlater had had to admit: 'Maddeningly, there is no exact record of what these plays *were*, or who produced them; but it seems certain that they were not by Shakespeare. In Cicely Hamilton's history of the theatre, she says it had "already adventured into plays" by 1911 . . . The dating is almost certainly wrong.'[48] But a scattering of playbills has now come to light[49] which provides a framework for this pioneer (if pedestrian) season. On 8 March 1913 for instance, there was: *The Unknown: A Sturdy Drama of American Life*; on 24 March *The Streets of London*, followed by films; and on 5 April the special engagement of Queenie Fraser-Brunner with her own company in *Lady Audley's Secret*. The innovation does not seem to have been a success, and by July 1913 the Governors were informed that the Charity Commissioners had given permission for the Hall to be let three times a week (presumably on Mondays, Wednesdays and Saturdays) 'for cinematographic purposes'.[50]

Welcome as these modest programming details are, they pose almost as many questions as they answer. What did Miss Fraser-Brunner and her colleagues do on the nights they were not wanted at the Vic? It must have been difficult to find other dates which allowed them to keep their Wednesdays and Saturdays clear for the Waterloo Road. Even odder, why, having finally obtained her dramatic licence, did Miss Baylis promptly sponsor just the sort of 'blood-and-thunder' drama from which her aunt had saved the theatre in 1880? The only explanation must be that there was no other choice readily available, and indeed *The Unknown* and *Lady Audley's Secret* were logical extensions to play-length of the quasi-dramatic sketches that had featured on the Variety bills for some years. But they were no solution to a pressing problem, and other approaches had to be tried.

Legitimate at last

The decision to let the Hall three nights a week 'for cinematographic purposes', leaving Tuesdays clear for the lectures, Thursdays for music and Fridays for Temperance, provided Miss Baylis with a breathing-space in which to ponder the next move. Staging melodrama had not been a financial success, and was in any case not a policy in itself but part of the Variety programme from which the Vic was distancing itself. Film shows, whether sponsored or sublet, were no longer rewarding, either financially or educationally. Full-blown theatre was now statutorily possible, but doubtless an unknown quantity to Lilian, whose background was in musical entertainment, and entertainment of an essentially mild and middle-brow sort. Such enquiries regarding the theatrical use of the Hall as had reached her (e.g. from William Poel, Bridges-Adams and more recently Philip Carr)[51] were essentially from 'high-brows', interested in staging 'pure' Shakespeare or something similar. No doubt Lilian could not see such intellectual fare appealing to the New Cut public. But towards the end of 1913 she received an overture from a rather different source. Rosina Filippi was a retired actress with a solid record in character parts who had conceived the notion of founding a 'People's Theatre' and sought house-room at the Vic. In personality she seems to have resembled Miss Baylis very closely – a circumstance that was to prove fatal to their harmonious collaboration – but this probably commended her on first acquaintance. And a 'People's Theatre–Opera House' was after all the goal to which Lilian's thoughts were constantly turning. The Governing body was persuaded that presenting high-class drama was in accordance with the Hall's purpose, and that Miss Filippi should have a shot at doing just that. In April 1914 the first 'resident' (albeit temporarily) drama company since 1880 took the Old Vic for two nights a week.

We know what plays were performed: *The Merchant of Venice* (with Hermione Gingold, aged sixteen, as Jessica); *Romeo and Juliet*; and *The School for Scandal*. We also know what play was not performed: *Candida*, which the Governors rejected as 'modern' (it was over twenty years old) and 'unsuitable'[52] (although it ends with a wife rejecting her aristocratic admirer and standing loyally by her clergyman-husband). Miss Filippi made no bones about the paucity of her resources, claiming to have staged the plays 'with art muslin, two changes of scenery and two hired orange-trees',[53] but hailed 'the Marconi-communication between the audience and the players that was never experienced in the West End'.

Marconi-communication there may have been, but audience in any visible quantity there obviously was not, and it seems doubtful if the season lasted its advertised eight performances. Even this limited encounter appears to have been too much for Miss Baylis. 'Rosina had *such* a temper, a terrible temper', according to Sybil Thorndike, 'and so did Lil. They got on very well as long as they were apart.'[54] So they parted.

Nevertheless the two evenings a week had to be filled. Variety was finished; the film shows were no longer profitable. Drama was at least newsworthy, and Miss Filippi had earned the Vic a good deal of publicity. When a Mr Shakespeare Stewart, who at least had the right first name, and had moreover acted with William Poel, offered his services towards a Shakespeare season that summer, he seemed a gift horse whose mouth should not be inspected too closely. He came; he tried his best with *Twelfth Night, As You Like It* and *Much Ado*, but apparently he too failed to the tune of £50 over three weeks.[55]

Just about this time the Bard spoke to Lilian in a dream, as his Maker (and hers) was to do in so many moments of crisis. He asked: 'Why have you allowed my beautiful words to be so murdered?' and when she not unreasonably answered that if they had been slaughtered, the fault was not hers but the actors', he replied: 'You must run the plays yourself as you do the operas.'[56] The identification – or was it confusion? – in Lilian's mind between Shakespeare, opera and the Almighty was thus established. On 9 September 1914 there appeared in the *Era* the following paragraph:

> *Wanted*: Experienced Shakespeare Actors for special performance at Royal Victoria Hall, Waterloo Road, certain of being in London till end of October. Apply by letters only to the Manager, Box 7, 194.

But meanwhile not only had Shakespeare and the Almighty spoken. War had been declared.

Voluntary service

The War of 1914–18 was – ultimately – to be the making of the Old Vic, transforming it from an obscure Hall devoted to improving works into a People's Theatre and Opera House well on the way to national and international fame. But initially it must have struck the management as disaster, coming as it did just when the historic decision had been taken to sponsor a resident Shakespeare company to share the stage with the steadily developing opera company. Obviously war would make the achievement of this end doubly difficult: manpower would be short as the services claimed their due; resources would be limited; night-time audiences inhibited from patronising entertainment of any kind, even if the dire threat of aerial attack did not immediately materialise.

But the die was cast: the plans were announced, and the programme had to go ahead. What was needed was a more experienced hand than Miss Baylis, even when inspired, could provide. Neither the quarrelsome Miss Filiippi nor the vague Mr Stewart who 'drove her up the wall' was acceptable as a coadjutor, but a soulmate did present herself in the person of Estelle Stead, actress and journalist's daughter, who was prepared to sacrifice her own ambitions to the needs of the Vic. More importantly she had the ear of the theatrical establishment, in particular that of actor-manager Matheson Lang, and his wife Hutin Britten. Lang, a matinee idol ten years earlier, was now well established in the stage hierarchy. He generously lent his name and experience to the all-too-vulnerable project at the Vic, directing the three opening productions (*The Merchant of Venice*; *The Taming of the Shrew*; *Hamlet*), encouraging his wife to play Portia and the Shrew, 'lending' scenery – a loan which seems to have turned into a gift and on which the company drew almost exclusively throughout the War years. Even more helpfully, the Langs set a precedent which others proved willing to follow. Constance Benson (wife of the cricketing Shakespearean) took on *She Stoops To Conquer*, and Andrew Leigh (a name never long absent from the Old Vic annals over the next fifteen years) *Twelfth Night*, *The Merry Wives* and *As You Like It*, with help from Estelle Stead.

So the season progressed, though still without one clearly acknowledged helmsman. But that voice – Shakespeare's or the Deity's – which had spoken to Lilian in the still of a summer's night, did not desert her. One evening at the end of the performance, a decidedly nautical-looking gentleman with a thatch of white hair approached her and offered his services. Not only did he look as though he could command the enterprise; he had the credentials and the experience to prove it.

He was Philip Ben Greet.

5

Seeking Shakespeare

1914–1933

The accidental meeting of Ben Greet and Lilian Baylis after an early Shakespeare performance at the Old Vic, and his offer to lend a hand, proved to be a momentous turning-point in the Theatre's history. It is difficult to see how the experiment of alternating opera with drama could have survived without his wealth of experience. An appeal for £5,000 in the summer of 1914 had foundered among the distractions of wartime, with only £800 contributed;[1] and the City Parochial Foundation luckily saved the day by providing a further £500 a year.[2] Matheson Lang and Hutin Britten had many other responsibilities; they were popular players with their own company and their own programme to fulfil. Lilian herself was totally without experience – or knowledge – of Shakespeare, and felt an innate distrust of the theatrical as opposed to the musical profession. There was as yet no ready-made audience for highbrow drama in the neighbourhood, and it would take several years to build up. Without Greet it appears that the autumn season of 1914 would have followed Rosina Filippi's and Shakespeare Stewart's on the scrapheap of good intentions.

But Ben Greet was made of sterner stuff than his predecessors. Born of nautical stock he had inherited a sailor's adaptability to wind and weather. By 1914 he was in his late fifties and had been running theatrical companies for thirty years, a good deal of his experience being in North America. It seems unlikely that he would have been given leading parts in anyone else's company, but his claim to play Shylock and Malvolio was founded not on overweening ambition but rather on his talents as captain of his crew. In fact he often played supporting parts or did not himself appear. Over the years he had recruited, trained and provided experience for hundreds of young hopefuls, and he was thus able to cast any Shakespeare play from personal knowledge of these performers – an expertise which Lilian Baylis at this stage of her managerial career totally lacked.

Above all his experience as an actor-manager had been gained not through running a West End theatre or on lucrative provincial and foreign tours, like such leading lights as Irving and Tree. Greet was essentially an impresario of the fit-up performance, offering instant Shakespeare within the limitations of a school or parish hall, or more often in the wide expanses of parks and gardens. He had founded his Woodland Players as early as 1886, and many of his public, hitherto ignorant or suspicious of the theatre itself, obtained their first taste for drama at these alfresco performances. The sheer necessity of getting the show on, however adverse the conditions, had endowed him with resources, both personal and psychological, which were to prove invaluable in his four years at the Vic, under conditions which, if they did not comprise inclement weather, certainly took in bombs and gun barrages. As Margaret Webster, herself born of a long theatrical line, noted when she played with him:

> He had done the plays so often, in so many extraordinary ways and places, that I don't think he took any of it seriously any more. In the face of some particularly fearful or ludicrous happening, his eyes would twinkle with enjoyment. Anything short of total disaster simply passed him by. He had become so accustomed to making his actors fend for themselves that he knew we would, between us, get the shows on somehow.[3]

He persevered, not from megalomania but from his belief that Shakespeare's plays provided spiritual comfort for all kinds and conditions of men, not exclusively or even essentially those with the education and aesthetic judgement needed to assess their finer points. His handling of the texts was indeed codified into a formula adaptable to any emergency with which his company was faced. His programme note for the Old Vic in 1917 makes it clear that he felt a full text to be beyond the capacity of his audience. What was needed was an immediately comprehensible experience, and to this end a good deal of doctoring was not only justified but desirable:

> We think The Old Vic is a good specimen of what they call in America 'Family Theatre'. It is jolly for the audience to get to know each other. We on the stage race to get our scenery set to make the plays act as closely and rapidly as possible. This brings us once more to the often disputed question as to how to present the great plays. Let us admit at

once that the best way is a plain stage representing as nearly as possible Shakespeare's own stage, and give as much as possible, all, in fact, of the text. This plan entails enormous study on the part of the actors and could not possibly be undertaken in any ordinary theatre, the Vic, for instance, where there is a weekly change of play. We can only give here with our limited means, carefully arranged 'Acting versions'; therefore we do them with changes of scenery to make them entertaining and interesting to ordinary audiences. The intellectual ones and the youngsters who study the plays can supply with their knowledge the omitted scenes. The regular playgoer can understand the plot as it stands and imagination will help him fill in the gaps.[4]

In other hands this rough and ready approach might result in artistic sterility. But Greet's actors and audiences were willing to make allowances because of the devotion – in the religious as well as the professional sense – that inspired his work.

Devotion to his task, without thought of any worldly gain or recognition, was a characteristic he shared with William Poel, and it is no coincidence that they should have been associated, above all, in spreading the gospel of *Everyman*. After Poel's initial production at Charterhouse in 1901, Greet took over responsibility for this newly discovered text, which so perfectly embodied his own belief in the spiritual power of the drama, and introduced it to American audiences in 1902. Not surprisingly it was to figure early and often in the Old Vic programme, being regularly performed in Lent, starting in 1915 (with Sybil Thorndike as Everyman, following Poel's practice of casting a woman in the title-role). Outside the Shakespearean canon it most completely answered the purposes of the Royal Victoria Hall and the faith in which it had been founded thirty years earlier.

Certainly Greet's experience of adapting his productions to every possible variant of location and vicissitude in performance was thoroughly tested at the Vic. Apart from the stage itself, virtually every other backstage facility had been taken over by Morley College, which remained firmly in occupation until 1923. Dressing-rooms as understood in other theatrs were non-existent; the men of the company crowded into two narrow slits without running water. The women dressed in the saloon, and all quick changes had to be made at stage level, while the stage-hands looked the other way. Principals were occasionally allowed to share Miss Baylis's office, and for large-cast plays the male supers were banished to an upper box, making their way backstage through the front of house and pass-door. The settings lent by Matheson

Lang turned into a permanent loan and were used with very little reference to play or period. Costumes were also interchangeable, and only hired (from nearby Raynes) in extreme necessity. Even these meagre facilities were of course shared with the opera company, who as the sitting tenants no doubt got first choice, particularly since they were Miss Baylis's special concern.

The limitations imposed on performance standards by the building itself were formidable. Winifred Isaac, writing in 1961 but from first-hand observation, has commented:

> It must be difficult to present-day audiences of the The Old Vic to realise what the auditorium *looked* like, *felt* like, and *smelt* like during the years when Ben Greet first worked there . . . The footlights were incandescent lamps until Rosina Filippi's time (1914) when electric footlights were installed because she wanted subdued coloured effects for her productions. The stage and auditorium were lit by gas . . . The exits and entrances were lit by naked gas jets in wire cages. (At one time there were oil lamps besides these in case the gas failed.) . . . The walls of the stalls and pit were lined with the remains of the Looking Glass curtain. The reflections interfered with the stage lighting and distracted the actors, so the glass was removed and the walls were afterwards covered with red paper . . . I have heard that in Emma Cons's time the staff wore long red coats and 'postmen's' hats; but by 1914 the usual navy blue uniform had been introduced.
>
> The audience sat on hard wooden benches covered with American cloth, with a bar at the back; the gallery seats were bare boards, with no backs; the floors were bare boards . . . it must be remembered that The Old Vic of Emma Cons's and Lilian Baylis's early days was intended for the working class who were used to nothing better.

She also paints a picturesque background to the scene. 'When the naphtha lights were lit over the vivid splashes of colour of the fruit and vegetables on the stalls, this was one of the most romantic spots in the whole of romantic London. Men from all parts of the world, back to town again, rubbed elbows with the costers and with the wind in a certain direction and a certain amount of imagination you could faintly smell the sea. A cynic suggested that the fried-fish shops of the neighbourhood were responsible for this phenomenon!' (*Ben Greet and the Old Vic* pp. 126–7). On the other hand Robert Atkins, who acted with the Company in 1915–16, suggests a darker side to the setting: 'Facing the theatre was the shop of Mr Hurry, the undertaker. Beside it was a gin palace, frightening on a Saturday night when no women in the

Vic company were allowed to leave without male escort' (*The Times* 30 March 1974).

All these limitations would have faced an Old Vic drama company whenever it had been founded, but these teething troubles were greatly exacerbated by wartime conditions and all the upheaval they involved. Resources, particularly human resources and above all able-bodied males, proved increasingly scarce. Casting women in male roles became a necessity of which Greet was characteristically to make a virtue, declaring 'It will do them good to put on beards and play some of those lovely parts.'[5] But the female conscripts who in a 1918 performance of *Henry V* played not merely Chorus, Orleans, Mountjoy, the Constable of France, the French Ambassador and the Dauphin (foreigners are, after all, *exotica*) but also the Dukes of Bedford, Gloucester and Westmoreland, Lord Scroop, Sir Thomas Grey and Sir Thomas Erpingham, must have felt they deserved the name-part as well.

Human resources were often in short supply in the auditorium, especially in the early days. The New Cut public was by no means instantly converted to Shakespeare, and at first the crowded opera houses were urged from the stage by leading figures, including Mrs Kendal, Frank Benson and Beerbohm Tree, to extend their patronage to the plays. The turning-point seems to have been reached with the successful introduction of schools matinees which, although ultimately disavowed by the LCC on the grounds that all education, including the drama, must be free, spread the Shakespearean gospel amongst local playgoers of all ages. Even so the bombing of 1917–18 sometimes reduced the houses to such pitiful proportions that proceeding with the performance was in doubt, although this threat in its turn sparked off a spirit of resistance from which the Shakespeare performances profited.

Nevertheless keeping the curtain up would have proved impossible without the astonishing spirit of loyalty which Ben Greet and Lilian Baylis between them inspired. Tales of going on without preparation of any kind abound in accounts by members of the Company. In 1916 Beatrice Wilson was summoned by telegram to play Viola in *Twelfth Night*. As she had been rehearsing elsewhere, she did not receive the summons until less than an hour before the performance. She sent a message suggesting she switch with Sybil Thorndike and play Olivia (who enters later). She reached the Theatre just as the curtain rose, dressed in Lilian Baylis's office, and was rewarded with a boiled egg in the interval and the news that Ellen Terry was in front.[6] Sybil Thorndike herself was fetched from a maternity bed to start rehearsing *Hamlet*, and protests that the infant in question (Ann Casson) had been late in arriving were brushed aside by Miss Baylis: 'That was her fault, not mine.' Dame Sybil's comment: 'I took it from her because it was all for the Old Vic, never for herself'[7] applied equally aptly to Ben Greet's appeals for assistance. They both inspired total dedication in their followers.

It was on this selflessness that their partnership rested. Greet's High Church principles were no less firm than Lilian's, and she was willing to forgive him much on their account. He on his side saw his work at the Vic as the war service for which he was too old, refused all payment in the early years, and only agreed to accept expenses under pressure. Since they had so many characteristics in common, friction was frequent, though never sustained. Both knew when to respect the other's need, as is best illustrated by the famous Nose-Pulling incident (inflicted by Greet on Baylis not once but twice). He himself was chiefly contrite because he had enjoyed it, and she was not concerned for her dignity but for his character, because 'wanting to pull someone's nose *is* a nasty tendency'.[8] Their most sensational quarrel seems to have arisen over the failure of a stage-manager, Madge Whiteman, to turn up the house lights fully. In the ensuing fracas Lilian called Madge 'a bloody liar', and Madge appealed to Greet who knew she was indispensable to him, as both actress and stage-manager. He bearded Miss Baylis, demanded an apology and got it by blocking her escape route and telling her she was 'too fat to get out of the window'.[9]

Despite the scarcity of early audiences and the vicissitudes of war-time, a loyal and responsive public steadily attached itself to the Shakespeare performances, for which additional time had to be found. The Friday Temperance Evenings were surrendered early on, but Thursdays and Saturdays were sacred to the opera company and pressure therefore built up on the Tuesday lectures which were cut down to once a fortnight, allowing for onstage rehearsals. Other familiar features began to emerge. Starting in 1915 the week of Shakespeare's birthday was suitably acknowledged, with additional matinees and a special Birthday Performance graced by visiting luminaries from more fashionable theatres: in 1915 these included Henry Ainley, Lilian Braithwaite and Constance Collier, and the following year Ellen Terry as Queen Katharine in an extract from *Henry VIII*. That year also saw the introduction of *Hamlet* in its entirety (with an Old Vic stalwart, William Stack, and Sybil Thorndike as Ophelia) which became a standard feature of the Birthday Week. A further mark of the Company's progress was the invitation to undertake the Tercentenary

Festival at Stratford, in the absence on war service of Frank Benson, whose company usually occupied the Memorial Theatre in the summer. They put on no less than twelve plays in four weeks, and their acting strength was augmented by guest appearances from Lilian Braithwaite as Queen Katharine, and Nancy Price sharing Lady Macbeth with Sybil Thorndike.

Ben Greet left the Old Vic at the end of the 1917–18 season, but he came back for a Gala matinee, graced by Queen Mary and her daughter, Princess Mary, on 25 October to celebrate the Centenary of the Theatre. The programme then offered to the Royal ladies did not lack for diversity. Besides extracts from Shakespeare and popular operas, it included impersonations of the Duke of Wellington making an (undocumented) appearance at the Coburg on opening night, and of Paganini giving his (authenticated) farewell performance there in 1834. The proceedings also drew attention to the Theatre's early history with an extract, perhaps unwisely chosen, from *Simon Lee; or The Murder in the Five Fields Copse*, a Dibdin Pitt piece staged by Osbaldiston at the Victoria in the 1840s. The extract took place in the condemned cell, with Greet as the accused and Athene Seyler as his wife taking poison minutes before his reprieve was announced. Amongst the guest artistes Ellen Terry contributed 'The quality of mercy' (which she still regularly included in her recitals) and Juliet's Potion Speech (a rarer offering by that time – she was seventy-one).

The Gala marked the first visit to the Theatre by a reigning British monarch since that of the controversial Queen Caroline almost a hundred years earlier, and the first Royal function which Lilian had had to organise without the tutelary presence of Aunt Emma. It also proved the occasion of two of the most endearing anecdotes about her. Richard Findlater tells of the attempt by her man-of-all-work, 'Old Bob' Robinson, to calm her nerves: 'Don't *worry* so much. The Queen knows she aint acomin' to Buckingham Palace' (*Lilian Baylis*, p. 185), and in *Old Vic Saga* Harcourt Williams records Lilian's explanation to the Queen of the relative size of the Theatre's portraits of George V and Miss Cons: 'Not quite so large as Aunt Emma's because your dear husband has not done so much for the Old Vic.' (p. 23). Queen Mary was attended by a 'Guard of Honour from the War Wounded Heroes at St George's Hospital', and the singing of the National Anthem at the end included a special verse:

> God save our splendid men,
> Bring them safe home again,
> God save our men.

> Keep them victorious,
> Patient and chivalrous,
> They are so dear to us,
> God save our men.

Ten days later this prayer was answered in the Armistice.

Enter Robert Atkins

Amongst the actors who answered Ben Greet's appeal, pending their call-up, was Robert Atkins who had served apprenticeships with both Tree and Forbes-Robertson, and who put their teaching to good use at the Vic in a round of leading Shakespearean parts. Atkins also made himself useful as an assistant director, in particular during the 1916 season at Stratford when Greet and Lilian were having one of their periodic feuds. He must have satisfied his manageress, for when he came to leave the Company for the Army, Lilian asked: 'Would you like to come back to me? If you would, I'd like to have you here.'[10]

She kept her word. After Greet's departure in 1918 *locum tenentes* were appointed: George Foss, a scholarly director of the Poel school for 1918–19, and two actors, Russell Thorndike (no less valuable to the Vic than his more illustrious sister) and Charles Warburton for 1919–20. By the summer of 1920 Atkins was a civilian once more and available. He opened the 1920–1 season with *The Winter's Tale*, and for the next five years responsibility for the Old Vic's plays rested firmly on his (fortunately solid) shoulders. Atkins was the first director whose methods were shaped by the singular needs of the Old Vic. Greet was too set in his ways to change, though luckily those methods admirably suited the requirements of the Theatre at the time, and his immediate successors were interim appointments. Atkins brought to his task dedication and a resolve to see the job through to its logical end, the presentation of all the plays in the First Folio, an end reached in *Troilus and Cressida* in November 1923, with a special performance before the Princess Royal and a First Folio displayed under glass in the orchestra pit.

In material terms the resources available to Atkins were little better than Greet's, but he saw the artistic absurdity of staging all the plays from an existing scenic stock, irrespective of its suitability for the piece in hand. Instead he employed mainly curtains, imaginatively lit, with a selective use of painted scenery, and built out a platform in front of the proscenium. In this transformation he was greatly assisted by the abolition (during the Thorndike–Warburton regime) of the Victorian grooves over and in the stage, which had served their time. Even these had to be removed clandestinely in the middle of the night, lest Lilian pronounce their demolition sacrilege, which she did – too late.[11] Atkins also introduced a false proscenium of black velvet which provided an aptly neutral framework for non-representational settings.

These changes proved a virtue not merely imposed by necessity since they gave an artistic unity to all his work. For the first time critics could write of 'Old Vic Shakespeare' and judge it, for better or worse, by recognisable standards. Moreover the scrapping of the hard-pressed Matheson Lang sets opened up the repertoire to a handful of plays by authors other than Shakespeare. Some of these were occasional pieces: the Christmas fare varied the Coventry Nativity Play and *A Christmas Carol* with Strindberg's *Advent* and *The Hope of the World*, a devout drama by Lilian's spiritual adviser, Father Andrew, whom she revered but the Company liked less. More importantly, Atkins used his new freedom of staging to mount several poetic dramas which called for as much imagination from the audience as the production. Chief amongst these was *Peer Gynt* in 1922, the first full English production, with Russell Thorndike as Peer. It is a measure of Atkins's enterprise and Lilian's trust in him that such a task should have been attempted at this point of the Theatre's evolution. Its success, both artistic and popular, inspired Atkins to tackle Goethe's *Faust* (in a much simplified version by Graham and Tristan Rawson) the following year, and Hauptmann's *Hannele* at Christmas 1924. The confidence which encouraged him to intersperse the Shakespearean programme with these ambitious choices was fed by the loyalty of steadily growing audiences. This loyalty was reflected not only in improved attendance but in the establishment of the *Old Vic Magazine* (in 1919) and of two 'supporters' clubs', the Old Vic Circle for the Galleryites and the more comprehensive Old Vic Association (in 1923).

During his five years in command Atkins relied on a group of leading actors who responded to his demands and sacrificed better-paid opportunities to share the camaraderie of the Vic. Ernest Milton was released in the middle of the 1921–2 season to create one of his most memorable characters, De Levis in Galsworthy's *Loyalties* for the prestigious Basil Dean management at the St Martin's, but he rallied to the Vic's call repeatedly. Actors like Ion Swinley, John Laurie, George Hayes and Wilfred Walter, on whom Atkins depended heavily, were dedicated Shakespeareans and rarely achieved comparable success in the hectic and often superficial world of the commercial theatre in the 1920s. This was equally true of the Company's leading actresses, such as Beatrice Wilson and Florence Saunders; the latter, universally loved by audiences and colleagues, was paid a unique tribute following her untimely death in 1926 at the age of thirty-five, in the form of a handsomely illustrated record of her work for the Vic.

The Company's identity and standing were increasingly recognised beyond the Waterloo Road. At the end of the 1920-1 season they were invited to appear at the Théâtre du Parc in Brussels, where they gave six plays in six days, and their audience for *The Tempest* included the King and Queen of the Belgians. The British Royal family also took a growing interest. Early in 1924 King George V and Queen Mary (who as Prince and Princess of Wales had provided a high point of Emma Cons's regime) graciously agreed to become the Theatre's Patrons; at the same time Princess Marie-Louise succeeded her mother, Princess Christian (Queen Victoria's daughter), as President. This Royal recognition represented a last benefaction from Lady Frederick Cavendish, who died in 1925, and whose help over thirty-five years had never faltered.

Recognition of a more pecuniary kind came from the Shakespeare Memorial Committee who in 1922 granted £1,000 a year for three years,[12] and from the BBC who undertook to pay fifteen guineas for the broadcast of an opera and ten guineas for a play.[13] A tribute Lilian appreciated even more highly was the invitation to perform *Everyman* in the Chapel of King's College, Cambridge, at Easter 1924. Another invitation – from a very different quarter – was accepted that summer: C. B. Cochran, the consummate showman, presented the Company in four Shakespeare plays at the New Oxford Theatre, their West End debut. The visit was recorded as 'an artistic success' in the Annual Report, and evidently did more for the Vic's prestige than Cochran's pocket.

On the crest of this wave came Oxford University's conferment of the degree of Master of Arts on Lilian. This event (although outdone by a later Doctorate from Birmingham, and above all her admission as a Companion of Honour in 1929) became something of a milestone in Old Vic history, partly because of the portrait of her in her robes by C. E. Butler, which hung in the foyer, but above all through her insistence on wearing the cap and gown on first and last nights, as well as other important occasions. This gesture – much mocked in certain quarters – was not one of self-importance. She herself commented characteristically: 'Somebody has to wear the things. You can't leave them hanging in the hall.'[14] But as the Governors' Minutes record,[15] they had paid for and presented the robes to her, and she was saying thank you to them, the Theatre and the public by wearing them.

Concurrently with Atkins's transformation of the play programme, an important development took place in the opera repertory. The leading soprano Muriel Pope, cast as Susanna in *The Marriage of Figaro*, persuaded Lilian to entrust the production to the team of Edward Dent (translator) and Clive Carey (producer), who had made a considerable impression at Cambridge with a pre-War staging of *The Magic Flute*. Their aims must have seemed impossibly perfectionist to such old hands as Charles Corri, and their methods ruinously expensive to Lilian, but they persevered, and the success of *Figaro* in January 1920 led to their being entrusted with *The Magic Flute* in December of that year, and *Don Giovanni* the following year (it was for this production that Lilian was recruited to play the offstage mandolin accompaniment to the Serenade, bravely if inaudibly).[16]

The artistic standards demanded by a Dent or a Carey were not consistently feasible in an opera company giving at most three performances a week, with minimal orchestral rehearsal and basic salaries for principals and (hithero unpaid) chorus. The work could only be accomplished at all by pragmatists such as Corri and his director of productions, Frederick Hudson, prepared to accept the possible instead of the desirable. But their minimum standards were steadily enhanced by lieutenants such as Lawrance Collingwood, brought in as Chorus Master in 1920, who dedicated himself to higher musical standards for next to no salary, and the singer-director Sumner Austin, a stalwart of the Company during these years.

If in some respects the repertoire was cautious to the point of timidity (even Dent and Carey decided against *Così Fan Tutte* for an Old Vic audience), it was consistently loyal to contemporary British composers, and Ethel Smyth's *The Boatswain's Mate* and *Fête Galante* and Nicholas Gatty's *Prince Fenelon* and *The Tempest* were introduced, then revived even when (as inevitably happened) the public stayed away. On the other hand there was a distinct reluctance to widen the range of Continental composers. Even Puccini remained unrepresented until *Madame Butterfly* was introduced in 1927, and favourites from the earliest days like *Fra Diavolo* and the 'English Ring Cycle' were retained long after their disappearance from other stages. The programmes continued to depend heavily on the more popular works of Verdi and Wagner, interspersed with the indestructible *Faust* and *Carmen*.

The collaboration of Robert Atkins and Lilian Baylis was subject to even greater strain than her partnership with Ben Greet. In the early years she looked to her producer for theatrical experience and guidance, and no matter how violent her quarrels with Greet, she recognised his dedication and sound religious principles. Atkins was cast in a different, secular mould, with a ripeness of language and gesture no doubt enriched by his time in the trenches. Greet and Lilian had had bouts of non-speaking, but Atkins's rows with her usually arose from his speaking all too plainly. Nevertheless she recognised his astonishing energy, resource and refusal to be beaten by conditions which would have defeated most other men, however sweetly spoken and behaved.

For the season 1923–4 a young writer in the making, Doris Westwood, joined the Company to walk on and more particularly serve as prompter; she kept a diary and from it compiled *These Players*, which fully substantiates Atkins's Herculean labours. She depicts him holding together the first night of a *Coriolanus* rehearsed in just over a week (while playing *The Rivals* and *Everyman*). 'At one moment he was in the centre of the crowd disguised in rough serge tunic and hood, at another he was giving the signal for the drum and trumpet, again pushing the soldiers into their places';[17] or raging at rehearsal: 'Carry that coffin straight, for God's sake';[18] 'Move your bodies, ladies; for God's sake look as though you were enjoying yourselves; take a little stimulant before you come on if you can't do it without.'[19] In between he finds the energy to play Cardinal Wolsey, Toby Belch and Caliban.

Her account is as valuable for the picture provided of life backstage as onstage, particularly since the season covered was the last for which the Company shared the premises with Morley College. There are frequent glimpses of those family occasions which marked out the Old Vic from other theatres, then or perhaps at any time. The supers shout at each other through the partition of their dressing-room ('Less noise there, do you hear?'); the girls are 'At Home' for tea during a mid-week matinee; some of the younger members help Miss Baylis serve five hundred local children at a party in the auditorium sponsored by the 'Jabberwocky Christmas Tree Fund'; the whole Company attends the Old Vic Circle dance at the Lambeth Baths to swell the funds, and mingles with the audience onstage to consume the Twelfth Night cake and lemonade; on the last night of the season they line up in their best clothes to receive the public's gifts.

Exit Morley College

The cramped quarters in which the Company were still working in 1923 may have stimulated that spirit of improvisation and camaraderie to which Doris Westwood pays tribute, but they manifestly impeded refinement and progress in performance standards. Tuesday nights, for long dedicated to lectures, were increasingly needed; the occasional free night was filled by recitals, such as 'Folk Songs and Old Ballads' or a 'Demonstration by the Folk Dance Society', and even these disappeared in 1923. All that remained of the Vic's further education programme were the introductory addresses before *Everyman* during the annual Lent performances. But more summary measures were needed; for several years the Old Vic Governors had been pressing their Morley College colleagues to look elsewhere for accommodation, and the College Governors (although protected by the Charity Commissioners' provisions) agreed to do so if the Old Vic found the funds. It seemed they had discovered an alternative home in the former Licensed Victuallers' School (a change of purpose which Emma Cons would have heartily approved), but the appeal launched in November 1921 to effect this move flagged, and when salvation appeared in the form of a cheque for £30,000, from George Dance, an impresario who had attended the old Old Vic as a boy (and understood correctly that his contribution would earn him a knighthood), the alternative site was no longer available.[20]

Undaunted, the College authorities persevered with their search and came upon the Yorkshire Society's disused school in the Westminster Bridge Road. After another alarm when it seemed the site would be undermined by an extension of the London Electric Railway,[21] the purchase proceeded, alterations began in the autumn of 1923, the College moved out piecemeal during 1924 and their new quarters were opened by the Prince of Wales (later Edward VIII) in December 1924. One of the corollaries of their migration was the issue by the Charity Commissioners in March 1925 of separate schemes for Morley College and the Royal Victoria Hall, replacing the Order in Council of 1891 which had recognised them as a single institution. The object of the latter was stated as 'to provide in the theatre high-class drama, especially the plays of Shakespeare, and high-class opera or lectures, musical and other entertainments and exhibitions suited for the recreation and instruction of the poorer classes of the former County of London'.[22] This was doubtless an accurate definition of the Hall's intended purpose, but it was already becoming outdated. The lectures, as has been noted, were finished and the exhibitions had scarcely ever begun. Those references to 'the poorer classes of the former County of London' were to prove increasingly intractable as the audience's standards of living and the Theatre's standards of presentation rose. Nevertheless such objectives were regularly cited when increased prices of admission were discussed, and became something of a stumbling-block after the opening of Sadler's Wells. They were also to figure decisively in the final debate on the Theatre's future when the Old Vic Trust had to relinquish possession.

Pressure to improve backstage conditions had long been exerted by the LCC who viewed the safety arrangements at the Vic with justified concern, and had only been resisted over the years by the unique combination of dedication and dogged obstruction inherent in both Emma Cons's and Lilian Baylis's characters. Work on the improvements was scheduled for the summer recess of 1924, but threatened by a national builders' strike. One category of building for which the workers were prepared to make exception was hospital construction, and it says much for the standing of the Old Vic that the contractors were able to persuade their men to include this work in the excepted category.[23]

The twin objects of reconstruction were safety and convenience for the Company, including backstage-staff. In the preceding years the wardrobe had operated from a former public house in nearby Oakley Street, later renamed Baylis Road in Lilian's honour. The former pub was always known as 'the stores', perhaps in deference to Emma Cons's memory, and much of the scenic construction had to be done on the stage itself, in the rare intervals when it was not being used by either the opera or drama companies. Now there were wardrobe and workshop facilities within the Theatre itself. There was also a big rehearsal room above the stage, replacing the cramped circle foyer and other *ad hoc* arrangements; purpose-built dressing-rooms ('with hot and cold water and even a bathroom', as Lilian proudly boasted);[24] a genuine stage-door, kept by 'Old Bob' Robinson, the Theatre's long-serving and outspoken guardian, and distinct from the public entrance which had hitherto served all comers; and designated, if minute, offices. But the main foyer was still bespoken for the catering activities of 'Pearce and Plenty', and the auditorium itself remained virtually untouched, while the LCC fretted and funds accumulated all too slowly.

With Morley College established elsewhere, the urge to carry the Vic's message further afield began to claim Lilian's attention, and in this she was seconded by one of her Governors, Reginald Rowe, a barrister dedicated to improving the lot of London's working classes, particularly their housing. Local outposts such as the Surrey Theatre (once a deadly rival to the Coburg, now struggling to survive as a cinema) and Canterbury Music Hall were considered but quickly dismissed as likely to poach the Vic's audience. But as early as 1924 the idea of linking with Sadler's Wells figured in Lilian's and Reginald Rowe's ambitions. Its location in Islington aptly counterpointed the Vic's in Lambeth; its history was even longer, since there had been some sort of theatre there since the middle of the eighteenth century. Indeed to some extent Sadler's Wells had anticipated the Vic's function, for in the 1850s under the actor-manager Samuel Phelps it had achieved remarkable success with seasons of respectful versions of Shakespeare and other Elizabethans in productions cherished by Islington audiences and envied by other theatre people. Its history as a playhouse had then declined, barely surviving into the twentieth century, and after an inglorious phase as a cinema, it had shut in 1914 and was derelict. Purchasing the site was not a great problem; a grant from the Carnegie Foundation of £14,200 in July 1925 made this possible.[25] But finding the money to rebuild the theatre was another matter; an appeal launched early in 1925 made slow progress. Reviving *Trelawny of the 'Wells'* under the author's supervision in May 1925 turned out to be more window-dressing than fund-raising; it lost £65 'owing to the hot weather'.[26] There would be much barrel-scraping and many set-backs before this particular mission could be accomplished.

The Pinero revival also proved to be the straw which broke the back of the unlikely though valuable partnership of Lilian and Robert Atkins, who wanted to add to his personal First Folio by doing *Cymbeline* instead. He had worked tirelessly to bring about his vision of the Old Vic as an arena for the exercise of a newly forged Shakespearean steel, and despite fearsome limitations in resources he had succeeded. If in the process he came to believe that he had built the Company and its public from nothing, it was perhaps his due reward, making up for the lack of material gain. It is notable that in his subsequent active career over forty years he was most regularly employed in directing at the Open Air Theatre, Regent's Park, a summer season (when the Old Vic was closed) of mainly Shakespeare comedies, simply set and swiftly staged in the Waterloo Road tradition he had established.

New faces

His successor from 1925 to 1929 was Andrew Leigh, an old friend of the Vic, having acted and directed in the very first season. He had played many of Shakespeare's clowns and possessed the comedian's gift for establishing an immediate rapport between himself and his fellow-men. There seems to have been none of the feuds which characterised both Greet's and Atkins's regimes, and when he resigned the *Annual Report* affirmed that 'he never lost the friendship and goodwill of a single one of those who have worked with him'. He also recognised that in casting the house tradition of using mostly home-grown ingredients might make for some decidedly plain cooking and that a dash of the exotic might add flavour. His first Company was led by Balliol Holloway, who had played Shakespearean leads with every kind of company, fashionable and unfashionable, and Edith Evans.

As a protégée of William Poel she was an apt choice for leading lady, and she generously recognised that the Old Vic was an apt academy for her at that stage of her career which had included West End success and brave endeavours in Restoration comedy (at the Lyric, Hammersmith) and Shaw (chiefly at the Birmingham Repertory Theatre). But she lacked confidence in her ability to play Shakespeare, and embraced the challenge of playing eleven leading parts in nine months. In the process she established the tradition of big names welcoming the demands of a season at the Vic; she was followed by Jean Forbes-Robertson in 1927, by Gielgud in 1929, and herself returned twice in the 1930s.

She also brought the Theatre financial success: the season 1925–6 earned a profit of £4,500.[27] Indeed the Company's fortunes steadily improved: Atkins's last season had shown a profit over £1,000,[28] and Leigh's second £2,700.[29] These figures were not of course clear profit; they took no account of the City Parochial Foundation's annual grants, nor of occasional lump sums from such bodies as the Carnegie Foundation and the Shakespeare Memorial Committee. Nor did they reflect the demands of such undertakings as rehousing Morley College or rebuilding Sadler's Wells. They were also gained by underpaying the entire Company on the grounds that working for the Old Vic brought its own reward. But they reflected the enthusiasm which the Company now inspired, and not only in the Gallery.

In the middle of his term of office Leigh had to grapple with exile from the Waterloo Road to Hammersmith. The LCC, having settled for half measures in 1924, now insisted that the auditorium be brought up to the standards of safety introduced backstage, and from the summer of 1927 to the following February the Theatre was closed for major renovation. It was during this work that the original foundation stone, with Leopold's and Charlotte's names, was rediscovered and reinstated.[30] More significantly for the audience's comfort, the main foyer was reclaimed from John Pearce whose contract had run out, to the management's relief, and henceforward the public entered the building from the front, as the architect intended. Catering became the Theatre's responsibility (and remained strictly teetotal); even so by the season of 1928–9 the profit on catering was £800, compared with £700 on the production programme.[31] The half-season at the Lyric, Hammersmith was greatly enhanced by the return of Sybil Thorndike and the first official appearances for the Old Vic of Lewis Casson, playing opposite each other in *The Merchant of Venice*, *The Taming of the Shrew*, *Much Ado About Nothing*, and *Henry V*. (Unofficially he had 'helped out' while on Army leave during the War.) Meantime the opera company played twice nightly at various outer London music halls, an interesting variation on the original operatic recitals of the early days.

Until his last season Leigh did not risk the excursions from the Elizabethan repertoire that Atkins had allowed himself, but in 1928–9 he ranged more widely. There was a brave attempt at Ibsen's *The Vikings* to mark the centenary of the playwright's birth, and another centenary tribute to T. W. Robertson, a very different writer, with a production of *Caste*. For the first time *Everyman* was not offered at Lent but replaced by Hebbel's *Maria Magdalene*. It proved 'surprisingly popular', according to the *Annual Report*, and *Everyman* never returned. Even more ambitious was the first production of an elaborate modern morality, *Adam's Opera*, by Clemence Dane, with music by Richard Addinsell, which lost the unprecedented sum of £600.[32] But its inclusion was perhaps an indication that the makeshift treatment of music-drama, accepted as a necessity for so many years, was becoming less appropriate to the increased status of the Theatre.

Many operas and plays, even in the simplified staging adopted at the Vic, required some form of dancing, and this had been put into the hands of a series of instructors whose aim was to conceal weakness rather than reveal strength. But by 1926 more consistency and continuity were needed, and that need moved Lilian to respond to an approach from the young Ninette de Valois who was using her experience with the Diaghilev ballet to set up her own Dance Academy. No doubt Miss Baylis saw this approach as a source of ready-made dancers and the versatile de Valois as offering a high rate of return on a modest investment. For some years yet the choreographer had to look to other outlets for her creative work, including such enterprising companies as the Festival Theatre, Cambridge, and the Abbey Theatre, Dublin. But Lilian had faith in her, and by 1928 she was being given stage space for a performance of *Les Petits Riens*, with other short ballets being offered as part of the operatic bill, particularly *Hansel and Gretel* at Christmas. For both there was always the prospect of a wider public and greater opportunities once Sadler's Wells was open, even if this must sometimes have seemed a mirage during these years.

New directions

In the early months of 1929 Lilian and her advisers were greatly taxed by the problem of a successor to Andrew Leigh. Several of those approached (including Raymond Massey and Reginald Denham) declined the honour,[33] and when eventually Harcourt Williams was offered the post, he was as surprised as anyone. Although an actor of wide experience and accomplishment, notably under Granville-Barker, his modest knowledge of production was chiefly derived from occasional performances with specially assembled casts. He had no experience at all of running a large company with an exhausting programme such as the Old Vic. Though loved and respected by his intimates, he was also a somewhat private and ascetic character for so bracing an atmosphere; his recourse in moments of stress to the health food Bemax contrasted strongly with Lilian's public prayer or Atkins's taste for liquor. What commended him to Lilian at least was his family association with the Vic; his wife, the singer Jean Sterling Mackinlay, with whom he had given recitals there, was the daughter of the redoubtable Antoinette Sterling, a pillar of the Royal Victoria Hall in its very early days.

Williams felt that Old Vic Shakespeare had developed certain characteristics as a result of the conditions it had had to overcome. He particularly disliked the practice of engaging a number of actors of proven ability, casting them to type, and then giving them their heads. As a break from this tradition he persuaded John Gielgud and Martita Hunt to lead his first Company. Neither was obvious Old Vic casting: although Gielgud had walked on there (none too auspiciously) at the age of seventeen, London audiences had seen him mostly in modern parts, and his great artistic successes had been in Chekhov under Komisarjevsky. Martita Hunt had no classical experience at all. Their selection was part of Williams's aim to transform the Vic's approach to Shakespeare, above all to the speaking of the verse. No doubt because the earliest Companies struggled to interpret the plays to audiences unfamiliar with anything of the kind, the pace of speaking had been established as measured and deliberate ('so damned explanatory' was how Granville-Barker put it to his pupil),[34] sometimes sacrificing variety of mood and subtlety of feeling.

Williams aimed for vitality in attack, matched by swiftness in scene-changing, with decors as imaginative and stimulating as the strained resources of the Vic allowed. In implementing these aims he may have confused spontaneity with sheer speed; certainly the first two productions, *Romeo and Juliet* and *The Merchant of Venice*, were charged with gabbled speaking and indecent haste, not only by the Old Vic regulars but by the Press, so that the hypersensitive director offered his resignation. This was rejected out of hand by Lilian, who proved the stoutest of allies, and in the course of the first season players, Press and public all came to appreciate Williams's intentions; acceptance grew with Gielgud's Richard II and Macbeth, and became unstinted with his Hamlet at the end of the season. Its reception tempted the impresario Maurice Browne to transfer it to the Queen's, the first Old Vic Shakespeare to be singled out for a West End run, though it had to compete with two other Hamlets – Henry Ainley's (in English) and Alexander Moissi's (in German) – and was quickly withdrawn.

Nevertheless the new director had made his mark. 'Early in the season' states the *Annual Report* 'it was made plain that in Harcourt Williams, whose first year as Producer of the Shakespeare Company has just been concluded, the Old Vic has found a revolutionary.' It notes that at the Birthday Performance 'when members of previous Shakespeare Companies took the stage, a great difference in the tempi, if such an expression may be used, was perceptible', and concludes stoutly: 'The Old Vic is pre-eminently the place for artistic experiment, even if some eggshells of prejudice have to be smashed in the process.'

Gielgud also showed his confidence by agreeing to return for the 1930–1 season, and the strength of the Company was much enhanced by the arrival of Ralph Richardson, whom Williams had seen at the Birmingham Repertory where he had detected the resources of humour and feeling behind the actor's deceptively homespun features. The two made a powerful combination as (amongst other parts) Hotspur and Hal; Richard and Bolingbroke; Prospero and Caliban; Antony and

Enobarbus; Malvolio and Toby Belch; and Lear and Kent in the last production of the season which replaced the conventional *Hamlet* – a sign that the 'revolution' had been widely accepted. Richardson then headed the Company for the following season, to win predictable success as Bottom and the Bastard Faulconbridge, less expectedly as Henry V, and struggle manfully as Brutus and Iago. Edith Evans returned to partner him as Emilia, and then shed years to play Viola.

Although Harcourt Williams saw the reformation of Shakespearean staging as his prime task at the Vic, he was anxious to bring forward plays by other writers. A particularly happy inspiration was the revival in 1932 of *The Knight of the Burning Pestle*, with Richardson as Ralph and Sybil Thorndike (returning to the Company in an hour of need, as so often) as the Citizen's Wife. Fittingly, since some of his most impressionable years had been spent playing Shaw for Granville-Barker, Williams also introduced the dramatist whose *Candida* had been vetoed at the very outset of the Vic's drama programme. For his first Easter (1930) programme he coupled *Androcles and the Lion* with *The Dark Lady of the Sonnets*, playing Shakespeare himself and voicing the plea for a National Theatre which could be sure of a warm response from the Old Vic audience.

The following season he included *Arms and the Man* (with Gielgud as Sergius and Richardson as Bluntschli, not for the last time), and in 1932–3 an ambitious *Caesar and Cleopatra* (with Peggy Ashcroft) and a light-hearted *Admirable Bashville*, with Roger Livesey as the boxer-hero and Alistair Sim as the Zulu chief, Cetewayo! Less happily he turned to John Drinkwater, whose work was closely associated with the early history of the Birmingham Repertory. In the 1932 revival of *Abraham Lincoln*, Drinkwater's first major success, Williams played the name-part; *Mary Stuart*, which he included the following year, did not equal that success, despite Peggy Ashcroft's performance in the title-role.

Double-billing

Williams's later seasons were made increasingly difficult by the reopening of Sadler's Wells. After the purchase of the site in 1924, this dream had repeatedly threatened to turn into a nightmare as the struggle for funds stretched on from year to year. There were moments of encouragement, such as a Farewell Performance given by Dame Nellie Melba in December 1926, which inevitably ruffled feathers, as she insisted on her own conductor, the enlargement of the orchestra pit and

Plates

1 On the way. 'The Half-Way House' Inn en route from Waterloo Bridge to the Coburg Theatre

2 Building up. The new Coburg Theatre 1818

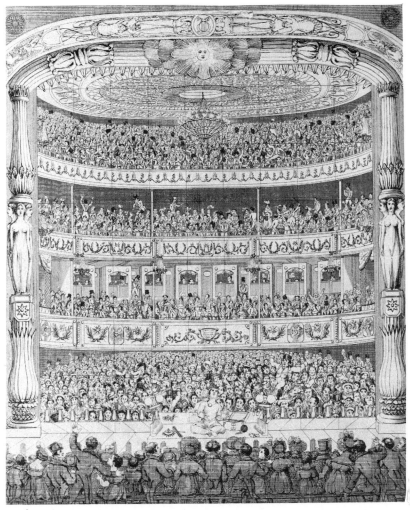

3 Mirror image. Interior of the Coburg Theatre, reflected in the Looking-Glass Curtain 1823

Mr T. P. COOKE, as Harry Hallyard.

4 First mate. T.P. Cooke

5b Partners. Eliza Vincent

5a Partners. David Webster Osbaldiston

VIEW IN THE NEW CUT

6 View of the New Cut 1871

1. Pit and Galleries: An Appreciative Audience.—2. Stalls and Boxes: Burnt-Cork Minstrelsy.—3. The Café: "The Cup which Cheers but not Inebriates."

THE ROYAL VICTORIA COFFEE PALACE AND MUSIC HALL

7 Coffee-house. The Royal Victoria Coffee-Tavern and Temperance Music Hall

8 Governing body. Emma Cons by William Rothenstein

9 London's Threepenny Opera. *Tannhäuser* 1914

1916   Memorial Theatre, Stratford-upon-Avon: The Old Vic Company in *The Comedy of Errors*.
[at top] Madge Whiteman (Æmilia) and Russell Thorndike (Ægeon).

Second row, from left: Florence Saunders (Courtezan), Mary Sumner (Luciana) [in front], Duncan Yarrow (Antipholus of Syracuse), Austin Trevor Solinus), Robert Atkins (Antipholus of Ephesus), Sybil Thorndike Adriana).
Front row: Orlando Barnett Angelo) [extreme left], W. R. Staveley (Dromio of Syracuse) [3rd from right] and Ben Greet (Dromio of Ephesus) [2nd from right].

10   Family album 1916.   The Old Vic Company at Stratford-on-Avon

11 Drama by degrees. Lilian Baylis MA Oxon. at a First Night

12 Lead, kindly lights. John Gielgud and Martita Hunt in *Hamlet* 1930

13 Lead, kindly lights. Ralph Richardson and Edith Evans in *Othello* 1932

14 Lead, kindly lights. Peggy Ashcroft and William Fox in *As You Like It* 1932

15 Stars in their courses. Charles Laughton and Flora Robson with Robert Farquharson and Marius Goring in *Henry VIII* 1933

16 Stars in their courses. Edith Evans and Michael Redgrave in *As You Like It* 1936

17b Stars in their courses. A Dream Cast. Robert Helpmann and Vivien Leigh as Oberon and Titania 1937

17a Stars in their courses. A Dream Cast. Ralph Richardson as Bottom 1937

18 Stars in their courses. Laurence Olivier and Sybil Thorndike in *Coriolanus* 1938

19 Last act. John Gielgud as Prospero and Marius Goring as Ariel in *The Tempest* 1940

20 War wounds. Old Vic Theatre 1941

21 Revival. Peggy Ashcroft and Alec Clunes in *Twelfth Night* 1950

22 First Folio favourites. Richard Burton and Claire Bloom as Hamlet and Ophelia 1953

23 First Folio favourites. Paul Rogers as Macbeth 1954

24b First Folio favourites. Barbara Jefford as
Viola 1958

24a First Folio favourites. John Neville as
Richard II 1954

25 First Folio favourites. Edith Evans and John Gielgud in *Henry VIII* 1958

26 National nights. Laurence Olivier as Othello 1964

27 National nights. Laurence Olivier in *The Dance of Death* 1967

28 National nights. Laurence Olivier and Joan Plowright in *The Merchant of Venice* 1971

29 National nights. John Gielgud and Ralph Richardson in *No Man's Land* 1975

30 The new Old Vic 1983

even her own choice of the bouquet she was to receive, but the occasion resulted in a profit of £300.[35] But after the site had been acquired no more major grants were forthcoming, and the rebuilding proceeded piecemeal as funds allowed, thanks to an extraordinarily accommodating firm of builders, F. G. Minter. Even when the work was completed, there was still a bill of £15,000 outstanding, which they did not press for settlement.[36]

Moreover the finished building itself presented problems. The capacity (1,500) was dictated by running costs, particularly of opera, but the style, exterior and interior, to the designs of F. G. Chancellor, was strongly influenced by contemporary cinema architecture, then riding the wave of the 'talkies' boom, and proved anything but sympathetic to Shakespeare. Gielgud, who played Malvolio in the opening *Twelfth Night* (appropriately on 6 January 1931), was outspoken: 'How we all detested Sadler's Wells when it opened first! The auditorium looked like a denuded wedding-cake and the acoustics were dreadful.'[37]

Equally serious was the lack of forethought which Lilian and her colleagues, in their missionary zeal to spread the gospel, had given to programme planning. Without the funds to double their output, it would be necessary to give twice as many performances of the existing repertory in order to keep both houses open. Moreover Islington showed no signs of providing a local audience, such as Emma Cons had wooed and won in Lambeth. Old Vic Shakespeare in particular was cold-shouldered when given away from the Waterloo Road. The Opera Company was able to find a new audience, not least by putting itself under new management and transforming its image. Edward Dent noted that whereas the frequently make-do-and-mend air lent itself to the time-honoured surroundings of the Old Vic, it lacked lustre in the brash surroundings of Sadler's Wells.[38] Charles Corri accepted that the new regime would prove too demanding for one of his years, and increasingly passed responsibility to Lawrance Collingwood, though he did not retire until 1935, after thirty-five years devoted service (without official recognition) to the Vic. Frederick Hudson had already resigned in 1930, and a pool of opera producers, including Clive Carey and Sumner Austin, were able to set a personal imprint on the staging. Geoffrey Toye was brought in to share responsibility for the planning of opera in 1932, and assumed sole control the following year.

But these developments took time and cost money. Significantly the feature of the programme which found an enthusiastic response at Sadler's Wells from the start was the ballet, first given a full evening in

1931, and allocated two a week the following year. It was custom-designed for the new situation and was valued accordingly. Ninette de Valois acquired an inspired assistant in the dancer-choreographer Frederic Ashton and a leading dancer in Alicia Markova. A little later two major artistes emerged in Robert Helpmann'and Margot Fonteyn. In the years between 1931 and 1939 the Vic–Wells Ballet Company acquired an exciting repertoire, international standing and a public loyal to the point of idolatry.

Rationalisation

However, this success was not achieved without setbacks and much anxiety. By the autumn of 1931 (a dark hour in the financial world everywhere) the Governors' Minutes were full of foreboding. At the end of October the season had already lost £600 at the Vic and £1,060 at Sadler's Wells, and Reginald Rowe predicted: 'If this rate of loss continues Sadler's Wells can hardly avoid closing down before the end of the present season.' A proposal that Sadler's Wells should go 'dark' for three nights a week was resisted by Lilian on the grounds that 'a part-time theatre is not really alive'.[39] The immediate threat was averted by a grant of £8,280 from the Carnegie Foundation,[40] but there were protracted (and damaging) experiments in the deployment of the Companies between the two Theatres in an attempt to meet their diverse demands and cut down the expense and effort of constant interchange.

From the opening of the Wells voices at Governors' meetings had urged the concentration there of opera and ballet, a solution resisted by Lilian and others from their missionary zeal to provide music and drama for those least likely to look for it elsewhere in Islington as in Lambeth. The compromise then adopted – two weeks of drama and one of opera/ballet at the Vic and vice versa – was only possible by cutting the run of each play from four to three weeks, and more seriously for artistic standards by reducing rehearsal accordingly. Later experiments included (in 1933–4) six weeks of drama at the Vic, followed by three at Sadler's Wells; and (in 1934–5) three months of drama at the Vic, followed by one at the Wells. Not until 1937 did the *Annual Report* finally admit: 'Henceforward drama must be restricted to the Old Vic, opera and ballet to Sadler's Wells.'

The 1932–3 season suffered particularly from the stresses of divided loyalties and increased demands which the two Theatres imposed. As leading lady Peggy Ashcroft experienced especial strain: she was required to play Imogen, Rosalind, Portia, Perdita, Juliet and Miranda (amongst other taxing parts), and not surprisingly lacked the necessary stamina. But other members of the Company were overstretched; *Macbeth* lived up to its reputation as accident-prone. When Malcolm Keen was injured in the battle-scenes, Marius Goring stood in for him until John Laurie could take over. The constant modifications imposed on the director's plans were reflected in Harcourt Williams's frequent appearances as an actor, including Prospero in the final *Tempest*, an apt character for a retiring director, but not one conducive to the highest standards of performance.

A junior member of the Company in this last season was Anthony Quayle, then at the outset of his career. Writing nearly fifty years later, he gives a distinctly jaundiced account of the experience: Harcourt Williams 'was as stale as an old crust . . . productions at the Vic that season were appalling'; on the evidence of the resident designer, Paul Smyth, the budget was £28 per production.[41] Even well-loved figures like Orlando Whitehead, the wardrobe master, appear mean and menacing: 'A monk's habit, there it is, that's your monk's habit. If it's too long or too short, well, get your mother to take a tuck in it.'[42] Of course Quayle is judging with the hindsight of the enormous improvements in standards achieved by companies like the later Old Vic and Royal Shakespeare, to which he contributed. He also remained dazzled by the recollection of Gielgud's production in this season of *The Merchant of Venice*. (In fact Williams had to take over when Gielgud was claimed by the film-studio, a characteristic crisis of the time.) 'It was, I think, the best concept of the play I have ever seen – inventive, amusing and gossamer-light', and since he was playing Morocco, he was especially thrilled with the clothes created by the newly formed team of Motley: 'Every costume had been designed and actually made to fit each individual actor.'[43] Under the conditions then obtaining at the Vic this had to be exceptional.

When Harcourt Williams broke his director's staff at the end of *The Tempest* in May 1933 he could also claim to have broken the mould of 'Waterloo Road Shakespeare', and to have given his audiences a glimpse of what might take its place. By coaxing artists such as Gielgud, Richardson and Ashcroft to the Company early in their careers he achieved from them some moments of insight and wonder which they were to extend and enrich on their later visits to the Vic. But for the Company to progress further a younger, tougher director was needed: sufficiently confident in himself to challenge a code of conducting an organisation honourable and even heroic at its inception but fifty years later increasingly unsuited to the Theatre and its potential audience; to demand adequate conditions of preparation; to seek and obtain sufficient funds for proper presentation, from outside sources if necessary; to attract performers who would compel the attention of the public and the Press, not primarily because of their reliability as Shakespearean stalwarts or regularity as churchgoers, but by their power to draw, delight (and inevitably sometimes disappoint) a wide and discerning audience.

It is greatly to the credit of Lilian Baylis and her advisers that they recognised these qualities in the man they chose as Harcourt Williams's successor.

6

Seeking the stars

1933–1940

At thirty-three Tyrone Guthrie was the youngest director the Vic had appointed. He was also far less steeped in theatrical tradition. His experience had been mostly with pioneering groups such as the Oxford Playhouse and the Cambridge Festival Theatre, and his knowledge of Shakespeare in production was slight. He had, however, recently caused something of a stir with a season of plays at the Westminster Theatre (newly converted from a cinema and once a chapel), including Pirandello and James Bridie, and had introduced J. B. Priestley to the West End with *Dangerous Corner*. More to the Governors' liking, his production at the Westminster of *Love's Labour's Lost*, then still regarded as a rarity, had been warmly received. His great height and commanding air gave him the appearance of a prophet, though whether his mission to the Vic was to coincide with Lilian's to Her People remained to be seen.

His first steps did not reassure her. He recruited as leading man Charles Laughton, an acclaimed West End actor in characters who were usually neurotic, often criminal, and sometimes both. Laughton was also on the verge of international fame, following his appearance in Alexander Korda's film *The Private Life of Henry VIII*. With him came his wife, Elsa Lanchester, an exotic talent, by no means easily employed in the classical repertory. Guthrie chose as leading lady Flora Robson, who was closely associated with his work and had been widely praised in Pirandello, James Bridie and O'Neill, though not notably in Shakespeare. Between them Guthrie and Laughton had persuaded the Pilgrim Trust to make a grant of £1,750 towards the staging of Shakespeare, something of a curate's egg to Lilian who preferred negotiating such gifts herself. Guthrie commissioned a 'permanent' set from the architect Wells-Coates, which proved altogether too restricting and in the event was not used for two of the plays (*Henry VIII* and *The Tempest*). The balance of the Company was provided by such experienced players as Athene Seyler, Leon Quartermaine and Roger Livesey (joined during the season by father Sam and brother Barry), and by a promising newcomer, Ursula Jeans.

Guthrie was unable to end the practice of presenting plays at Sadler's Wells. His 'clearly reasoned letter' was turned down by the Governors on 26 April 1934 because they 'felt it would be breaking faith with those who helped to open the Wells if plays were not available at both theatres'. On the other hand he did achieve an extended six-week run of *The Cherry Orchard*, thus challenging the tyranny of the 'green leaflet' (setting out the programme for the season) which had inhibited all his predecessors, and he established a tradition of using different designers which gave the productions individuality. He also reduced the number of productions to seven (Williams had averaged ten; Atkins had tackled as many as twenty, and in his last two seasons Greet attempted twenty-six).

The success of these innovations was overwhelming: as early as 15 January 1934 the Governors were informed of a profit of £6,083 on drama so far (four months), though this was balanced by a loss of £1,281 on opera and £1,291 on ballet to the same date. This diversity of return was to rankle with Lilian; the Box-Office bonanza for the plays derived from an influx of 'West Endy' audiences she had not sought to see artistes she found suspect, and there was to be trouble with Laughton when she understandably offset the surplus on drama against the deficit on opera and ballet.

Guthrie's level of artistic achievement was clearly variable. Of the Shakespeare plays *Measure for Measure* suited Laughton best: his Angelo powerfully projected those dark currents of doubt and menace which always lurked behind his flaccid features and measured tones, and Flora Robson's disciplined emotion lent conviction to Isabella. As Shakespeare's Henry VIII Laughton could not hope to satisfy admirers of his Rabelaisian film creation, and Guthrie himself described *The Tempest* as 'the worst production ever achieved',[1] though it had in Elsa Lanchester's Ariel a dazzling if inappropriate first sketch for her Peter Pan three years later. *Macbeth*, which was to be the climax of the season, was marked by Laughton's first night failure, compounded by Lilian's assurance: 'I'm sure you did your best. And I'm sure that one day you may be quite a good Macbeth.' Guthrie's comment: 'He never forgave her. He believed it was her vengeance for the affair of the Pilgrim Trust' highlights the suspicion which soured the atmosphere, though he insists: 'In that I am sure he was wrong. She was not a petty person.'[2]

The non-Shakespeare plays fared better. Guthrie's courage in risking
Chekhov (hithero regarded as a 'coterie' author for the specialised
audiences of Barnes and Hammersmith) was wholly vindicated. Athene
Seyler and Leon Quartermaine were firmly in command as Ranevsky
and Gaev, the director deemed Laughton 'extremely subtle and
interesting'[3] as Lopakhin (the public agreed), Lanchester fitted in as
Carlotta and Flora Robson made much of Varya. *Love for Love* (a daring
choice after twenty years' restriction to Sheridan and Goldsmith, but
one which succeeded) added a further degree of titillation to Congreve
in the Tattle–Miss Prue scenes, when played by Mr and Mrs Laughton.
Guthrie dismissed his handling of *The Importance of Being Earnest*
(Wilde's introduction to the Vic) as 'galumphing and uninteresting',[4]
but since it drew the crowds and tempted Laughton into making Canon
Chasuble the leading character, it cannot have been uninteresting,
however wrong.

What clearly was not working was the Lilian–Guthrie partnership. As
with the early Harcourt Williams productions, there was a spate of
vitriolic letters from the diehards, and Lilian chose to show the most
poisonous of these to its subject. The contrast with her protection and
championing of Williams is pointed, and Guthrie threw in his hand. As
early as 8 March 1934 (immediately after *Love for Love* had opened, and
almost a month before the ill-starred *Macbeth*) the Governors were
informed: 'For family reasons Mr Guthrie has to be in Ireland most of
the summer which would preclude his returning.' This sounds suspiciously like face-saving, and certainly the 'family reasons' did not
prevent Mr Guthrie undertaking two West End productions that
autumn. Another implied criticism was the staging of a Birthday
Matinee of *Hamlet* in its entirety at Sadler's Wells, directed by Ben Greet
(now seventy-seven and knighted) with Ernest Milton, Sybil Thorndike
and a cast of Old Vic alumni. There had been no such move when
Harcourt Williams omitted *Hamlet* from two of his seasons. In searching
for Guthrie's successor Lilian was determined to maintain a firmer
control. At the Governors' meeting on 12 April 1934 'It was agreed on
Mrs Lang's suggestion that when the post was offered it should be for
part of the season only, the management retaining the option to prolong
the contract should this be advisable.'

The *Annual Report* for 1933–4 affirmed that Guthrie 'had been
instrumental in bringing into the theatre many of the younger
generation, particularly the definitely artistic section, which might
otherwise have never entered it', but the truth was that neither Lilian nor
Guthrie had yet come to appreciate the other's quality. It would take an

older Miss Baylis and a more experienced Guthrie to find a shared vision
for the Vic.

Losing ground

After a predictable reaction in favour of a safe appointment (Lewis
Casson turned them down)[5] the Governors bravely chose another
young man, Henry Cass, with a background not dissimilar to Guthrie's:
he had been running an ambitious programme of unfamiliar plays at the
Croydon Repertory Theatre, but was even less practised in staging
Shakespeare. He showed judgement in bringing forward Maurice Evans
(hitherto a successful juvenile lead), and first as Richard II, then as
Euripides' Hippolytus, and finally as Hamlet Evans achieved such wide
acclaim that he was asked to play Romeo on Broadway, remained in
America, and never appeared on the British stage again. But Cass was
less fortunate in his other casting, and the Shakespeare plays suffered at
the Box-Office. The *Annual Report* for 1934–5 admitted: 'The management now resorts to the plays of Mr Bernard Shaw not only with
admiration but relief. It is unlikely that they will be performed to meagre
houses', and both *St Joan* and *Major Barbara* (with American-born Mary
Newcomb in the title-roles) figured in Cass's first season.

His second season employed William Devlin, still in his early
twenties, as a leading actor. Remarkably he played Richard III, Leontes
and Lear, and even more remarkably challenged memories of one of
Robert Atkins's and Russell Thorndike's greatest achievements by
tackling Peer Gynt. Cass also followed Guthrie's lead by including *The
Three Sisters* in a production which preceded the memorable St
Denis–Gielgud version by three years, and showed courage by tackling
a new play, *St Helena*. Such novelties as had previously appeared on the
Old Vic stage were usually commissioned for special occasions,
particularly Christmas and Easter, but this was R. C. Sheriff's account of
the journey's end of another soldier, Napoleon. It has something of a
succès d'estime, particularly after Winston Churchill wrote enthusiastically
about it in *The Times*, and was briefly transferred to the West End.

The 1935–6 season also reduced the showing of plays at Sadler's Wells
to a minimum: one week of *King Lear* and two of *Peer Gynt*. Nevertheless
neither the solid support of the earlier years nor the feverish interest of
the Laughton season was forthcoming. The *Annual Report* summed up
the year as 'peculiarly and rather unfortunately instructive', and Cass
confessed long afterwards: 'It was either make or break at the Vic; it

broke me professionally'⁶ – an unduly damning assessment, since he was gainfully if not glamorously employed as a director of plays and films for the next thirty years. Perhaps his lasting legacy to the Vic was convincing Lilian that Guthrie had a great deal more in him than she had previously allowed. Always as quick to forgive as upbraid, she welcomed him back two years after she had helped him to go.

Gaining the lead

For the next ten years Tyrone Guthrie was to guide the fortunes of the Old Vic, *de facto* after Lilian's death in 1937, *de jure* from February 1939 when his existing title of 'Director of Drama' was enlarged to 'Director of the Old Vic and Sadler's Wells Theatres'.⁷ His return was greatly eased by Lilian's acceptance that at her age and in her state of health she needed to share responsibility and that Guthrie had the energy and flair for this undertaking. Their relationship was not always smooth – for example, there was the famous dispute over his extravagance in hiring taxis for the entire Company after a late night dress rehearsal of *Henry V* in 1937 – but increasingly she trusted and depended on him. Their understanding certainly deepened during the preparations for *Hamlet* with Olivier at Elsinore in the summer of 1937, the first time a British company had performed there. Both during the rehearsals in the courtyard of Kronborg Castle, where she sustained Her People with sandwiches, lemonade and even rum, and in the frantic transfer of a rain-soaked first night, attended by the Danish Royal family, to the Ballroom of the Marjienlist Hotel, she recognised her director of drama as a man after her own heart. In 1938, when Guthrie had to defend his decision to present *Hamlet* in modern dress before a sceptical Board of Governors, he acknowledged her trust: 'Miss Baylis was always prepared to support her producer, even against her personal inclination, when she felt his point of view was a matter of conviction and sincere thought.'⁸

During the years before the outbreak of War Guthrie was therefore able to transform the Vic's standing, whether consciously or not, towards the nucleus of a National Theatre. This was not a goal which appealed to Lilian Baylis, who regarded her Vic–Wells empire as a *de facto* National Theatre, made all the more important by its location on the perimeter of theatrical London. But Guthrie saw that it could not stand still and without incentive must regress (as it had under his predecessor). He made the necessary provisions; the consolidation of the drama programme at the Vic was finally accepted and before he resumed direction he persuaded the Governors, on 6 May 1936, to agree to 'open' runs of not less than three and not more than six weeks.

He also greatly increased the use of 'special' engagements, so that the leading actors were not overworked, as for example Ion Swinley, Ralph Richardson, Edith Evans and Peggy Ashcroft had been, and important supporting parts could be appropriately cast. The limitation of a leading actor's tour of duty meant that one season could offer a range of major performers: in 1936–7, for example, Edith Evans dominated the first half and Olivier the second; in 1937–8 Emlyn Williams appeared as Angelo and Richard III in the early part, and Olivier and Richardson played leads in the later plays. Leading actors could also be engaged for a single production, as Diana Wynyard and Robert Morley were for *Pygmalion* in 1937, and Judith Anderson for Lady Macbeth the same season.

Assistance from outside was forthcoming. Just before he took over, both Theatres had finally been exempted from Entertainment Tax on the grounds of their educational objects. One of his first moves was to persuade the Governors to agree to co-production of *The Country Wife* (an altogether stronger brew than *Love for Love*) with the American impresario Gilbert Miller, and an American star, Ruth Gordon. Miller commissioned the elegant sets and costumes from Oliver Messel, and transferred them, with the star, to Broadway after the run. For *A Midsummer Night's Dream*, the 1937 Christmas production (also designed by Messel), the resources of Sadler's Wells were added to those of the Vic: full orchestra for Mendelssohn's music, Ninette de Valois to choreograph and supply dancers, Robert Helpmann as Oberon and Vivien Leigh as Titania, with Ralph Richardson adding to the ripeness of his earlier performance as Bottom the Weaver. The result was the most universally popular production of Guthrie's term of office, chosen for the Princesses Elizabeth's and Margaret's first visit to the theatre.

Not all his choices of play were as shrewd as this. To ask Michel St Denis, still a stranger to the English theatre, to undertake a little-known Elizabethan piece, *The Witch of Edmonton*, the previous Christmas invited the incomprehension it earned. *Ghosts*, tried out at Buxton in the summer of 1937, was 'thought unsuitable to the Vic'⁹ (and promptly secured by Bronson Albery for the West End). James Bridie's satire on Fascist dictators, *The King of Nowhere*, was as rash an offering in the uneasy spring of 1938 as *Henry V* was apt for the Coronation attraction in 1937. Both name-parts were played by Olivier, but with very different responses.

Nevertheless the choice of plays and players was mostly and overwhelmingly vindicated. Even controversy could be employed to the Vic's advantage, as Olivier's appearances proved. His Hamlet, early in 1937, was played in its entirety throughout the run, a feat only an actor of his stamina could accomplish. Its violence and speed seemed to many achieved at the cost of depth and feeling. Similarly his Macbeth in 1937 was more effective in battle than soliloquy: more warrior than worrier, reluctant to yield to Macduff and disabling the actor originally cast during the run. Despite the criticism both productions drew packed houses. Olivier's Iago, later in 1938, owed much to Freud, a debt Richardson as Othello was totally unwilling to pay. The most satisfying interpretation Olivier gave was his last: Coriolanus (under Lewis Casson's direction) to the Volumnia of Sybil Thorndike, a fascinating foreword to their stage partnership and relationship in Sophocles' *Oedipus* eight years later.

Passing on

Olivier's *Macbeth* attracted more than its due of that play's expected disasters. Directed by Michel St Denis with his customarily ruminative manner and leisured pace, it was manifestly unready at the dress rehearsal, and before the delayed opening night Lilian Baylis suffered a massive heart attack and died on 25 November 1937. She was sixty-three, and had devoted almost forty years of her life to the Theatre. It can truly be said that at least since Emma Cons's death in 1912 Lilian had represented the Old Vic for hundreds of performers and thousands of the public who knew her far better than almost any other audience knew any other manager in theatre history. Her character, with its strong contrasts of shrewdness and simplicity, piety and penny-pinching, good intentions and bad temper, and her idiom, richly rewarding to imitate, have become the subject of countless anecdotes, some substantiated, most funny and endearing, all particular to Lilian. Her dedication (however trying to colleagues on occasion) drove her to the verge of martyrdom. To conclude that without her the Theatre and the Company would not have survived is the barest tribute that can be paid her. Perhaps it is best to let her have the last word (as her associates always came to do). To her entry in *Who's Who in the Theatre* (5th Edition, 1925) Lilian added the claim:

> In 1914 she made the boldest experiment in theatrical history; against the advice of every London manager consulted she essayed what was regarded as the impossible task, in the conditions and at the low prices

charged, of producing Shakespeare permanently throughout the long annual season; since then there have been performed at the 'Old Vic' and under her direction, all the works in the first folio of Shakespeare, with the addition of Pericles, a feat which has never been equalled in the history of the stage, and this within a period of nine seasons . . .

Anyone who knew her would surely add: 'She was blowing the Old Vic's trumpet, not her own.'

Guthrie's pursuit of big 'names': Olivier, Richardson, Helpmann, Edith Evans, Judith Anderson, Sybil Thorndike, Vivien Leigh – to draw the crowds justified itself at the Box-Office, but it is notable that the productions succeeded as part of a programme. When *As You Like It*, with Edith Evans as an improbable but enchanting forty-eight-year-old Rosalind and Michael Redgrave as Orlando, and Olivier's *Macbeth* transferred to the West End, they failed to find a wider audience. Nor was his programme planning always proof against unforeseen circumstance. The opening of the 1938 season coincided with the Munich Crisis, during which the Underground lines beneath the Thames were closed as a precaution against air attack. The takings for the first production (*Trelawny of the 'Wells'*) dropped from £115 to £15 on consecutive nights.[10] Guthrie offered to scrap the modern-dress *Hamlet* (with Alec Guiness) then in preparation, and rehearse *Fanny's First Play* in ten days, but the Governors bravely insisted that *Hamlet* go ahead.[11] It made a considerable critical impact but did not draw the public. ('The poor Old Vic . . . the Westminster Bank rings up – but literally *every morning* – to say what about the overdraft' wrote Guthrie to his mother.)[12] *Man and Superman*, with Anthony Quayle as John Tanner, followed, and Shaw turned the corner, not for the first time.

In the years following Lilian Baylis's death the Vic–Wells organisation seemed increasingly destined to be more than a National Theatre, rather a National Performing Arts Association. With Sadler's Wells Opera steadily finding a public, and Sadler's Wells Ballet moving from national to international recognition, the goal appeared in sight. The Old Vic itself was also widening its sphere of activity: in the summer of 1937, following the visit to Elsinore, the Company established a precedent by undertaking a season at Buxton, running in the plays for the autumn. Early in 1939 a three-month Mediterranean tour, directed by Lewis Casson, was undertaken with an extensive repertory: all four productions staged so far that season (including *The Rivals*), together with *Henry V*, *I Have Been Here Before*, *Viceroy Sarah*, and *Libel*. There had been considerable debate about the inclusion of Fascist Italy on the itinerary; one correspondent had threatened to jump from the Gallery on the eve of their departure if the Italian commitment was kept. He did not do so ('a teeny bit disappointing for those of us who were all ears for the thud of a body landing in row L 76' was Guthrie's comment[13]), and in fact the Company was warmly received everywhere, the modern-dress *Hamlet* being particularly popular. The spring of 1939 seemed a season of promise for the Old Vic. The new resident Company won support for a strongly comic programme, including the revival of *A Midsummer Night's Dream* in Messel's designs, *The Taming of the Shrew*, and *She Stoops To Conquer*, though for *An Enemy of the People* (which Guthrie thought one of his best productions) 'the business in an otherwise prosperous season was the lowest within living memory at the Vic'.[14]

Nevertheless the Vic–Wells organisation seemed poised to move forward to truly national status. Guthrie's appointment as Director of both Theatres prompted a transfer of headquarters to Sadler's Wells, and in fact at this time the Old Vic building was under sentence of demolition by the LCC as part of a plan to build a Charing Cross road bridge across the Thames. This was abandoned in the summer, but meanwhile important negotiations had taken place between the Governors and the Shakespeare Memorial National Theatre Committee. On 10 March 1939 the Governors minuted:

> If the National Theatre authorities would accept the Old Vic Company as their planners and the Old Vic could accept the National Theatre as their building when the Old Vic was demolished, these two could become one.

– an ironic comment, with the hindsight that the Old Vic building (but not Company) and the National Theatre were to become one twenty-four years later.

The programme for the Buxton season that summer included *Romeo and Juliet*, *The Devil's Disciple* and *St Joan*, with Robert Donat as Romeo and Dick Dudgeon, and Constance Cummings as Juliet and Joan. It coincided with the outbreak of War and the closing of London theatres as a safety measure. Guthrie struggled to keep the Company together, but they got no nearer the Waterloo Road than Streatham Hill and Golders Green, and then disbanded. Save for a few weeks in the spring of 1940 the Old Vic Theatre remained closed for the duration, and from May 1941 onwards suffered increasing damage. The Old Vic Company was to play away for the next ten years.

7

Seeking shelter

1940—1944

The off-on regulations issued to theatres in the autumn of 1939 by a Government expecting massive air raids, if not actual invasion, left managements in a state of uncertainty approaching panic. Gradually London theatres were allowed to reopen, but the Governors of the Old Vic and Sadler's Wells, conscious of their responsibility for funds provided by charitable bodies, were more cautious than most. The Vic remained closed; the Wells began to offer occasional performances, and early in November the Governors authorised increased opening, from one to three nights a week. In fact Guthrie seems to have believed that wartime conditions, even those of the 'phoney' War, favoured the provision of opera and ballet, as an antidote to the darkness and drabness of the blackout, rather than the intellectual demands of the classical repertory. The importance of musical theatre to the capital's morale was recognised by a 'Jubilee Performance of Wartime Opera', attended by the Queen and Princess Marina, Duchess of Kent, at Sadler's Wells on 31 January 1940.[1]

But pressure to reopen the Vic built up, and an offer from John Gielgud to head the Company in a spring season of three plays was welcomed.[2] It was made all the more attractive by the promise of guidance from the man who many believed should have directed the National Theatre years before: Harley Granville-Barker. By this time he was in charge of the British Centre in Paris and very chary of theatrical responsibility. He would only agree to supervise the first production, *King Lear*, if Lewis Casson, a pupil of his twenty-five years earlier, was billed as director and undertook the early rehearsals. He did come to London to discuss the production with Gielgud and Casson, but then returned to Paris, while a distinguished Company was assembled: Casson himself (Kent); Nicholas Hannen (Gloucester); Fay Compton (Regan); Catherine Nesbitt (Goneril); Jessica Tandy (Cordelia); Jack

Hawkins (Edmund); Robert Harris (Edgar); and Harcourt Williams returning to his former duchy as Albany. Casson, having set the production in motion, had the dubious satisfaction of seeing the play re-directed by Granville-Barker over the last ten days of rehearsal. The experience was immensely educative for the Company, but the results predictably lacked clarity and speed, and since Granville-Barker left before the first night on 15 April, could not be tightened up during the run.[3]

In any case the European stage was rapidly becoming more gripping than that in the Waterloo Road or any other theatre. The German drive to the French coast cut off not only the British Expeditionary Force but the Sadler's Wells Ballet on a goodwill tour to Holland. At their meeting on 10 May the Governors were informed that the dancers were 'under the protection of our Legation in Holland', and in fact they only escaped at the last minute, leaving all their scenery and costumes behind. At the Old Vic *Lear* survived such hazards as losing Stephen Haggard (the Fool) when he went to Harwich to visit a Naval friend, found himself taken to sea on an emergency mission and disappeared without trace for a week.[4]

Against this background *The Tempest*, directed by George Devine and Marius Goring, which opened on 29 May had to compete with more urgent marine matters such as the Dunkirk evacuation. Lewis Casson, playing Gonzalo, heard just as he went on at a matinee that his son in the Fleet Air Arm had been shot down over Norway and was missing, believed killed. He bore up through the early scenes (including Alonso's cruelly relevant line: 'My son is lost') but broke down at the sight of Ferdinand and Miranda (played by Alec Guinness and Jessica Tandy) happily engaged at chess. (Mercifully John Casson was no more lost than Prince Ferdinand; he survived five years in a Prisoner of War Camp and returned to prosper in his theatrical career.)[5] But the time was not propitious for *The Tempest*, which closed early on 22 June, the day France fell. The third play in the programme was abandoned, the Old Vic went dark and the Old Vic Company left the Waterloo Road for a decade.

In August the Battle of Britain began and London braced itself for air raids. At a meeting on 13 September, held at the New Theatre because of transport difficulties, the Governors learnt that the Borough of Finsbury had commandeered Sadler's Wells as a Reception Centre, and 'during the meeting there was a bomb explosion, followed by an air raid warning' (in that order). 'The Governors moved to the basement to complete the business.' Nevertheless the Opera and Ballet Companies, with the musical support of two pianos, toured extensively to crowded houses. Finance for these and other activities was provided by the newly established Council for the Encouragement of Music and the Arts (CEMA), funded by the government to bring the evidence of enduring values to those on work of national importance. The Old Vic was immediately signed up to mount a tour of the South Wales mining areas with Lewis Casson and Sybil Thorndike in *Macbeth*, and of the North West with *Twelfth Night* and *She Stoops to Conquer*. The itinerary for this tour included the Victoria Theatre, Burnley, a date of more than usual significance since the warm reception there inspired Guthrie to suggest moving the Company headquarters and administrative offices to Burnley until further notice. This proved a wise decision and set the pace for much touring in the next three years. In the autumn of 1941, for example, there were three Old Vic Companies in action: the Cassons in South Wales with *Candida* and *Medea* (no concessions to light relief but overflowing houses); *The Merchant of Venice* with Frederick Valk and Sonia Dresdel in the North West; and *The Cherry Orchard* with Athene Seyler and Nicholas Hannen touring major theatres. A year later an Old Vic Company was established at the Liverpool Playhouse, where the resident company had had to disband because of the Blitz, and operated with artistic and commercial success for the next four years.

But meanwhile disaster had struck in the Waterloo Road. On 10 May 1941 enemy action caused extensive damage to the Theatre. At their next meeting the Governors learnt that:

a The roof needs to be replaced entirely.
b Back-stage walls are partly down; the remainder of the walls may have to come down.
c The lift needs repairing.

The surveyor who gave this report added: 'The damage does not justify complete rebuilding. There is therefore no claim against the Government for the replacement of the building.'⁶ It is perhaps not too fanciful to detect a note of regret in this last statement. For some years those Governors who looked to the Old Vic's emergence as the National Theatre Company had been troubled by the limitations of the Old Vic building for such a metamorphosis. The proposed demolition for a bridge-building scheme in 1939 had offered one solution. Total destruction by air raids might have offered another. Certainly there appears to have been some doubt in the Governors' minds as to the feasibility of patching up the Theatre. At this same meeting they concluded: 'As it seemed impossible that the Vic would reopen during the War in any case it would be wrong to spend a large sum of money on repairs which might easily be wasted through enemy action', a judgement confirmed when the cost of repairs was estimated at £6,000.[7] It was probably this point of view which allowed further deterioration in the Theatre over the next four years: the leaking roof let in the rain, and a hard winter froze the pipes which subsequently burst, causing further damage.

Although committed to touring Guthrie felt that Old Vic productions should still be seen in London, if only briefly, and accordingly *King John* (with Ernest Milton) and *The Cherry Orchard* were played at the New Theatre in 1941; *Othello* (with Frederick Valk and Bernard Miles) and *The Merry Wives of Windsor* (with Freda Jackson and Rosalind Atkinson) in 1942, and *The Merchant of Venice* (with Valk) in 1943. The New Theatre was made available through the good offices of its Managing Director, Bronson Albery, and served also as a London base for the Opera Company (now under Joan Cross) and the Ballet. Albery was appointed Joint Administrator of the organisation in October 1942, and his knowledge and resources proved invaluable to Guthrie during these years. By the summer of 1943 the latter felt confident enough to mount a 'Salute to the Allies' season at the Playhouse, the Allies in question being the USA (with Drinkwater's *Abraham Lincoln*, in which Harcourt Williams, the Lincoln of the Vic's 1932 revival, changed sides and played Robert E. Lee); the USSR (with *The Russians* by Konstantin Simonov); and Britain, represented by a very young Peter Ustinov's very early play, *Blow Your Own Trumpet*, directed by Michael Redgrave. But this Second Front proved decidedly premature, and the season folded precipitately.

If the Old Vic were to establish themselves in the West End, several major names were clearly desirable. A move in this direction was Guthrie's revival (with the assistance of Michael Benthall) of *Hamlet* at the New early in 1944, with Robert Helpmann, a mainstay of the Ballet Company throughout the War, showing he could play as well as dance the Prince, and Leslie Hurry designing, as he had the ballet two years earlier. Flora Robson also returned from Hollywood to play Thérèse Raquin (in an adaptation entitled *Guilty*) at the Lyric, Hammersmith in April 1944.

A much more ambitious scheme was in the making. The Admiralty were persuaded to release Ralph Richardson and Laurence Olivier (who suggests in his autobiography that 'the speediness and lack of reluctance with which their Lordships let us go was positively hurtful')[8] from the Fleet Air Arm to lead a distinguished Company in an open-ended programme at the New Theatre. John Burrell, hitherto a radio producer, was assigned to second Guthrie; the veterans in the Company included Sybil Thorndike, Nicholas Hannen, Harcourt Williams and George Relph; and the two discoveries were Margaret Leighton and Joyce Redman. The first three productions were to be *Peer Gynt*, with Richardson, Sybil Thorndike as Aase, Joyce Redman as Solveig, and Olivier as the Button-Moulder; *Arms and the Man*, with Olivier as Sergius, Richardson as Bluntschli again, and Margaret Leighton as Raina; and *Richard III* with Olivier. The plays were to be presented in repertory, a rare achievement for a British company in the West End. Rehearsals began just as the first VI missiles ('doodlebugs') struck London, but D Day had dawned, attack was the password, and the capitulation of four years earlier was inconceivable.

Peer Gynt opened on 31 August, and the remaining two productions within a fortnight. All three were were triumphs, individually and corporately, with both critics and public. The Box-Office was besieged, and the glamour attaching to the enterprise greatly enhanced by Olivier's subsequent success as both director and star of the film *Henry V*. Although CEMA had originally undertaken to guarantee the New Theatre season against loss up to £10,000,[9] there was no need to call on them while Olivier and Richardson led the Company.

So began the most illustrious chapter in the history of the Old Vic Company, though not strictly part of the history of the Old Vic Theatre.

8

Seeking supremacy

1944–1976

Between August 1944 and April 1947 the Old Vic Company at the New Theatre mounted productions of *Peer Gynt*; *Arms and the Man*; *Richard III*; *Uncle Vanya*; *Henry IV*: 1 and 2; *Oedipus Rex* and *The Critic*; *King Lear*; *An Inspector Calls*; *Cyrano de Bergerac*; *The Alchemist*; and *Richard II*. Olivier triumphed in leading roles (Richard III; Astrov; and – more controversially – King Lear), and in astonishing 'doubles' (Hotspur and Justice Shallow; Oedipus and Puff). Richardson was outstanding as Peer Gynt; Vanya; Falstaff; Cyrano; Inspector Goole; Face, besides stealing a scene as Lord Burleigh. Alec Guinness, still in the Navy when the Company was formed, made his mark as De Guiche; the Fool; Abel Drugger and – less certainly – Richard II. The Company blazed the British trail in Europe immediately after VE Day, when they played in such vastly disparate venues as Hamburg, Belsen, and the Comédie Française, in New York, and again in Paris, in 1946. In terms of actor-managers' theatre the era was enthralling, except that, unlike the Victorian model, there were two actor-managers at the same theatre, working in harmony and with equal standing.

But for the Old Vic–Sadler's Wells organisation these years were less halcyon. The very success of the New Theatre seasons exacerbated the inevitably complex issues with which the end of the War confronted the Governors. Should they return to the *status quo*? Guthrie and others were strongly opposed. Even before the War was over Guthrie had argued at a Governors' meeting on 12 January 1945 that 'since the Old Vic charter was granted in 1880 social conditions had changed: the theatres' most valuable contribution could now be made in high artistic standard, not in cheap seats as a form of social service'. Then there was the problem occasioned by the Opera and Ballet Companies' extraordinary wartime popularity. The tenure of the New Theatre by the Old Vic had driven them temporarily to the Prince's, but with peace approaching Sadler's

Wells would be available once more. Should they return to the theatrical perimeter? Edward Dent, a senior spokesman, declared at the same meeting that 'both theatres stand for moral ideas, not bricks and mortar', and made it clear that his preference would be to house both Opera and Ballet Companies at Covent Garden. This illustrious edifice had been downgraded to a dancehall during the War, but the lessees, Boosey and Hawkes, were planning to reopen it and indicated their interest in some sort of understanding with the Vic–Wells Companies. As for Sadler's Wells itself, Dent suggested that it should become an opera and ballet school.

Meanwhile the idea of the Old Vic's involvement in the National Theatre was revived. At a 'Private and Confidential Meeting' of the Shakespeare Memorial National Theatre Committee and Old Vic representatives on 21 February the Chairman, Oliver Lyttelton, then a member of the Wartime Cabinet, proposed the purchase of a 'freehold site of one acre midway between Waterloo Bridge and Hungerford Bridge' (in part exchange for the existing South Kensington site) and suggested that the name of the new building should be 'The National Theatre, incorporating the Shakespeare Memorial National Theatre and the Old Vic'.[1]

Perhaps it was these strongly felt but potentially conflicting views that made Guthrie aware what problems lay ahead; and how exhausted six year of sustaining the Vic–Wells under wartime conditions had left him. Bronson Albery had resigned as Joint Administrator in April 1944, no doubt foreseeing that the new Old Vic Company would have too many chiefs for these particular Indians. Guthrie himself records that

> The Shakespeare Company was now being operated by a triumvirate – Olivier, Richardson and John Burrell. I had agreed to the arrangement and already had misgivings about it. Burrell, considerably younger and less experienced than the other two, could not be expected to have the authority and weight to stand up against their towering reputation and powerful personalities.[2]

More specifically the planning of the 1945–6 season ran into trouble when Olivier insisted that *Oedipus* (which Guthrie was to direct) should be twinned with *The Critic*. The director's response was: 'Over my dead body',[3] and when it became clear that Olivier would not yield, resigned. At their meeting on 1 June 1945 the Governors accepted a recommendation 'that the dramatic activities of the Old Vic be under a Panel of Directors, consisting of John Burrell, Laurence Olivier, and Ralph

Richardson, of which Mr Burrell will be Chairman', and at a subsequent meeting, on 27 July, heard that 'the Old Vic Drama Panel under the Chairmanship of Mr Burrell had accepted responsibility for all Old Vic dramatic activities. The replacement of Mr Guthrie as Administrator was not therefore necessary.'

Michel St Denis, who had spent the War rallying his fellow-countrymen on the Free French radio, took over *Oedipus*, and Miles Malleson directed *The Critic*. When the double bill opened on 18 October 1945 it proved the most sensational success of the Olivier–Richardson years. Guthrie would (and did) return to direct *Cyrano de Bergerac*, but for the time being looked to the New World to redress the balance of the Old and went to America. The meeting of Governors on 12 October records:

> The Governors of the Old Vic and Salder's Wells Theatres desire to record their great regret that Mr Tyrone Guthrie has decided to resign his post as Administrator, to take up other work in the US, and their gratitude and appreciation of the splendid services he has rendered to the three activities of the two Theatres – Drama, Opera and Ballet – for over ten years.
>
> After the death of Lilian Baylis in 1937, it was due to the combined efforts of Sir Reginald Rowe and Tyrone Guthrie that the continuity of her work was maintained, and that the high standard of all three activities was not only maintained unimpaired but even raised still higher.

Meanwhile the decision to base the Ballet on Covent Garden was confirmed, and the Company reopened the Royal Opera House with a performance of *The Sleeping Beauty* on 20 February 1946. Sadler's Wells Opera on the other hand returned to its old home before Guthrie's departure, marking that return with great distinction by staging the world premiere of *Peter Grimes* only a month after VE Day. Nevertheless the decision to fund publicly a permanent opera company at Covent Garden presented Sadler's Wells with powerful competition both for Arts Council (as CEMA became) support and for leading singers.

The departure of the Ballet left a gap which was gradually filled by the Sadler's Wells Opera Ballet, at first providing the necessary support in the operas but ultimately finding a public and a repertoire of its own. Meanwhile the Old Vic Company was itself expanding. Although a resident company had returned to the Liverpool Playhouse after the War, the Arts Council invited the Vic to provide a company for the historic Theatre Royal, Bristol, which CEMA had restored and reopened (with a touring Old Vic production of *She Stoops to Conquer*) in 1943. In February 1946 the Bristol Old Vic was launched under the direction of Hugh Hunt, and their success was such that nine months later their production of *Tess of the D'Urbervilles* with Wendy Hiller occupied the New Theatre while *King Lear* played in Paris.

Splendid as the achievements of the Old Vic were in these years, their rapturous reception at the outset was at least partly due to the spirit of the times: the knowledge that the tide of War had turned and victory was within sight. There was real hope for a nation that could mount *Peer Gynt* and *Richard III* concurrently with the return to Europe, and mark VJ Day by the two parts of *Henry IV*. Such heroic feats could not be sustained indefinitely, particularly by two actors whose fame (and income) depended on their film rather than their theatrical careers. After *King Lear* Olivier took leave of absence to make his film of *Hamlet*, and did not return to the New Theatre for two years. Richardson completed the 1946–7 season and then started filming *Anna Karenina* with Vivien Leigh. He was to make only one further appearance for the Old Vic Company, as Timon of Athens nine years later. The burden of running the Company fell on John Burrell, and both the quality of the productions and the warmth of audience response suffered. As early as 16 January 1947 (three days after the premiere of *The Alchemist*) Kenneth Rae, Secretary of the Old Vic Trust, wrote to Mary Glasgow, Secretary of the Arts Council:

> The Old Vic Sub-Committee does not altogether like the look of the theatrical sky. In its opinion the boom is over and account must be taken of the fact that we have returned to more normal times when everything touched by the producer cannot be expected to turn to gold.[4]

He went on to plead for a £15,000 guarantee against loss on the 1947–8 season.

There remained the problem of the Old Vic Theatre itself. The Company's success in the West End had lent weight to the prospect of a new role in a newly built National Theatre, and this development became the objective of Viscount Esher, a long-standing member of the National Theatre Committee, and a Governor from 1946. He became Chairman in 1948, following the death in 1947 of the Earl of Lytton, who had served the Old Vic so long and so valiantly, and of his successor, Viscount Hambledon, early in 1948. An acceptable use for the Waterloo Road building presented itself in 1946 when a proposal was put to the Governors by three distinguished theatre practitioners, Michel St Denis, George Devine and Glen Byam Shaw. Their aim was to reopen the damaged building as a Theatre Centre, encompassing an Experimental Stage, a Theatre School and the base for a Children's Theatre Company, the 'Young Vic'. St Denis was to be in overall control, Byam Shaw to run the School, and Devine the Young Vic, but all three would teach at the School and contribute to the Theatre Centre. The Governors viewed this concept as an exciting development which would exonerate them from the charge of abandoning the Waterloo Road house, with its faithful public and stirring history. Funding was precarious, but the Arts Council offered £9,500 annually, to be reviewed every two years,[5] minimal repairs were carried out, and the School inaugurated on 24 January 1947.

The opening ceremony was performed by Ellen Wilkinson, Minister of Education, and Olivier (in a final Old Vic appearance before starting to film *Hamlet*) addressed the students in these striking if somewhat daunting words:

> An actor, above all, must be a great understander, either by intuition, observation, or both, and that puts him on the level with a doctor, a priest or a philosopher. If I can get more from him than just belief, then I feel fortunate and overjoyed . . . There are many dimensions in the art of acting, but NONE of them . . . are good or interesting . . . unless they are invested with the appearance, or complete illusion, of truth. The difference between the actual truth and the illusion of truth is what you are about to learn. You will not finish learning it until you are dead.[6]

The actual opening ceremony coincided with the onset of a major fuel crisis due to bitterly cold weather. The patched-up Theatre was heated only by an oil stove, and the consequent chill may have had a fatal effect on poor Ellen Wilkinson, who died shortly afterwards. Nevertheless the School began its work in good heart and St Denis commissioned a French architect, Pierre Sonrel, to plan the transformation of the bruised and battered Vic into an Experimental Theatre space by constructing a substantial and accessible thrust-stage.

At the same time the Young Vic Company under Devine was launched with a Christmas production of *The King Stag* at the Lyric, Hammersmith. It was conceived as a Children's Theatre Company, playing to young audiences in schools or similar locales, but the lack of response from education authorities forced a change of policy. Throughout its five years of existence the Young Vic performed a repertoire mostly of Elizabethan comedies in conventional theatres to mixed age-groups. It twice played at the Old Vic itself: in December 1948, with *The Snow Queen*, and in January 1949 with *As You Like It*. In 1949 a smaller group, the Young Vic Players, did take their mixed bill and mobile productions to theatreless areas, but the Company's biggest successes were achieved in Shakespeare (*A Midsummer Night's Dream*; *The Merchant of Venice*) and, paradoxically, abroad on tour to Scandinavia, Belgium and Holland.

Unhappily the Theatre Centre Scheme, which promised to please all parties in 1946, when the Old Vic Company was riding high, looked very different two years later. The National Theatre was still on the drawing-board (after three changes of site and architect), and though legislation was finally passed in February 1949 authorising the expenditure of £1 million on a South Bank site to be provided by the LCC, there was no promise of when the money would be made available. Without Olivier and Richardson the 1947–8 season at the New Theatre proved an inevitable anticlimax: the leading actors engaged (Trevor Howard as Petruchio; Celia Johnson as St Joan; John Clements as Coriolanus) did not entirely find the measure of their parts, and the major personal success was achieved by Alec Guinness in a supporting role (the Dauphin) and as Gogol's Government Inspector in a play not then widely known or popular. The season lost £9,000.[7]

It was clear to some members of the Governing body that placing the direction of the Company in the hands of actors with world-wide reputations and commitments was a risky business. The solution appeared to them to be a long-term Administrator and a short-term Artistic Director. The outcome of these deliberations was the notorious 'dismissal' of Olivier, Richardson and Burrell (in fact letters pointing out that their contracts, due to expire in 1949, would not be renewed). The task, which fell to Lord Esher, was made all the more invidious since Olivier was abroad at the time, leading an Old Vic Company with Vivien Leigh on an enormously successful tour of Australia and New Zealand, with *Richard III*, *The School for Scandal* and *The Skin of Our Teeth*. As a further twist of the screw Olivier's reappearance at the New (and Vivien Leigh's first appearances there) for the second part of the 1948–9 season in *Richard III*, *The School for Scandal* and the British premiere of Anouilh's *Antigone*, were hugely popular, and the British Council, who had sponsored the Australasian tour, handed over the profits (£20,000) to an embarrassed board of Governors.[8]

Their embarrassment was compounded by the drubbing which the resident Company had received in the early part of the season. Cedric Hardwicke, a leading British actor twenty years earlier, returned from Hollywood to play Toby Belch, Doctor Faustus and Gaev, but filming had dulled his acting edge. In particular his Faustus lacked all magic and the production had to be withdrawn. Edith Evans as Lady Wishfort could not raise *The Way of the World* to the level remembered by those who saw her as Millamant long ago and far away at the Lyric, Hammersmith, and only Hugh Hunt's production of *The Cherry Orchard* matched the inspiration of her Ranevsky. At their meeting on 4 November 1948 the Governors were warned that the Company was likely to lose £18,000 by January, and a tour of North America was cancelled. New brooms seemed called for; Llewellyn Rees, at that time Drama Director of the Arts Council and a Governor some years earlier, was appointed Administrator, and Hugh Hunt's success at Bristol recognised by his promotion to be Artistic Director of the parent Company.

It was also clear that economy was called for. One prudent measure suggested itself: cutting out the expensive rent of a West End theatre and heading back home. This move was encouraged by the Arts Council's offer of an earmarked grant of £50,000 to restore the Waterloo Road building (conveniently placed for the Festival of Britain site) in time for the 1951 festivities. The Company's return would inevitably affect the Theatre Centre. There was distrust in some quarters of the intuitive and analytical emphasis of the School's teaching (inherited from the London Theatre Studio, which St Denis had run before the War), rather than rigorous technical exercises which would prepare the students to play as cast. In any case the Company could not function fully in the same building as the School, and after a frustrating search for alternative premises near the Theatre it moved in November 1949 to the former Dulwich High School for Girls, purchased for £8,500. In January 1950 work on the Theatre itself began, after agreement that responsibility for alterations to the stage and backstage area should rest with St Denis and his architect Sonrel, while the auditorium and front of house were to be Hugh Hunt's preserve. These plans had received a set-back two months earlier, when the Governors learnt that the Arts Council, while still offering help towards the Company's opening productions, could not find the £50,000 promised for rebuilding. This sum had therefore to be borrowed, apart from modest grants from the Carnegie and Pilgrim Trusts and the City Parochial Foundation.[9]

The choice of Michael Redgrave to lead the 1949–50 season was propitious. He extended his comic range as Berowne and Young Marlow, and consolidated his tragic standing as Hamlet. Hugh Hunt's production of *Love's Labour's Lost* was acclaimed, Tyrone Guthrie returned to direct an adaptation of *The Miser* by and with Miles Malleson, and only *A Month in the Country*, directed by St Denis, seemed to some an eternity in the theatre. With the move back to the Waterloo Road now imminent, the relationship of the Old Vic to the elusive National Theatre and Company acquired a new dimension. In December 1949 the then Chairman of the Arts Council, Sir Ernest Pooley, took exception to a statement by the Governors that they had a 'legal right' to be the first occupants of the projected building, and in March 1950 an exchange of letters between Hugh Hunt and Viscount Esher suggested that the future role of the Old Vic Theatre would be as a 'second house' for the National. To Esher's misgivings about the geographical separation of the two, Hunt pointed out that in Paris the Comédie Française and the Salle Luxembourg were even further apart but managed to cooperate.[10]

Of more immediate concern was the line of command at the reopened Old Vic Theatre. Rees, Hunt, St Denis, Devine and Byam Shaw were all to be Directors of the Company, but their respective status was not defined and misunderstandings proved inevitable. Rees as Administrator insisted that he should attend Governors' meetings and speak for the other Directors; Hunt as Artistic Director, made a similar claim, and the three 'boys' found themselves cut off from direct communication with the Board.[11] The withdrawal of the earmarked Arts Council grant and consequent need to borrow impressed the importance of economy on the Governors, who suggested that Byam Shaw should relinquish his post at the School, on the understanding that he would succeed Hunt as Artistic Director in due course. But the effective date for this change remained uncertain, and the operation of the building as an Experimental Theatre Centre looked increasingly improbable. Meanwhile the reopening had been set for 14 November 1950 with a Royal visit from King George VI, Queen Elizabeth and Princess Margaret on 6 December. The first production was to be *Twelfth Night*, with Peggy Ashcroft as Viola, Roger Livesey as Sir Toby, Paul Rogers as Malvolio, and (on the first night) Edith Evans to speak a specially written Prologue. The Young Vic offered an adaptation of Stevenson's *Black Arrow* for Christmas, Devine directed *Bartholomew Fair*, Peggy Ashcroft appeared as Sophocles' Electra in a production by St Denis that aimed to display the thrust-stage, and Byam Shaw directed *Henry V* with Alec Clunes.

But there was more drama backstage than onstage. The three men at the Centre felt the proposal regarding Glen Byam Shaw was the first move in a divide-and-destroy policy, and wondered who would go next. In particular St Denis's position as overall director of the Centre seemed threatened. Rightly or wrongly they believed his French nationality to be held against him. It has been claimed that 'Esher could never understand St Denis's broken English, and dismissed him accordingly as a foreigner whose proper place was somewhere else'.[12] When Byam Shaw was asked to attend an Emergercy Meeting of the Governors, he affirmed:

> The personal view of the two other Directors was that it was immoral not to allow someone in whom they themselves believed to be the top authority simply because he was French and not English. The decisions made at the last few meetings had reduced M. St Denis from Director of the Centre to a Director of the School, and this was fundamentally wrong.[13]

Early in May 1951 the Centre trio decided to force the issue by submitting their resignations. If they hoped thereby to compel the Governors to admit them to their confidence, they were disappointed. Lord Esher accepted the resignations on 7 May, and despite vociferous protests from the Press, the profession, the School and ultimately the House of Commons, the Governors stuck to their decision. Some of them, however, did feel that Rees's obduracy had contributed to the impasse, and his resignation was also requested.[14] In his place Tyrone Guthrie was persuaded to return as Administrator, leaving Hugh Hunt awkwardly designated Administrative Director. Not surprisingly his production of *The Merry Wives of Windsor*, opening in the midst of the maelstrom, proved less merry than Shakespeare intended, despite the talents of Peggy Ashcroft and Ursula Jeans as the Wives and Roger Livesey as Falstaff.

The Experimental Theatre Centre was clearly doomed and the Young Vic Company disbanded at once. The School was not immediately closed; obligations to the students were honoured, and the courses continued until the summer of 1952. It is not true that 'St Denis was too tired . . . Everything had been taken away from him, and he'd had such a battering that he did not want to fight any more.'[15] Records of the

Governors' meetings show that as late as March 1952 he was negotiating for the School, independently funded, to continue in its Dulwich premises.[16] But the money was not forthcoming, and instead St Denis returned to France to become Directeur of the Centre Dramatique Nationale de l'Est at Strasbourg. Byam Shaw had already transferred his allegiance to Stratford, first as Assistant Director and then as Director. Devine picked up the threads of his free-lancing career until, three years later, he was able to establish the English Stage Company at the Royal Court. The Dulwich premises proved something of a liability; efforts to sell them failed and they had to be let to an independent school.

Guthrie's return was hailed with relief by the Governors, particularly when he announced that Donald Wolfit would head the new Company, opening as Tamburlaine in what was claimed as the first professional production of Marlowe's play for three hundred years. Both Guthrie and Wolfit lived up to expectations, Leslie Hurry's designs were aptly stunning, and the Old Vic's fortunes again looked fair. But Wolfit had led his own company too long to take his allotted place in an ensemble. He rapidly began to assume actor-managerial airs and habits, which were greatly resented by his colleagues. The breaking-point was reached in October, when the Company performed *Tamburlaine* at Stratford-on-Avon, and Wolfit, safe from Guthrie's eyes and ears, played the tyrant on and off the stage. An SOS brought Guthrie to remonstrate, and Wolfit rashly resigned (and then characteristically gave a superb performance as Lord Ogleby in *The Clandestine Marriage*).[17]

His departure meant the withdrawal of these two productions and left two leading roles, Lear and Timon of Athens, to fill. To add to the Old Vic's woes Guthrie's way with the Christmas attraction, *A Midsummer Night's Dream*, left audiences unseasonably critical. No doubt he aimed for something as different as possible from the Mendelssohnian splendours of his pre-War productions. If so, he succeeded at the expense of the Box-Office. Predictably disasters multiplied. Stephen Murray, recruited for Lear, carried out an exhausting Scandinavian tour but collapsed shortly after the London opening, and his understudy, John Colicos, took over for the remainder of the run. *Timon of Athens* was not the play to restore the audiences' spirits, nor was a new play about François Villon, *The Other Heart*. Guthrie had already begun to look elsewhere, arranging for Alfred Francis, an able entrepreneur from Liverpool, to take over as Administrative Director, and suggesting Michael Benthall as Hugh Hunt's successor.

But man proposes and the public disposes. At a meeting of the Old Vic Trust on 12 June 1952 it was agreed 'in view of the serious financial position' to accept Guthrie's offer to surrender his salary from 31 May until his resignation took effect on 30 June. A Mr Shovelton, representing the City Parochial Foundation, subsequently reminded the Governors that 'the purpose for which the Old Vic existed was to serve the poor people of London and not necessarily to aim at West End standards'.[18] In fact the position had become so serious that the Arts Council advised the Old Vic not to enter into any commitments beyond Christmas, and at an Emergency Meeting of the Governors on 30 May Hugh Hunt demanded – and received – a vote of confidence. The Theatre's future seemed to depend on his production of *Romeo and Juliet*, which was (despite Hunt's misgivings as to its suitability) to open in the Church of Scotland's Assembly Hall at the Edinburgh Festival, before coming to the Old Vic in September. The casting (Alan Badel; Claire Bloom, bathed in her *Limelight* success; and Peter Finch as Mercutio) was propitious, the production stirring, and the Box-Office so healthy that the run had to be extended. The Arts Council withdrew its warning, the Governors breathed again. Success continued: in February 1953 Hugh Hunt told the Governors that his production of *The Merchant of Venice* (with Paul Rogers and Irene Worth) had sold out for its entire seven-week run,[19] and *Murder in the Cathedral* proved both a critical and Box-Office favourite, largely due the Becket of Robert Donat. The season ended with an apt Coronation choice, *Henry VIII*, directed by Guthrie, with Rogers and Gwen Ffrangçon Davies, and the Queen and the Duke of Edinburgh present on the first night. Hunt then handed over to Michael Benthall. He was not to work for the Old Vic again, but he has left a fitting memorial in the shape of his book *Old Vic Prefaces*.

Long-term planning

Before 1953 Michael Benthall had had only a modest connection with the Old Vic Company, helping Guthrie to direct *Hamlet* during the War, and directing *She Stoops to Conquer* in the last season at the New Theatre. But he had undertaken a number of Shakespeare productions at Stratford and elsewhere, and on appointment announced a Five-Year Plan to present all the plays in the First Folio. In fact Shakespeare claimed the Old Vic stage from September 1953 to July 1958. The last Old Vic production by another author was *Murder in the Cathedral* in

April 1953 and the next Schiller's *Mary Stuart* in September 1958. For the first time in thirty years rarities like *Troilus and Cressida*, *Titus Andronicus* and *Henry VI* appeared on the Old Vic bills.

Benthall's decision to make the Old Vic an exclusively Shakespearean company parallels Robert Atkins's programme in the early 1920s, though Atkins did of course intersperse Shakespeare with other fare. Benthall's plan had the great virtue of stabilising the situation after the upheavals of the previous three years. It also recognised the need for a London base offering Shakespeare throughout the year. Commercial managements had begun to find classical productions too costly, and the Stratford company was still confined to the summer months and had no permanent London home. During these years the Old Vic found an audience corresponding to (though by no means identical with) its earliest public: lacking the cosmopolitan glitter of the following who packed the New Theatre for a glimpse of Olivier and Richardson, but dedicated, if no longer local, strongly supported by the younger generation, and recognising the Company as 'their' Company and the Theatre as 'their' alma mater.

Benthall was regularly seconded by the versatile dancer-actor-choreographer Robert Helpmann, who directed *The Tempest* (1954), *As You Like It* (1955), *Romeo and Juliet* (1956), *Antony and Cleopatra* (1957) and played leading roles (Shylock, Richard III – and on overseas tours Angelo and Petruchio), as well as some supporting parts (Launce, Dr Pinch, Saturninus in *Titus Andronicus*). Old favourites returned from time to time: Ralph Richardson played Timon of Athens in 1956, and John Gielgud and Edith Evans Wolsey and Queen Katharine in *Henry VIII*, the last play to be presented in the cycle; but the emphasis was on new faces.

As in the 1930s the Company helped to launch some new stars into wider firmaments. Richard Burton, still on the threshold of international film celebrity, led Benthall's first ensemble, playing (predictably) Hamlet and Coriolanus, but also (less predictably) Toby Belch, Caliban and the Bastard Faulconbridge. He returned for the 1955–6 season to play Henry V and alternate Othello and Iago with John Neville. The latter was very much a star of the Old Vic's making; he had appeared there with the Bristol Old Vic in *Two Gentlement of Verona* and *Henry V* before joining the London Company in 1953. In the course of the next three years he played amongst other parts Richard II, Romeo, Antony (in *Julius Caesar*), Troilus, Othello, Iago, Hamlet and Angelo. Another Old Vic alumnus who achieved prominence at this period was Keith Michell, trained at the Old Vic School, who played Antony (in *Antony and Cleopatra*), Benedick and Aaron in the 1956–7 season, while Eric Porter appeared as Banquo, Navarre, Henry IV, Bolingbroke and Jacques in 1954–5, before going on to play leads, first with the Bristol Old Vic and then at Stratford.

But the lion's share of leading roles during these five years was assumed by two artistes who, like Ernest Milton, Ion Swinley and Sybil Thorndike thirty years earlier, returned to tackle major parts when summoned. Paul Rogers (whose association with the Old Vic went back to the New Theatre seasons) played Macbeth (twice), Lear, Brutus, Falstaff (in both *Henry IV* and *The Merry Wives of Windsor*), Leontes, Petruchio, Mercutio, Touchstone and other parts. Amongst the ladies Barbara Jefford was the mainstay of the later years, undertaking not only Viola, Imogen, Portia and Beatrice, but also Regan, Queen Margaret (in all three parts of *Henry VI*), as well as supporting roles like Lady Anne, Julia (in *Two Gentlemen of Verona*) and Tamora in *Titus Andronicus* followed by the Courtesan in *The Comedy of Errors* on the same evening, a double only less impressive than Olivier's as 'Oedipuff'.

To undertake so extensive a programme it was necessary not only to rely on a nucleus of actors whose first loyalty was to the Old Vic but (since each season's plays were performed in repertoire) to mount the productions simply and not too expensively. For his first season Benthall commissioned from James Bailey a permanent setting of three Palladian arches with balconies. Like Guthrie twenty years earlier he found this solved fewer problems than it created, and the permanent setting did not survive its initiation. By contrast Stratford during these years embarked on a series of star-studded seasons with each production elaborately and individually designed and directed. Barry Jackson's pioneering work after the War was advanced by his successors, Anthony Quayle and Glen Byam Shaw (an exile from the Old Vic organisation). International names like Gielgud, Laurence Olivier and Vivien Leigh, Ralph Richardson, Michael Redgrave, Paul Robeson, Diana Wynyard, Peggy Ashcroft and Margaret Leighton were glad to fit a six-month season at Stratford into their film and other commitments. During the 1950s therefore the role of the Old Vic as heir apparent to the National Theatre, which it had assumed since the amalgamation of the Shakespeare Memorial and National Theatre Committees, was increasingly challenged by the glamour and attention which the Stratford seasons engendered. By 1959 the Governors were sufficiently alarmed to pass a resolution that:

the Objects of the Trust are

a the preservation of the Old Vic organisation.
b the upholding of the Old Vic as the nucleus of the National Theatre, as acknowledged by the agreement between the Governors of the Royal Victoria Hall and the Trustees of the Shakespeare Memorial and National Theatre Committee, dated 25 January 1946.[20]

Another legacy of the Five-Year Plan was the creation of a vacuum once it had been achieved. To substantiate the Vic's claim to be the National Theatre Company-elect Benthall widened the representation of both British and foreign drama. Examples of the former included *Doctor Faustus*; Congreve's *The Double Dealer*; *The Cenci* (with Barbara Jefford); Pinero's *The Magistrate*; *What Every Woman Knows* for the Barrie Centenary in 1960; and *St Joan*. The foreign playwrights included Aeschylus (*The Oresteia*); Molière (a double bill of *Scapin* and *Tartuffe*); Schiller (*Mary Stuart* in a new translation by Stephen Spender); Ibsen (*Ghosts* with Flora Robson); Chekhov (*The Seagull*); and O'Neill (*Mourning Becomes Electra*). But the unpalatable fact remained that the Old Vic was firmly established in the public's mind as a Shakespearean Company, and forays outside the Folio, however enterprising, often played to alarmingly empty benches.

There was also the problem of attracting big names to offset lesser-known plays. In the 1930s, when the dominance of Shakespeare was first relaxed, Guthrie and others had built their seasons round leading actors (Laughton, Olivier, Richardson, and later Peggy Ashcroft and Donald Wolfit), but these were less inclined to trek out to the Waterloo Road in the late 1950s. There was still the occasional 'prestige production', for example a stunning *Romeo and Juliet* in 1960, designed and directed by Franco Zeffirelli, with John Stride and Judi Dench, but in general the Shakespeare productions seemed somewhat routine after the lofty concept of the Five-Year Plan, with actors cast because they were members of the Company rather than commensurate with the part.

Lacking established names, the alternative course of creating the Old Vic's own stars proved a great deal more difficult to sustain against the demands and opportunities of film and television. There were exciting discoveries: Judi Dench went straight from drama school in 1957 to play Ophelia, and stayed for four seasons. Maggie Smith, hitherto known as a revue artiste, staked a claim to wider recognition as Maggie Wylie in *What Every Woman Knows* and was to make good that claim. Alec

McCowen moved purposefully towards pre-eminence with his Algernon in *The Importance of Being Earnest*, the Dauphin in *St Joan*, and Mercutio in Zeffirelli's *Romeo*. But there was no longer continuity in either casting or directing. Benthall, with his term of office drawing to a close, looked elsewhere for his opportunities. Understandably he did not direct a single Shakespeare play in the Waterloo Road between *Henry VIII*, with which the Plan ended in 1958, and leaving the Theatre in 1961. Douglas Seale, whose work at Birmingham (notably with *Henry VI*) achieved wide recognition, took charge for the 1958–9 season, and Oliver Neville during 1961–2, but recourse to so many different directors during these later years did not make for maintenance of style or standards.

Indeed the status of the Old Vic seemed increasingly higher abroad than at home. North American tours were regularly undertaken; in 1954 *A Midsummer Night's Dream*, with Helpmann, Moira Shearer and Stanley Holloway; in 1956–7 with Paul Rogers, John Neville, Claire Bloom and Coral Browne in *Macbeth*, *Richard II*, *Romeo and Juliet* and Guthrie's 'Ruritanian' *Troilus and Cressida*; in 1958–9 with Neville, Laurence Harvey and Barbara Jefford in *Hamlet*, *Henry V* and *Twelfth Night*; and in 1961 with John Clements, Barbara Jefford and Judi Dench in *Macbeth*, *St Joan* and the Zeffirelli *Romeo and Juliet*. There were several shorter European tours, and more controversially the Old Vic's name was invoked for companies whose connection with the Waterloo Road seemed tenuous at best. Helpmann and Katharine Hepburn led such a company to Australia in 1955, and Helpmann directed another tour to Australia, New Zealand and South America in 1961, with Vivien Leigh and John Merivale in *Twelfth Night*, Giraudoux's *Duel of Angels*, and *The Lady of the Camellias*. These tours earned profits and provided funds for the Old Vic Annexe, built at a cost of £90,000 on the corner of Webber Street to house the workshops and wardrobe. This was inaugurated on 18 March 1958 when the Queen unveiled a plaque, and with the Duke of Edinburgh attended a performance marking the climax of the Five-Year Plan, with extracts from five plays and appearances by such favourites as Paul Rogers as Falstaff, John Neville as Hamlet, Judi Dench as Ophelia, Coral Browne as Gertrude, Barbara Jefford and Keith Michell as Katharina and Petruchio, Robert Helpmann as Launce and Moira Shearer as Titania. But the inevitable dispersal of energy between the Waterloo Road and overseas tours was not always beneficial. The Governors' *Report* for 1961–2 admits:

> However low the fortunes of the organisation might appear to be from
> Waterloo Bridge, the view taken from a similar construction in
> Sydney Harbour was quite different.

which sounds suspiciously like whistling in the dark.

By contrast the period 1958–62 was one of remarkable progress at Stratford. Peter Hall's appointment as Director in 1958 lent great impetus to their bid for recognition as the National Theatre Company in waiting. In January 1960 they received the title of the Royal Shakespeare Company, and acquisition of a London base at the Aldwych in December 1960 made possible a 'permanent' ensemble and a wider variety of plays. Planning the organisation as well as the architecture of the National Theatre now became a matter of concern to the Committee responsible. By 1958 Laurence Olivier had already been unofficially chosen as its Director. During a weekend house party at Notley Abbey (Olivier's country home) in 1959 attended by leading figures on the Shakespeare Memorial National Theatre Committee approval was given to the Stratford Company's participation with the Old Vic in the operation of a future National Theatre.[21] A memorandum submitted to the then Chancellor of the Exchequer, Selwyn Lloyd, in December 1960 envisaged a National Theatre Company consisting of three groups (one at the new building, one at Stratford, and one touring), with the Old Vic occupied by a young company offering experimental work (shades of 1946!).[22] Nevertheless this document adds under a heading 'The problem of the Old Vic' a warning that 'the present building is not in good condition and will need a great deal of money spent on it if it is to continue in regular use. For this reason we believe that in the long run the Old Vic premises will have to be abandoned as a theatre.'[23] All this planning seemed abortive when in March 1961 the Chancellor announced that no National Theatre would be built with government funds, but after an extraordinary volte-face he confirmed in June of that year that the £1 million voted in 1949 would now be available, provided the LCC met its promise to contribute £1.3 million.

The pace of planning now accelerated. The key figures in the National Theatre Committee were Lord Chandos (formerly Oliver Lyttelton), whose family representation on it went back to its inception in 1908, and Lord Esher, whose membership long predated his Chairmanship of the Old Vic Governors and who had resigned that post in favour of Lord Wilmot two years earlier. A third force was Lord Cottesloe, also an Old Vic Governor but more importantly Chairman of the Arts Council. The spokesmen for the Old Vic organisation were Michael Benthall, by now at the end of his directorate, and Alfred Francis. It has been claimed that 'they sat mum on the sidelines throughout',[24] and even that their dilatoriness could be described as 'la tragédie anglaise'.[25] Whatever the accuracy of such comments, the Old Vic's representatives clearly carried less weight than the Lords Chandos, Esher and Cottesloe. The Old Vic Company were being steadily edged off the stage.

In the end the Royal Shakespeare Company's participation foundered when the National Theatre Committee insisted it should surrender its autonomy as a condition of entry. In July 1962 the establishment of a National Theatre Board, under the Chairmanship of Lord Chandos, was announced, and the following month the choice of Olivier as the Theatre's first Director made public. Meanwhile he had taken charge of the Chichester Festival Theatre with its bold thrust-stage. The opening season, in 1962, was distinguished more by the Company (Olivier, Redgrave, Lewis Casson, John Neville, Keith Michell, Sybil Thorndike, Athene Seyler, Fay Compton, Joan Plowright, Joan Greenwood) than the productions, but redeemed by a memorable *Uncle Vanya*. The way forward emerged: a National Theatre Company directed by Olivier and drawn from the Chichester ensemble. They would need a temporary home until the South Bank building was ready, and the Old Vic Governors accepted what seemed their only chance of taking part in the project by making their Theatre available for this purpose. At their meeting on 25 April 1962 they adopted a resolution that 'The Old Vic Theatre, with the Governors as Landlords, will continue in use as the proscenium theatre of the National Theatre for some years.'[26] The unstated corollary of this was of course the end after nearly fifty years of the Old Vic Company.

In a bid to give that Company a coherent and dignified final season Michael Elliott, who had been a moving force behind the ambitious and admired Theatre 59 seasons at the Lyric, Hammersmith, was appointed Artistic Director. He authorised a new apron stage and the modification of the proscenium to a 'tunnel' design. For his first production he challenged memories of the New Theatre years by choosing *Peer Gynt*, in which Leo McKern gave a performance of growing stature. The rest of the programme was drawn entirely from the Elizabethan drama: *The Merchant of Venice* (with Lee Montague): *Othello* (with McKern as Iago); *Measure for Measure*; and *The Alchemist*, aptly directed by Guthrie, with McKern as Subtle and Montague as Face.

The last performance, on 15 June 1963, was *Measure for Measure*, and the last words spoken for the Old Vic Company after half a century were those of the Duke of Vienna:

> I have a motion which imports your good;
> Whereto if you'll a willing ear incline,
> What's mine is yours, and what is yours is mine.
> So bring us to our palace, where we'll show
> What's yet behind, that's meet you all should know.

The lines are cryptic in their context and were doubly cryptic on this occasion. Would the 'palace' which the National Theatre Board promised really show what's theirs would also be the Old Vic's? Who could guess 'what's yet behind' (or before), however 'meet you all should know'? Time alone would tell.

Landlords and tenants

The four months between the last performance by the Old Vic and the first night of the National Theatre Company at the Old Vic were taken up with frantic reconstruction and redecoration. The 'tunnel proscenium' and forestage were both replaced by more open and functional designs from Sean Kenny, the Irish architect-designer who also introduced a revolve (familiarly known as 'Kenny's Revolt' because of its perverse behaviour). Max Adrian, a leading member of the new Company, gives a vivid account of the preparations:

> I remember when we got on to the stage at the Old Vic to rehearse the *Hamlet*, the whole place was still littered with rubble and mortar, and there was a bloody enormous hole in one wall which allowed the wind to blow straight in from the Waterloo Road. It was frightfully uncomfortable and chaotic. Then to add to the problems we had a very complicated, overpowering set by Sean Kenny . . . a delightful and talented Irishman, but I think he went too far on that occasion. I said to him after falling over bits of the set for the hundredth time: 'I suppose this is your revenge on the English.' There were moments during rehearsals for that very first production when I thought we'd never open.[27]

By a cruel coincidence Viscount Esher, who had worked indefatigably for a National Theatre, died two weeks before the opening, which took place on 22 October.

The first production, *Hamlet*, with Peter O'Toole, Michael Redgrave as Claudius, Diana Wynyard as Gertrude, Max Adrian as Polonius and

Rosemary Harris as Ophelia, was respectfully if not rapturously received. It was swiftly followed by two transfers from Chichester: *St Joan* with Joan Plowright, and *Uncle Vanya*, with Redgrave and Olivier, both popular and critical successes. The remainder of the season (*The Recruiting Officer*; *Hobson's Choice*; *Andorra* (Frisch); *Play* (Beckett) and *Philoctetes* (Sophocles); *Othello*; and *The Master Builder* accurately reflected the range and quality of production at which Olivier, his Literary Manager, Kenneth Tynan, and Assistant Directors, John Dexter and William Gaskell, were aiming.

Nevertheless if the National Theatre Board had known in the Spring of 1963 that it would be fourteen years before the National Theatre building would be fully operational, they would probably have made other arrangements, or at least postponed any move into temporary quarters. The lease of the Old Vic was originally for five years. It was in fact more than six years before work began on the Theatre (at the fourth and final site, east of Waterloo Bridge; to the designs of the fifth and final architect, Denys Lasdun). For all its history and traditions, the Old Vic was neither large enough nor flexible enough for an operation as multiple as the National Theatre under Olivier's command became. Throughout its period of tenancy at the Vic the National Theatre's offices were established in temporary huts at Aquinas Street, half a mile from the Theatre. There was of course only one auditorium, and all the plans had envisaged at least two. Thus a second company was established in the West End (at the Queen's in 1966, at the Cambridge in 1970, and the New in 1971), and individual productions transferred: *A Flea in Her Ear*, 1966; *Jumpers*, 1972; *Equus*, 1973; *No Man's Land*, 1975. From 1970 the Young Vic, a converted butcher's shop in the Cut, equipped with a wide thrust-stage, offered the classics in productions reminiscent of the earlier Young Vic Company; later it became independent and operated as an experimental theatre. There were also occasional seasons elsewhere, for example of plays by women writers at the Jeanetta Cochrane Theatre in 1968. In 1973 and 1974 there were 'mobile' productions of (surprisingly) *'Tis Pity She's a Whore*, and (predictably) *Twelfth Night*, *Romeo and Juliet* and *Measure for Measure*.

The first ten years of the National Theatre Company unquestionably bear the imprint of Laurence Olivier. He was by no means the *sine qua non*, in the sense that Irving and Tree were essential to the bills at the Lyceum or His Majesty's. During the decade of his directorate Olivier played twelve parts (and *hors série* Chebutikin in *The Three Sisters* for the American trip), of which only six could be called leads (Astrov; Othello;

Solness; Edgar in *The Dance of Death*; Shylock; James Tyrone in *Long Day's Journey into Night*); four were important supporting parts (Brazen in *The Recruiting Officer*; Tattle in *Love for Love*; Antonio in *Saturday, Sunday, Monday*; John Tagg in *The Party*); and two were 'jokes' (A. B. Raham in *Home and Beauty*; Plucheux in *A Flea in Her Ear*, for the Canadian tour). But at least four of these performances (Othello, Edgar, Shylock, Tyrone) were masterly, and in addition Olivier directed nine plays during this period, some – *Uncle Vanya*; *The Crucible*; *The Three Sisters* – with great distinction. He was above all the link between the fabled New Theatre seasons and the new National Theatre Company, and it was his reputation that ensured the publicity, crowded houses and controversy that the Company engendered.

It would, however, be entirely wrong to assess the National Theatre's achievements as wholly or even principally due to Olivier's acting and direction. He was able to recruit major names for individual plays (O'Toole for the opening *Hamlet*; Gielgud for Seneca's *Oedipus*; Edith Evans for *Hay Fever*), and greatly extend the range of others, notably Geraldine McEwan who was regarded as essentially a comedienne until cast as Alice in *The Dance of Death* and Vittoria in *The White Devil*. He aimed to build an ensemble, not a series of strongly cast productions, and the careers at the National of those who played supporting roles in the opening *Hamlet* amply demonstrate his success in this aim. Robert Stephens (Horatio) was to become a leading actor for the next eight years; Derek Jacobi (Laertes), John Stride (Fortinbras), Frank Finlay (First Gravedigger), Colin Blakely (Captain), Lynn Redgrave (Court Lady), all graduated to principal parts with distinction. In the first season Maggie Smith established her claim to the important roles (including Desdemona, Beatrice, Hilda Wangel and Hedda Gabler) which she subsequently played. There were also actors in that first season who, without achieving star status, gave the Company invaluable service over many productions: Anthony Nicholls; Robert Lang; Edward Petherbridge; Edward Hardwicke.

There were of course lows as well as highs in the National Theatre Company's fortunes, often occasioned by Olivier's ill health, which he resisted heroically. It was his advancing years which decided him against sticking out the recurrent building delays so as to take his Company into the Promised Land of the South Bank. Peter Hall's accession to that role in 1974 presented problems which his first production (*The Tempest* with Gielgud) did little to resolve; but his *John Gabriel Borkman*, with Ralph

Richardson, Peggy Ashcroft and Wendy Hiller, *Happy Days* with Peggy Ashcroft, and *No Man's Land*, with Richardson and Gielgud, restored confidence and renewed the glitter of Olivier's regime. Hall's *Hamlet* with Albert Finney in December 1975 gave the impression of completing the cycle which Olivier had begun twelve years earlier, even if the first performance at the new complex was delayed for another three months, the official opening for a further six months, and the opening of the Cottesloe Theatre (and with it the whole complex) for six months after that.

In retrospect, therefore, the National Theatre Company's residence in the Waterloo Road brought high achievement and sustained prestige. For the Old Vic Theatre and its supporters that prestige was tinged with a certain foreboding. The interest that the productions aroused looked back to the pre-War Guthrie years, and by extension to the Olivier–Richardson seasons at the New Theatre. There was, however, both a sense of present achievement and future promise about those chapters in the Old Vic's history. The nearer the National Theatre Company came to possessing a home of its own, the more uncertain grew the prospect for the Old Vic Theatre itself. Its function, once the National Theatre had opened, began to occupy the Governors' attention as soon as the final site had been decided in 1967. Lord Wilmot, who had succeeded Lord Esher as Chairman in 1959, died suddenly five years later. His colleagues chose Alfred Francis, Administrator of the Old Vic Company from 1952 to the completion of the Five-Year Plan in 1958, as his successor. When Francis resigned in 1972, Colin Benham became Chairman for what were to prove ten anxious and sadly conclusive years.

Work on the National Theatre finally began in 1969 and was expected to be completed by 1973. Since the Old Vic Trust had been wound up in 1963 and the Governors of the Royal Victoria Hall Foundation lacked the experience and resources to run a theatre company, their hopes were pinned on leasing the building to an organisation which could take that responsibility from them. The most promising candidate seemed to be the English Stage Company, cramped in their Royal Court quarters and looking for a second house in which to mount large-scale productions and transfers. By September 1972 agreement had been reached that the English Stage Company would take a twenty-one-year lease of the Old Vic once the National Theatre Company moved out, and a press release announcing this agreement was issued on 1 November.[28] The idea did not meet with all the Governors' approval; the ESC's repertoire was hardly what Emma Cons and Lilian Baylis had seen as the Old Vic's mission (one of the 'specimen' plays put forward was Osborne's *A Patriot for Me*), but the proposal solved more problems than it posed.

Man proposes but the workman disposes. Delays in building postponed the opening year after year, and the English Stage Company could not wait indefinitely. Early in 1974 they withdrew their offer to lease the Old Vic.[29] Another candidate in the field was the Young Vic; originally founded as part of the National Theatre, they had become independent, with their own Arts Council grant. Their repertoire was certainly closer to Old Vic fare, but they were firmly committed to the open-staging of their adapted building, and there was suspicion amongst the Governors that architectural changes would be required if the Young Vic took over, and also doubts if they could obtain the funding for a full-scale programme in the Waterloo Road.

Another solution considered at this time was known as the 'Tripartite Scheme': a plan to house three companies, one operatic, one a dance group and the third offering classical drama. This idea appealed particularly to supporters of the 'lyric theatre' which had briefly found a place on the drawing-board of the National Theatre architect in the shape of a South Bank opera house, a proposal scrapped on the grounds of expense in 1967. The three most likely claimants were the English Music Theatre (which had grown out of the English Opera Group, responsible for introducing much of Britten's work); the Royal Ballet touring group (later the Sadler's Wells Royal Ballet); and Prospect Productions, a company mainly devoted to the English classics, which had been touring at home and abroad since 1963.

There were serious practical difficulties in the way of this scheme: chiefly on the score of the Theatre's size, including the stage, backstage and orchestra pit, and capacity (bravely given as 1,500 in various works of reference but nearer 850 under the National Theatre Company). Nevertheless in 1975 the Arts Council commissioned a report (the Godley Report) into the feasibility of the Tripartite Scheme at the Old Vic which concluded that the proposal would require an annual subsidy of £250,000 but was the most desirable use to which the Theatre could be put. No sooner had the Report appeared than the Arts Council announced it

> could not, in present circumstances, contemplate finding the money needed to finance the tripartite scheme discussed in Mr Godley's report.[30]

Of the three candidates Prospect Productions remained in the field. Ten years of touring had convinced their Director, Toby Robertson, that the Company could not progress without a London base, that the Old Vic would best meet their need and the Old Vic's name add lustre to their reputation. For the next two years Prospect sustained a campaign to move into the Waterloo Road.

Meanwhile matters were at last moving to a conclusion for the National Theatre Company. Peter Hall arrived in April 1973, initially sharing responsibility with Olivier and taking control at the end of the year. An announcement that 'the official opening [of the new building] can take place in the first half of 1975' proved premature yet again. In the end it was opened piecemeal: the Lyttelton Theatre in March 1976, the Olivier in October 1976 (in the presence of the Queen to mark the official opening) and the Cottesloe Theatre in March 1977.

The last performance by the National Theatre Company at the Old Vic was given on 28 February 1976. *Tribute to The Lady*, an affectionate account of Lilian Baylis, had been devised by Val May to mark the centenary of her birth and first staged in May 1974. For this occasion Peggy Ashcroft repeated her memorable interpretation of the Lady herself, and several more of those who had served her were present, either onstage (Richardson and Gielgud) or in the audience (Sybil Thorndike, aged ninety-three). It was an apt and touching gesture on the part of the National Theatre who donated the proceeds (over £4,000) to the Old Vic,[31] but for the Theatre itself and those who cared for it the occasion was bitter-sweet. The triumphs and tribulations of the past were richly recalled, but there was no pointer to the future. Despite all the debate and detailed planning of the past five years there was still no company ready to take over. In her curtain speech Peggy Ashcroft repeated Lilian's threat to come back and haunt the Old Vic should her and Aunt Emma's work seem at risk. It was a threat the Governors would have increasingly in mind.

9

Seeking an identity

1976–1983

Under the terms of their lease the National Theatre Board had to make good wear and tear of the past thirteen years, but chose instead to pay compensation, assessed by the surveyors, Clutton, at £96,000. Meanwhile, as discussions with Prospect and other companies continued, a short-term solution offered itself. Bullfinch Productions, a new commercial company, undertook to mount a season of plays, starting in August with Glenda Jackson in *The White Devil*, and this was accepted. It had become clear that will they, nill they, the Governors would have to make arrangements, at least temporarily, for the running of the Theatre, and in April James Verner, an impresario who had managed touring companies for the Old Vic in the past, was engaged as Business Manager. Those Governors who doubted the wisdom of such arrangements were soon proved right. *The White Devil* was coolly received, Bullfinch Productions could not complete the scheduled run and the last two weeks had to be financed by the Governors themselves.[1]

Worse was to follow; lacking alternatives, the Board found themselves forced to accept an offer from Verner to mount a series of plays, beginning with a programme called *The Frontiers of Farce* and following this with *The Ghost Train* for Christmas. Response to both was minuted as 'extremely disappointing',[2] Verner ceased his operations early in January 1977 and was subsequently declared bankrupt.[3] Even more seriously, many of his debts had been incurred in the name of the Old Vic who therefore found themselves involved in litigation to limit their responsibility. In this situation Prospect Productions' bid to play in the Waterloo Road could not be resisted. They opened a three-month season there in May 1977 with a distinguished programme, including *Hamlet* with Derek Jacobi; *Antony and Cleopatra* with Alec McCowen and Dorothy Tutin; and *St Joan* with Eileen Atkins, and these plays formed the core of the autumn programme in November and December.

Welcome as such visits proved to be, the affiliation between Prospect and the Old Vic presented grave problems. Prospect had been started as a touring company and their Arts Council funding insisted on this role, the Council's Touring Department booking and managing their itinerary. All requests for further funds to cover London seasons were refused; the Arts Council was heavily involved in the National Theatre and the RSC's programme at the Aldwych, and could see no case for supporting a third classical repertoire in London. This meant that Prospect could only appear at the Old Vic under the Governors' auspices, with the financial outcome largely dependent on Box-Office returns. The first season ended 'all square' but left nothing in hand for the future.[4]

If finances were stretched during Prospect's season, they were strained to breaking point afterwards. A week's visit by the African dance company *Umbatha* lost £4,000,[5] and a projected six-week season by the Nottingham Playhouse Company, with two experimental productions, *Touched* and *White Suit Blues*, had to be terminated after two weeks.[6] Prospect returned in November, but the losses by the end of the year were calculated at £71,941.[7] Failing Arts Council funds, these could be met in only two ways: by public appeal (started in the autumn of 1977) and assistance from local councils. The GLC and Southwark and Lambeth Councils did respond, though not until 1978 and in under-standably modest amounts (a total of £63,400 in 1978–9).[8]

Apart from the ever-present and pressing financial difficulties, two problems increasingly concerned the Governors in the winter of 1977–8: the need to reconstitute the Old Vic Trust as the body immediately responsible for running the Theatre, and the sustained pressure exerted by Prospect to take the name Old Vic and role of resident company. The former had the Governors' solid support; meeting only quarterly, they were not constituted or qualified to make the numerous decisions a major theatre demands. In April 1978 agreement was reached to set up a new Old Vic Trust (wound up in 1963) under the Chairmanship of the experienced drama critic J. W. Lambert, with representatives of Prospect sitting beside a nucleus of Governors.

There was less unanimity about the overture from Prospect, whose grant from the Arts Council still precluded funding for London. Nevertheless they played a five-month season at the Vic from January to May 1978, adding *Twelfth Night* to their repertory, and another four months from September to December, with a programme which included *The Rivals* and *The Lady's Not For Burning* (with Eileen Atkins) and culminated in Anthony Quayle's King Lear. Their audiences remained constant at between 60 per cent and 70 per cent of capacity, whereas attempts to fill the Theatre without them were uniformly unsuccessful (the Governors were informed in September 1978 of a 'calamitous fall in Box Office receipts', with 45 per cent capacity during the four months since the end of Prospect's season).[9] In December therefore the Governors agreed to enter into a five-year contract with Prospect, and approved a Press announcement, aptly timed for 23 April 1979, that they would henceforward be styled: 'Prospect Productions Ltd., trading as the Old Vic Company'.[10]

Ironically Prospect's touring commitments kept them away from the Waterloo Road for the first half of 1979. The Young Vic Company played a six-week season to modest Box-Office returns, and the Theatre then closed for four months, with the result that by May 1979 the Old Vic Trust was £170,000 in debt,[11] and in September a debt of £398,000 by the following March was projected.[12] A proposal to sell the Annexe was therefore mooted, but limitations laid on its use by the local authority inhibited possible buyers, and instead it had to be let – to the Royal Shakespeare Company!

In July Prospect returned with the indispensable Jacobi Hamlet (on its way to China), followed by Romeo and Juliet and The Government Inspector with Ian Richardson. The autumn programme proved much more controversial: in particular a double bill (The Padlock and Miss in her Teens) to mark the Bicentenary of Garrick's death, and a revival of Orton's What the Butler Saw were rejected by the Arts Council as unsuitable for touring.[13] The Prospect board found themselves in disagreement with their Artistic Director, Toby Robertson, 'as to whether' (in the words of their own report) 'Prospect can any longer satisfy the triple task of filling the Vic, of satisfying the Director of Touring's requirements for product of a certain familiar sort, and of realising the vision of Toby Robertson'.[14] When early in November the Arts Council announced that 'The Council will need to consider Prospect's submission on the specific merits of each individual touring project proposed, and will only offer subsidy to the Company on this basis', a change of Artistic Director became inevitable. Timothy West, who had played an important part in the Company's development almost from its inception, succeeded Toby Robertson.[15]

West's brief was to prepare a programme for the autumn of 1980 which would satisfy the Arts Council's touring requirements and prove acceptable at the Old Vic. His mainstay would clearly have to be the major classics with major performers. *Macbeth* with Peter O'Toole, which had been planned for September before Robertson's replacement, would fully answer this description. Meanwhile the Old Vic had eight months to fill, a daunting task. The most attractive offering proved to be the Bristol Old Vic in *A Midsummer Night's Dream* in June 1980, but hosting foreign companies met with little response, and audiences during this period fell to 20 per cent average of capacity.[16] Nevertheless the Governors pinned their faith to the autumn season which for the first time was to be on a subscription basis, with over 6,000 subscriptions sold before September.[17]

The production of *Macbeth* with which the new season began proved to be sensational even by the standards of that fateful play. It suffered a change of director and a performance from O'Toole which left critics and public gasping with disbelief. That it sold out before opening and played to 98 per cent capacity on its subsequent tour was a further turn of the screw.[18] The season proceeded more decorously with Timothy West as Shylock and a production of *Trelawny of the 'Wells'*, including an 'Eightieth Birthday Gala Performance' for the Queen Mother, Patron of the Old Vic, on 18 December. But the troubles of the previous months had exhausted the Arts Council's patience. Four days after the Gala they informed the Company that their grant was to be ended.[19] Without Arts Council support Prospect clearly could not continue.

In January 1981 the Company presenting *The Merchant of Venice* and *Trelawny of the 'Wells'* left for Hong Kong and Australia as arranged. The last Old Vic Company production was Vanbrugh's *The Relapse* (an ominous title, comparable to the National Theatre's last offering at the Vic, Osborne's *Watch It Come Down*), which was followed by two visiting companies, from the Baxter Theatre, Cape Town (with *Waiting for Godot*), and the Centaur Theatre, Montreal, with *Balconville*. There were further performances of *The Merchant* on the Company's return from their Far Eastern tour, and the season ended in May. All appeals to the Arts Council having been rejected, the Old Vic Company completed a European tour with *The Merchant*, giving its last performance in Rome on 14 June, and disbanded.

The Governors now faced the bitter truth that only by selling both the Theatre and Annexe could they discharge their debts. The GLC as the planning authority made it clear that no change of function would be allowed; the purchaser would have to undertake its continuance as a theatre. On the other hand the Charity Commissioners, responsible for the conduct of all registered charities, pointed out that 'under the

Scheme of 11 September 1925, Clause 30 and 31, the income of the Charity and the theatre was to be used for the recreation and instruction of the poorer classes in the former County of London',[20] and insisted that the building be offered to the highest bidder. Discrimination between suitable and less suitable purchasers might result in the sale price being lowered. The key issue was the residual funds available for charitable purposes once the Governors' debts had been settled.

Before these decisions were reached the Old Vic completed a melancholy yet apt assignment. For six months, between July and December 1981, the Theatre was used for rehearsing and shooting the nine-hour television version of the RSC's production of *Nicholas Nickleby*, staged earlier in the year at the Aldwych. Thus Dickens's most theatrical novel, with its scenes of an early nineteenth-century touring company and references to the Royal Coburg Theatre, found its largest audience after being performed in that Theatre, which Dickens himself knew and wrote about.

In April 1982 sealed bids for the freehold of the Theatre were invited. Amongst several potential purchasers whose names appeared in the Press the most publicised was certainly Andrew Lloyd Webber with a proposal to turn the Vic and Annexe into a school and shop-window for musical theatre which caught the public's imagination. One name which did not appear in print at all was that of Ed Mirvish, proprietor of the Royal Alexandra Theatre, Toronto, who remained unaware of the sale until 8 June, three days before the bidding closed. His representatives visited the Old Vic next day, and when the bids were opened on 11 June his at £550,000 was the highest. Andrew Lloyd Webber had bid £500,000. An announcement of the sale to Mirvish was made on 23 June, and on 5 August the legal formalities were completed.[21]

Between that date and 31 October 1983 the Old Vic was completely renovated, at a cost to the new proprietor of more than £2 million. The principle on which the consultants, Renton, Howard, Wood and Levin, worked was the restoration of the Theatre to its mid-Victorian identity, drawing on the available plans and details of its appearance during the 1870s as the Royal Victoria Palace Theatre.[22] The boxes, removed in 1950, were replaced and the decorative motifs returned to their Victorian origins. The consultants' main consideration was the 'unification' of the Theatre, ensuring that all parts of the house could be reached from the foyer, whereas previously the Gallery (now renamed the 'Lilian Baylis Circle') was approached from Webber Street. To achieve this object the builders, Kyrle Stewart, installed a single staircase with cast-iron balustrade copied from an even earlier (1830) design. An enlarged orchestra pit was achieved by cutting back the front of the stage, and the stage area widened to the full breadth of the building.

By an ironic twist of theatrical fortune the opening production was a musical, *Blondel*, with script and lyrics by Tim Rice, who had been Andrew Lloyd Webber's colleague on a number of enormously successful British musicals.

10

The search continues

The years since the Old Vic reopened have demonstrated the many difficulties of operating it as a theatre without a resident company. Mr Mirvish's original plan, inspired by the success and standing of the Royal Alexandra, Toronto, under his direction, was to offer its stage to visiting managements for limited runs, usually of four to six weeks. This plan was combined (as in Toronto) with a subscription scheme, encouraging patrons to support each production on advantageous terms.

However, the choice of the Royal Alexandra as a model led to a number of problems. The Old Vic is not well placed as a 'try-out' theatre: its productions are treated by the Press and public as West End offerings, and received accordingly, without the allowances which can be made for a 'fringe' or provincial production. A four-week run offered visiting managements little prospect of breaking even on a production mounted to West End standards, and only an outstanding success held out any prospect of a transfer or other continued existence. Such transfers did occur (for example *Masterclass* by David Pownall in 1984, with Timothy West as a formidable Stalin bullying Shostakovitch and Prokoviev), but they were exceptional.

Nor did the subscription scheme meet the Old Vic's requirements as happily as it had suited the Royal Alexandra's. A large proportion of London's theatregoers are visitors from other parts, many of them from overseas, and are more likely to see four plays in one week than one play every four weeks. Visiting managements also have strongly contrasted tastes in the work they choose to mount, making a coherent programme difficult to sustain. West End theatres can and do operate as shop-windows to a public making up its mind at short notice which entertainment to patronise. That public is unlikely to cross Waterloo

Bridge to press its noses against the plate glass of the Old Vic before settling either for or against the play offered.

In 1987 therefore Mr Mirvish decided to enter into production himself and engaged Jonathan Miller as his Artistic Director. This brave gesture has provided patrons of the Old Vic with a bill of fare as variable as might be expected from so individual a *chef de cuisine*. Amongst its highlights have been a production of *King Lear* in 1989, with Eric Porter, and several bold attempts to provide viable English-language versions of foreign classics by authors such as Racine, Corneille and Ostrovsky. There have also been profitable co-productions with the Scottish National Opera (*Candide* 1988), the Royal Shakespeare Company (*Kiss Me Kate* 1987), the English Shakespeare Company (the *Henries* 1987), and a commercial management (*Kean* with Derek Jacobi 1990). Other choices have proved less popular and Jonathan Miller's term of office concluded at the end of 1990.

It is remarkable that in a theatrical scene for which subvention from both State and Local Authority has become essential for all but the most popular entertainment, Mr Mirvish's conduct of the Old Vic has been entirely at his own expense. The contrast, not merely with the National Theatre and Royal Shakespeare Company but with such leading provincial theatres as the Bristol Old Vic at Bristol's Theatre Royal, the Royal Exchange, Manchester and the Citizens' Theatre, Glasgow, is striking. If the unhappy events preceding the sale of the Theatre in 1982 should be repeated, it is difficult to predict where another individual might be found to preserve the building and continue its traditions unaided.

The Old Vic has survived through the nineteenth and twentieth centuries and is within hailing distance of the twenty-first. If its early history was more colourful than cultured, it remains the only theatre in London first opened during the Regency and still operating. Its function as the Royal Victoria Hall was unique and deserves a living memorial. Its achievements as the home of the first English 'grand' opera company in London and its contribution to British theatre through the fifty years' record of the Old Vic Company cannot be overestimated. Its survival against bankruptcy, enemy action and population movements seems little less than miraculous and supremely ordained.

But theatres cannot exist as museums. Unlike the stately home, in which can be recreated the way of life it once sustained, a theatre only lives fully when a performance is being given to an audience. Even those

theatres which do attract tourists without regularly mounting performances (the Court Theatres at Versailles, Schönbrunn, or Drottningholm,
for example) do so because of their non-theatrical associations and
locations in the Palaces of the French, Austro-Hungarian and Swedish
Royal families.

The Old Vic Theatre remains a viable home for a programme
designed to its particular needs. Over the past hundred years it has
proved itself receptive to the classical repertory and to musical theatre
which does not make too great demands in terms of stage and orchestral
space. In return it offers intimacy, atmosphere and a unique tradition. A
theatre's historic past offers no security for its future, as the destruction
of George Alexander's St James's and the plight of Henry Irving's
Lyceum demonstrate. Given the present and future uncertainties for
private enterprise in the arts, the Old Vic's vulnerability is self-evident.
The guardians of our national heritage should not be allowed to ignore
those risks.

Appendix 1

The Royal Victoria Hall Foundation

Presidents

1890	1st Duke of Westminster PC, KG
1899	2nd Duke of Westminster GCVO, DSO, CLH
1914	HRH Princess Christian
1924	HRH Princess Marie-Louise
1957	HRH Princes Marina
1969	Viscountess Hambledon

Chairmen of the Governors

to 1906	W. T. Warry
1906	C. T. Harris
1913	E. G. Thorne
1921	Sir Wilmot Herringham KCMG, CB
1928	2nd Earl of Lytton KG, PC, GCSI, GCIC
1947	3rd Viscount Hambledon
1948	3rd Viscount Esher GBE
1959	1st Baron Wilmot of Selmeston PC
1964	Alfred Francis OBE
1972	Colin S. K. Benham OBE
1982	Tom H. Vaughan

Plays presented by the Old Vic Company at the Old Vic Theatre 1914–1963

This list draws on Harcourt Williams's *Old Vic Saga* (Winchester Publications, London, 1949) and on succeeding volumes of *Who's Who in the Theatre*, 11th Edition (1952) and 12th Edition (1957), both edited John Parker, 13th Edition (1960) and 14th Edition (1967), both edited Freda Gaye (Pitman, London).

For the years 1914–40 the term 'producer' to denote artistic responsibility for a play has been retained.

For the years 1950–63 the term 'director' (Dir.) which superseded it has been used and the names of the designer (Des.) and costume-designer (Cost.) where appropriate have been added.

The list does not include productions by the Old Vic Company at other theatres.

1914–15

The Merchant of Venice
The Tempest
The Merry Wives of Windsor
The Taming of the Shrew
King René's Daughter
The Comedy of Errors
Twelfth Night
A Midsummer Night's Dream
She Stoops to Conquer
As You Like It
The Winter's Tale
The School for Scandal
Othello
Hamlet
Macbeth
Julius Caesar

Producers : MATHESON LANG and HUTIN BRITTON (*The Merchant of Venice, The Taming of the Shrew, Hamlet*); BEN GREET (*The Tempest, King René's Daughter, The Comedy of Errors, A Midsummer Night's Dream, The Winter's Tale, Othello, Macbeth*); ANDREW LEIGH (*Twelfth Night, As You Like It* and – with ESTELLE STEAD – *The Merry Wives of Windsor*); LADY BENSON (*She Stoops to Conquer*); MRS EDWARD COMPTON (*The School for Scandal*); J. FISHER WHITE (*Julius Caesar*).

1915–16

As You Like it
The Merchant of Venice
Henry V
The Rivals
The Tempest
Othello
Richard III

A Midsummer Night's Dream
Julius Caesar
The Winter's Tale
She Stoops to Conquer
The Star of Bethlehem
Romeo and Juliet
Hamlet
Much Ado About Nothing
Macbeth
The Taming of the Shrew
Twelfth Night
Everyman
The School for Scandal

Producer: BEN GREET

1916–17

The School for Scandal
The Rivals
Henry VIII
The Comedy of Errors
As You Like It
The Merchant of Venice
Julius Caesar
The Tempest
Othello
Richard II
The Two Gentlemen of Verona
King René's Daughter
She Stoops to Conquer
The Star of Bethlehem
A Christmas Carol
Twelfth Night
The Taming of the Shrew
Macbeth
Everyman
Henry V
St Patrick's Day
The Critic
Much Ado About Nothing
The Lady of Lyons
The Merry Wives of Windsor
Hamlet

Producer: BEN GREET

1917–18

King John
The Merchant of Venice
Richard II
As You Like It
Henry IV: 2
Julius Caesar
The Tempest
The Taming of the Shrew
A Christmas Carol
Seaman's Pie
The Star of Bethlehem
The School for Scandal
She Stoops to Conquer
A Midsummer Night's Dream
The Winter's Tale
Romeo and Juliet
King Lear
Cymbeline
Henry VIII
The Merry Wives of Windsor
Henry V
Twelfth Night
Everyman
Richard III
Masks and Faces
Hamlet

Producer: BEN GREET

1918–19

The Merchant of Venice
Hamlet
Measure for Measure
Much Ado About Nothing
Macbeth
Twelfth Night
The Tempest
Henry V
As You Like It
Love's Labour's Lost
The Coventry Nativity Play
The Taming of the Shrew
A Midsummer Night's Dream
The Winter's Tale
Julius Caesar

Everyman
Henry IV: 1

Producers: G. R. Foss, all plays with the exceptions of *The Coventry Nativity Play*, PATRICK KIRWAN; *Everyman*, BEN GREET.

1919–20

The Merry Wives of Windsor
The Tempest
Richard II
As You Like It
Henry V
Macbeth
She Stoops to Conquer
The Hope of the World
A Christmas Carol
The Taming of the Shrew
The Merchant of Venice
Julius Caesar
A Midsummer Night's Dream
Hamlet
Everyman
The Rivals
Othello
Coriolanus
Henry IV: 1 and 2
The Land of Heart's Desire
The Proposal
Michael
Gallant Cassian

Producers: RUSSELL THORNDIKE and CHARLES WARBURTON, all plays with the exceptions of *The Land of Heart's Desire*, BETTY POTTER; *The Proposal*, STOCKWELL HAWKINS; *Gallant Cassian*, ERNEST MILTON. The producer of *Michael* is not recorded.

Costumes and settings for all productions by WILFRED WALTER.

1920–1

The Winter's Tale
The School for Scandal

As You Like It
Twelfth Night
King John
The Taming of the Shrew
The Hope of the World
The Comedy of Errors
Pantaloon
The Merchant of Venice
Julius Caesar
A Midsummer Night's Dream
Romeo and Juliet
Everyman
The Tempest
Hamlet
Richard III
Warrior's Day
King Lear
Pericles

Producer: ROBERT ATKINS

Costumes for *The School for Scandal* by TOM HESLEWOOD; for all other productions by NEIL CURTIS. Settings for all productions by WILFRED WALTER.

1921–2

Much Ado About Nothing
Richard II
As You Like It
Macbeth
Henry V
Wat Tyler
All's Well That Ends Well
Advent
The Merchant of Venice
Othello
Twelfth Night
Peer Gynt
King Lear
Everyman
Love Is the Best Doctor
The Comedy of Errors
Hamlet
Timon of Athens
She Stoops to Conquer
Vic Vicissitudes

Producers: ROBERT ATKINS, all plays with the exception of *She Stoops to Conquer*, RUPERT HARVEY.

Costumes for *Richard II, Macbeth*, and *Wat Tyler* by JOHN GARSIDE. Settings for *Macbeth* and *Peer Gynt* by ROBERT ATKINS; for all other productions by WILFRED WALTER.

1922–3

The Merry Wives of Windsor
The Taming of the Shrew
Henry IV: 1 and 2
Julius Caesar
A New Way to Pay Old Debts
Britain's Daughter
Antony and Cleopatra
The Hope of the World
The Cricket on the Hearth
The Merchant of Venice
Henry VI: 1, 2 and 3
Richard III
King Arthur
Everyman
Twelfth Night
Hamlet
A Midsummer Night's Dream

Producer: ROBERT ATKINS.
Costumes and settings for all productions by ALBERT HINE.

1923–4

Love's Labour's Lost
Titus Andronicus
Henry V
Troilus and Cressida
The Two Gentleman of Verona
As You Like It
The Play of the Shepherds
A Christmas Carol
The School for Scandal
Henry VIII
The Tempest
Faust

The Rivals
Coriolanus
The Merchant of Venice
Everyman
Hamlet
Twelfth Night

Producer: ROBERT ATKINS

Costumes for all productions by TOM HESLEWOOD; settings by HUBERT HINE.

1924–5

Othello
A Midsummer Night's Dream
Hannele
The Play of the Shepherds
She Stoops to Conquer
Richard II
Much Ado About Nothing
The Winter's Tale
Macbeth
Everyman
Hamlet
Twelfth Night
Trelawny of the 'Wells'

Producer: ROBERT ATKINS

Costumes for *Trelawny of the 'Wells'* by TOM HESLEWOOD; for all other productions by JOHN GARSIDE. Settings for *Hannele* by CHARLES MARFORD; for *The Play of the Shepherds* by HUBERT HINE; for all other productions by JOHN GARSIDE.

1925–6

The Merchant of Venice
Richard III
The Taming of the Shrew
Measure for Measure
Antony and Cleopatra
The Child in Flanders
Harlequin Jack Horner
The Merry Wives of Windsor
She Stoops to Conquer
Julius Caesar

As You Like It
The Shoemaker's Holiday
Everyman
Romeo and Juliet
Much Ado About Nothing

Producer: ANDREW LEIGH

Costumes and settings for all productions
by JOHN GARSIDE.

1926–7

King John
A Midsummer Night's Dream
Henry V
The Tempest
Macbeth
The Play of the Shepherds
Christmas Eve
Twelfth Night
Richard III
The Winter's Tale
Othello
Everyman
St Patrick's Day
The Comedy of Errors
Hamlet
The Two Shepherds

Producer: ANDREW LEIGH

Costumes and settings for all productions
by JOHN GARSIDE.

1927–8

The Taming of the Shrew
The Merchant of Venice
Much Ado About Nothing
Henry V
Romeo and Juliet
The Two Noble Kinsmen
The School for Scandal
Everyman
Hamlet
King Lear

Producer: ANDREW LEIGH

Costumes and settings for all productions
by JOHN GARSIDE.

The first four plays in this season were
given at the Lyric Theatre, Hammersmith,
while the Old Vic was closed for rebuilding.

1928–9

Love's Labour's Lost
The Vikings
As You Like It
Twelfth Night
Adam's Opera
Macbeth
Caste
The Merry Wives of Windsor
Mary Magdalene
Henry VIII
The Rivals
Hamlet

Producer: ANDREW LEIGH

Costumes for *Henry VIII* by CHARLES
RICKETTS and PAUL SMYTH; settings by
PAUL SMYTH. Costumes and settings for all
other productions by PAUL SMYTH.

1929–30

Romeo and Juliet
The Merchant of Venice
The Imaginary Invalid
Richard II
A Midsummer Night's Dream
Julius Caesar
As You Like It
The Dark Lady of the Sonnets
Androcles and the Lion
Macbeth
Hamlet

Producer: HARCOURT WILLIAMS

Costumes and settings for all productions
by PAUL SMYTH.

1930–1

Henry IV: 1
The Tempest
The Jealous Wife
Richard II
Antony and Cleopatra
Twelfth Night
Arms and the Man
Much Ado About Nothing
King Lear

Producer: HARCOURT WILLIAMS

Costumes and settings for all productions by PAUL SMYTH.

1931–2

King John
The Taming of the Shrew
A Midsummer Night's Dream
Henry V
The Knight of the Burning Pestle
Julius Caesar
Abraham Lincoln
Othello
Twelfth Night
Hamlet

Producer: HARCOURT WILLIAMS; and with JOHN DRINKWATER for Abraham Lincoln.

Costumes for The Taming of the Shrew by FARQUHARSON SMALL; for Abraham Lincoln, Twelfth Night, and Hamlet by PAUL SMYTH and PETER TAYLOR-SMITH; for other productions by PAUL SMYTH. Settings for all productions by PAUL SMYTH.

1932–3

Caesar and Cleopatra
Cymbeline
As You Like It
Macbeth
The Merchant of Venice
She Stoops to Conquer
The Winter's Tale

Mary Stuart
The Admirable Bashville
Romeo and Juliet
The School for Scandal
The Tempest

Producer: HARCOURT WILLIAMS; and with JOHN GIELGUD for The Merchant of Venice.

Costumes for The Merchant of Venice by MOTLEY; for other productions by PAUL SMYTH. Settings for Macbeth by EDWARD CARRICK; for The Merchant of Venice by JOHN GIELGUD; for other productions by PAUL SMYTH.

1933–4

Twelfth Night
The Cherry Orchard
Henry VIII
Measure for Measure
The Tempest
The Importance of Being Earnest
Macbeth

Producer: TYRONE GUTHRIE

Costumes and settings for The Cherry Orchard and The Importance of Being Earnest by MOLLY McARTHUR; for Henry VIII by CHARLES RICKETTS; for The Tempest by JOHN ARMSTRONG. Costumes for Twelfth Night by ELIZABETH and MARSH WILLIAMS; for Measure for Measure and Macbeth by JOHN ARMSTRONG. Settings for Twelfth Night, Measure for Measure, and Macbeth by WELLS-COATES.

1934–5

Antony and Cleopatra
Richard II
Much Ado About Nothing
St Joan
The Taming of the Shrew
Othello
The Two Shepherds
Hippolytus

Major Barbara
Henry IV: 2
Hamlet

Producers: HENRY CASS, all plays with the exception of *The Two Shepherds*, MICHAEL MACOWEN,

Costumes for *St Joan* by CHARLES RICKETTS; settings by DAVID FFOLKES. Costumes and settings for *Henry IV: 2* by FRANCIS BAKER-SMITH and DAVID FFOLKES; for *Othello*, adapted from E. McKNIGHT KAUFFER's designs for Ernest Milton. Costumes and settings for other productions by DAVID FFOLKES.

1935–6

Peer Gynt
Julius Caesar
The Three Sisters
Macbeth
St Helena
The School of Scandal
Richard III
The Winter's Tale
King Lear

Producers: HENRY CASS, all plays with the exceptions of *The School for Scandal* and *The Winter's Tale*, MICHAEL MACOWAN.

Costumes for all productions by BETTY DYSON. Settings for *Peer Gynt* and *Richard III* by ERIC NEWTON and BAGNALL HARRIS; for other productions by BAGNALL HARRIS.

1936–7

Love's Labour's Lost
The Country Wife
As You Like It
The Witch of Edmonton
Hamlet
Twelfth Night
Henry V

Producers: TYRONE GUTHRIE, all plays with the exceptions of *As You Like It*, ESME CHURCH; *The Witch of Edmonton*, MICHEL ST DENIS.

Costumes and settings for *Love's Labour's Lost, As You Like It*, and *Twelfth Night* by MOLLY McARTHUR; for *The Witch of Edmonton* and *Henry V* by MOTLEY; for *The Country Wife* by OLIVER MESSEL. Costumes for *Hamlet* by OSBORNE ROBINSON, settings by MARTIN BATTERSBY.

1937–8

Pygmalion
Measure for Measure
Richard III
Macbeth
A Midsummer Night's Dream
Othello
The King of Nowhere
Coriolanus

Producers: TYRONE GUTHRIE, all plays with the exceptions of *Macbeth*, MICHEL ST DENIS; *The King of Nowhere*, ESME CHURCH; *Coriolanus*, LEWIS CASSON.

Costumes and settings for *Pygmalion* and *The King of Nowhere* by MOLLY McARTHUR; for *Richard III* by OSBORNE ROBINSON; for *Macbeth* by MOTLEY; for *A Midsummer Night's Dream* by OLIVER MESSEL; for *Othello* by ROGER FURSE; for *Coriolanus* by BRUCE WINSTON. Costumes for *Measure for Measure* by JOHN ARMSTRONG; settings by FRANK SCARLETT.

1938–9

Trelawny of the 'Wells'
Hamlet
Man and Superman
The Rivals
A Midsummer Night's Dream
She Stoops to Conquer
An Enemy of the People
The Taming of the Shrew

Producers: TYRONE GUTHRIE, all plays with the exceptions of *Man and Superman*, LEWIS CASSON; *The Rivals*, ESME CHURCH; *She Stoops to Conquer*, FRANK NAPIER (with Tyrone Guthrie).

Costumes and settings for *Trelawny of the 'Wells'*, *Man and Superman*, and *An Enemy of the People* by RUTH KEATING; for *Hamlet* and *The Taming of the Shrew* by ROGER FURSE; for *The Rivals* by STEWART CHANEY; for *A Midsummer Night's Dream* by OLIVER MESSEL; for *She Stoops to Conquer* by DAVID HOMAN.

1940

King Lear
Producers: LEWIS CASSON and HARLEY GRANVILLE-BARKER

Costumes and settings by ROGER FURSE.

The Tempest
Producers: GEORGE DEVINE and MARIUS GORING

Costumes and settings by OLIVER MESSEL.

1950–1

Twelfth Night (Dir. HUGH HUNT; Des. ROGER FURSE). *Bartholomew Fair* Jonson (Dir. GEORGE DEVINE; Des. MOTLEY). *Henry V* (Dir. GLEN BYAM SHAW; Des. MOTLEY). *Electra* Sophocles, trans. J. T. Sheppard (Dir. MICHEL ST DENIS; Des. BARBARA HEPWORTH). *The Wedding* Chekhov (Dir. GEORGE DEVINE; Des. MOTLEY). *Captain Brassbound's Conversion* Shaw (Dir. HUGH HUNT; Des. VOYTEK). *The Merry Wives of Windsor* (Dir. HUGH HUNT; Des. ALAN BARLOW)

1950–2

Tamburlaine the Great Marlowe (Dir. TYRONE GUTHRIE; Des. LESLIE HURRY). *Othello* (Dir. MICHAEL LANGHAM; Des.

REGINALD WOOLLEY). *The Clandestine Marriage* Garrick and Colman (Dir. HILTON EDWARDS; Des. ALAN BARLOW). *A Midsummer Night's Dream* (Dir. TYRONE GUTHRIE; Des. TANYA MOISEIWITSCH). *King Lear* (Dir. HUGH HUNT; Des. REECE PEMBERTON). *The Other Heart* James Forsyth (Dir. MICHAEL LANGHAM; Des. HUTCHINSON SCOTT). *Timon of Athens* (Dir. TYRONE GUTHRIE; Des. TANYA MOISEIWITSCH)

1952–3

Romeo and Juliet (Dir. HUGH HUNT; Des. ROGER FURSE). *An Italian Straw Hat* Labiche, trans Thomas Walton (Dir. DENIS CAREY; Des. ROGER FURSE). *The Merchant of Venice* (Dir. HUGH HUNT; Des. ROGER FURSE). *Julius Caesar* (Dir. HUGH HUNT; Des. TANYA MOISEIWITSCH). *Murder in the Cathedral* Eliot (Dir. ROBERT HELPMANN; Des. ALAN BARLOW). *Henry VIII* (Dir. TYRONE GUTHRIE; Des. TANYA MOISEIWITSCH; Cost. ALAN TAGG)

1953–4

Hamlet (Dir. MICHAEL BENTHALL; Des. KENNETH ROWELL). *All's Well That Ends Well* (Dir. MICHAEL BENTHALL; Des. OSBERT LANCASTER). *King John* (Dir. GEORGE DEVINE; Des. MOTLEY). *Twelfth Night* (Dir. DENIS CAREY; Des. JAMES BAILEY). *Coriolanus* (Dir. MICHAEL BENTHALL; Des. AUDREY CRUDDAS). *The Tempest* (Dir. ROBERT HELPMANN; Des. LESLIE HURRY)

1954–5

Macbeth (Dir. MICHAEL BENTHALL; Des. AUDREY CRUDDAS). *Love's Labour's Lost* (Dir. FRITH BANBURY; Des. CECIL BEATON). *The Taming of the Shrew* (Dir. DENIS CAREY; Des. KENNETH ROWELL). *Richard II* (Dir. MICHAEL BENTHALL; Des.

LESLIE HURRY). *As You Like It* (Dir. ROBERT HELPMANN; Des. DOMENICO GNOLI). *Henry IV: 1 and 2* (Dir. DOUGLAS SEALE; Des. AUDREY CRUDDAS)

1955–6

Julius Caesar (Dir. MICHAEL BENTHALL; Des. AUDREY CRUDDAS). *The Merry Wives of Windsor* (Dir. DOUGLAS SEALE; Des. PAUL SHELVING). *The Winter's Tale* (Dir. MICHAEL BENTHALL; Des. PETER RICE). *Henry V* (Dir. MICHAEL BENTHALL; Des. AUDREY CRUDDAS). *Othello* (Dir. MICHAEL BENTHALL; Des. LOUDUN SAINTHILL). *Troilus and Cressida* (Dir. TYRONE GUTHRIE; Des. FREDERICK CROOKE). *Romeo and Juliet* (Dir. ROBERT HELPMANN; Des. LOUDUN SAINTHILL). *Richard II* (Dir. MICHAEL BENTHALL; Des. LESLIE HURRY)

1956–7

Timon of Athens (Dir. MICHAEL BENTHALL; Des. LESLIE HURRY). *Cymbeline* (Dir. MICHAEL BENTHALL; Des. AUDREY CRUDDAS). *Much Ado About Nothing* (Dir. DENIS CAREY; Des. PETER RICE). *The Merchant of Venice* (Dir. MICHAEL BENTHALL; Des. LOUDUN SAINTHILL). *Two Gentlement of Verona* (Dir. MICHAEL LANGHAM; Des. TANYA MOISEIWITSCH). *Antony and Cleopatra* (Dir. ROBERT HELPMANN; Des. LOUDUN SAINTHILL). *Titus Andronicus* and *The Comedy of Errors* (Dir. WALTER HUDD; Des. PAUL MAYO). *Richard III*: (Dir. DOUGLAS SEALE; Des. LESLIE HURRY)

1957–8

Hamlet (Dir. MICHAEL BENTHALL; Des. AUDREY CRUDDAS). *Henry VI: 2 and 3* (Dir. DOUGLAS SEALE; Des. LESLIE HURRY). *Measure for Measure* (Dir. MARGARET WEBSTER; Des. BARRY KAY). *A Midsummer Night's Dream* (Dir.

MICHAEL BENTHALL; Des. JAMES BAILEY). *King Lear* (Dir. DOUGLAS SEALE; Des. LESLIE HURRY). *Twelfth Night* (Dir. MICHAEL BENTHALL; Des. LOUDUN SAINTHILL)

1958–9

Mary Stuart Schiller, trans. S. Spender (Dir. PETER WOOD; Des. LESLIE HURRY). *Julius Caesar* (Dir. DOUGLAS SEALE; Des. BERKELEY SUTCLIFFE). *Ghosts* Ibsen, trans. N. Ginsbury (Dir. JOHN FERNALD; Des. NEIL HOBSON). *Macbeth* (Dir. DOUGLAS SEALE; Des. DESMOND HEELEY). *Sganarelle* Molière, trans. M. Malleson (Dir. MILES MALLESON; Des. PATRICK ROBERTSON; Cost. MICHAEL BALDWIN). *Tartuffe* Molière, trans. M. Malleson (Dir. DOUGLAS SEALE; Des. PATRICK ROBERTSON; Cost. MICHAEL BALDWIN). *The Magistrate* Pinero (Dir. DOUGLAS SEALE; Des. MOTLEY). *The Cenci* Shelley (Dir. MICHAEL BENTHALL; Des. LESLIE HURRY). *The Tempest; or The Enchanted Island* adapted J. Dryden and W. Davenant (Dir. DOUGLAS SEALE; Des. FINLAY JAMES)

1959–60

As You Like It (Dir. WENDY TOYE; Des. MALCOLM PRIDE). *The Double Dealer* Congreve (Dir. MICHAEL BENTHALL; Des. DESMOND HEELEY). *The Importance of Being Earnest* Wilde (Dir. MICHAEL BENTHALL Des. DESMOND HEELEY). *Richard II* (Dir. VAL MAY; Des. RICHARD NEGRI). *The Merry Wives of Windsor* (Dir. JOHN HALE; Des. CARL TOMS). *St Joan* Shaw (Dir. DOUGLAS SEALE; Des. LESLIE HURRY). *What Every Woman Knows* Barrie (Dir. PETER POTTER; Des. PATRICK ROBERTSON; Cost. ROSEMARY VERCOE). *Henry V* (Dir. JOHN NEVILLE; Des. JOHN BURY; Cost. MARGARET BURY).

1960–1

The Seagull Chekhov, trans. J. P. Davis (Dir. JOHN FERNALD; Des. PAUL DAVIS). *Romeo and Juliet*. (Dir. and Des. FRANCO ZEFFIRELLI; Cost. PETER J. HALL). *She Stoops to Conquer* Goldsmith (Dir. DOUGLAS SEALE; Des. OSBERT LANCASTER). *A Midsummer Night's Dream* (Dir. MICHAEL LANGHAM; Des. CARL TOMS). *Henry IV: 1* (Dir. DENNIS VANCE; Des. TIMOTHY O'BRIEN). *Twelfth Night* (Dir. COLIN GRAHAM; Des. ALIX STONE). *The Merchant of Venice* (Dir. PETER POTTER; Des. FELIX KELLY; Cost. ROSEMARY VERCOE)

1961–2

Doctor Faustus Marlowe (Dir. MICHAEL BENTHALL; Des. MICHAEL ANNALS). *King John* (Dir. PETER POTTER; Des. AUDREY CRUDDAS). *The Oresteia* Aeschylus, trans. E. Hamilton and M. Volanakis (Dir. MINOS VOLANAKIS; Des. YOLANDA SONNABEND). *Mourning Becomes Electra* O'Neill (Dir. VAL MAY; Des. LESLIE HURRY). *Macbeth* (Dir. OLIVER NEVILLE; Des. MICHAEL ANNALS). *Twelfth Night* (Dir. COLIN GRAHAM; Des. ALIX STONE). *Richard III* (Dir. COLIN GEORGE; Des. PATRICK ROBERTSON; Cost. ROSEMARY VERCOE). *Julius Caesar* (Dir. MINOS VOLANAKIS; Des. NICHOLAS GEORGIADIS). *The Tempest* (Dir. OLIVER NEVILLE; Des. LESLIE HURRY)

1962–3

Peer Gynt Ibsen, trans. M. Meyer (Dir. MICHAEL ELLIOTT; Des. RICHARD NEGRI). *The Merchant of Venice* (Dir. MICHAEL ELLIOTT; Des. MALCOLM PRIDE). *The Alchemist* Jonson (Dir. TYRONE GUTHRIE; Des. TANYA MOISEIWITSCH). *Othello* (Dir. CASPER WREDE; Des. RICHARD NEGRI). *Measure for Measure* (Dir. MICHAEL ELLIOTT; Des. MALCOLM PRIDE)

Appendix 3

Plays presented by the National Theatre Company at the Old Vic Theatre 1963–1976

This list draws on *Who's Who in the Theatre* 14th Edition (1967) edited by Freda Gaye, 15th Edition (1972) and 16th Edition (1977) edited Ian Herbert (Pitman, London), and on *Britain's Royal National Theatre: The First 25 Years*. Written and compiled Tim Goodwin (National Theatre in association with Nick Hern Books London, 1988). It does not include plays first presented by the Company at other London theatres and subsequently staged at the Old Vic. I am most grateful for the assistance I have received from the Publications Office of the Royal National Theatre.

1963–4

Hamlet (Dir. LAURENCE OLIVIER; Des. SEAN KENNY). *St Joan* Shaw (Dir. JOHN DEXTER; Des. MICHAEL ANNALS). *Uncle Vanya* Chekhov, trans. C. Garnett (Dir. LAURENCE OLIVIER; Des. SEAN KENNY; Cost. BEATRICE DAWSON). *The Recruiting Officer* Farquhar (Dir. WILLIAM GASKILL; Des. RENE ALLIO). *Hobson's Choice* Brighouse (Dir. JOHN DEXTER; Des. MOTLEY). *Andorra* Frisch, trans. M. Bullock (Dir. LINDSAY ANDERSON; Des. JOHN BURY; Cost. JOHN BURY and UNA COLLINS). *Play* Beckett (Dir. GEORGE DEVINE; Des. JOCELYN HERBERT). *Philoctetes* Sophocles, adapt. K. Johnstone (Dir. WILLIAM GASKILL; Des. SAM KIRKPATRICK). *Othello* (Dir. JOHN DEXTER; Des. JOCELYN HERBERT). *The Master Builder* Ibsen, adapt. E. Williams (Dir. PETER WOOD; Des. RUDOLF HEINRICH).

1964–5

The Dutch Courtesan Marston (Dirs. WILLIAM GASKILL and PIERS HAGGARD; Des. ANNENA STUBBS). *Hay Fever* Coward (Dir. NOEL COWARD; Des. MOTLEY). *The Royal Hunt of the Sun* P. Schaffer Dirs. JOHN DEXTER and DESMOND DONOVAN; Des. MICHAEL ANNALS). *The Crucible* Miller (Dir. LAURENCE OLIVIER; Des. MICHAEL ANNALS). *Much Ado About Nothing* (Dir and Des. FRANCO ZEFFIRELLI; Cost. PETER J. HALL). *Mother Courage and Her Children* Brecht, trans. E. Bentley (Dir. WILLIAM GASKILL; Des. JOCELYN HERBERT)

1965–6

Armstrong's Last Goodnight Arden (Dirs. JOHN DEXTER, WILLIAM GASKILL and ALBERT FINNEY; Des. RENE ALLIO). *Love for Love* Congreve (Dir. PETER WOOD; Des. LILA DE NOBILI). *Trelawny of the 'Wells'* Pinero (Dir. DESMOND O'DONOVAN; Des. MOTLEY). *A Flea in Her Ear* Feydeau, trans. J. Mortimer (Dir. JACQUES CHARON; Des. ANDRE LAVASSEUR). *Miss Julie* Strindberg, trans. M. Meyer (Dir. MICHAEL ELLIOTT; Des.

RICHARD NEGRI). *Black Comedy* P. Shaffer
(Dir. JOHN DEXTER; Des. ALAN TAGG).
Juno and the Paycock O'Casey (Dir.
LAURENCE OLIVIER; Des. CARMEN
DILLON). *A Bond Honoured* de Vega, adapt.
J. Osborne (Dir. JOHN DEXTER; Des.
MICHAEL ANNALS)

1966–7

The Storm Ostrovsky, adapt. D. Lessing
(Dir. JOHN DEXTER; Des. JOSEF SVOBODA;
Cost. RUTH MEYERS). *The Dance of Death*
Strindberg, trans. C. D. Locock (Dir.
GLEN BYAM SHAW; Des. MOTLEY). *Rosen-
crantz and Guildenstern Are Dead* Stoppard
(Dir. DEREK GOLDBY; Des. DESMOND
HEELEY). *Three Sisters* Chekhov, trans. M.
Budberg (Dir. LAURENCE OLIVIER; Des.
JOSEF SVOBODA; Cost. BEATRICE DAWSON)

1967–8

As You Like It (Dir. CLIFFORD WILLIAMS;
Des. RALPH KOLTAI). *Tartuffe* Molière;
trans. R. Wilbur (Dir. TYRONE GUTHRIE;
Des. RENE ALLIO). *Volpone* Jonson (Dir.
TYRONE GUTHRIE; Des. TANYA
MOISEIWITSCH). *Oedipus* Seneca, trans.
D. A. Turner, adapt. Ted Hughes (Dir.
and Des. PETER BROOK; Associate Des.
GEOFFREY REEVES; Cost. JEAN MONOD).
Edward II Brecht, trans. W. E. Smith and
F. Mannheim (Dir. FRANK DUNLOP; Des.
CARL TOMS). *The Covent Garden Tragedy*
Fielding (Dir. ROBERT LANG; Des. TONY
WALTON). *A Most Unwarrantable Intrusion*
J. M. Morton (Dir. ROBERT STEPHENS;
Des. TONY WALTON). *In His Own Write* J.
Lennon; A. Kennedy; V. Spinetti (Dir.
VICTOR SPINETTI; Des. TONY WALTON)

1968–9

The Advertisement N. Ginzburg, trans. H.
Reed (Dirs. DONALD MACKECHNIE and
LAURENCE OLIVIER; Des. PATRICK

ROBERTSON). *Home and Beauty* Maugham
(Dir. FRANK DUNLOP; Des. TOM
LINGWOOD). *Love's Labour's Lost* (Dir.
LAURENCE OLIVIER; Des. CARL TOMS). 'H'
C. Wood (Dir. GEOFFREY REEVES; Des.
MICHAEL ANNALS). *The Way of the World*
Congreve (Dir. MICHAEL LANGHAM; Des.
DESMOND HEELEY). *Macrune's Guevara* J.
Spurling (Dirs. FRANK DUNLOP and
ROBERT STEPHENS; Des. CAROLINE
MAXWELL; Cost. ELIZABETH COMPTON
and PETER MUMFORD). *Rites* M. Duffy
(Dir. JOAN PLOWRIGHT; Des. JOHN
HALLE; Cost. BARBARA KIDD). *Back to
Methuselah* Shaw (in two parts) (Dir.
CLIFFORD WILLIAMS with DONALD
MACKECHNIE; Des. RALPH KOLTAI)

1969–70

The National Health P. Nichols (Dir.
MICHAEL BLAKEMORE; Des. PATRICK
ROBERTSON). *The White Devil* Webster
(Dir. FRANK DUNLOP; Des. PIERO
GERHARDI). *The Travails of Sancho Panza* J.
Saunders (Dirs. DONALD MACKECHNIE
and JOAN PLOWRIGHT; Des. TONY
WALTON). *The Beaux' Strategem* Farquhar
(Dir. WILLIAM GASKILL; Des. RENE
ALLIO). *The Merchant of Venice* (Dir.
JONATHAN MILLER; Des. JULIA
TREVELYAN OMAN). *The Idiot* Dos-
toievsky, adapt. S. Gray (Dir. ANTHONY
QUAYLE; Des. JOSEF SVOBODA; Cost.
BEATRICE DAWSON)

1970–1

Mrs Warren's Profession Shaw (Dir.
RONALD EYRE; Des. ALAN TAGG). *The
Architect and the Emperor of Assyria* F.
Arrabal, trans. J.Benedetti (Dir. VICTOR
GARCIA; 'Visual concept': VICTOR
GARCIA and MICHAEL LAUNAY). *The Cap-
tain of Köpenick* C. Zuckmayer, adapt. J.
Mortimer (Dir. FRANK DUNLOP; Des.
KARL VON APPEN and MANFRED GRUND).

A Woman Killed with Kindness T. Heywood (Dir. JOHN DEXTER; Des. JOCELYN HERBERT). *Coriolanus* (Dirs. MANFRED WEKWERTH and JOACHIM TENSCHERT; Des. KARL VON APPEN with ANNA KASHDEN-CLARE)

1971–2

The Good Natur'd Man Goldsmith (Dir. JOHN DEXTER; Des. WILLIAM DUDLEY). *Jumpers* Stoppard (Dir. PETER WOOD; Des. PATRICK ROBERTSON; Cost. ROSEMARY VERCOE). *Richard II* (Dir. DAVID WILLIAM; Des. MICHAEL ANNALS). *The School for Scandal* Sheridan (Dir. JONATHAN MILLER; Des. PATRICK ROBERTSON; Cost. ROSEMARY VERCOE). *The Front Page* B. Hecht and C. MacArthur (Dir. MICHAEL BLAKEMORE; Des. MICHAEL ANNALS). *'Tis Pity She's A Whore* Ford (Dir. ROLAND JOFFE) Mobile Company

1972–3

Macbeth (Dir. MICHAEL BLAKEMORE; Des. MICHAEL ANNALS). *Twelfth Night* (Dir. PETER JAMES; Des. BRENDA HARTILL MOORES) Mobile Company. *The Misanthrope* Molière, trans. T. Harrison (Dir. JOHN DEXTER; Des. TANYA MOISEIWITSCH). *The Cherry Orchard* Chekhov, trans. R. Hingley (Dir. MICHAEL BLAKEMORE; Des. ALAN TAGG). *Equus* P. Shaffer (Dir. JOHN DEXTER; Des. JOHN NAPIER). *The Bacchae* Euripides, adapt. W. Soyinka (Dir. ROLAND JAFFE; Des. NADINE BAYLIS)

1973–4

Saturday, Sunday, Monday E. da Filippo, trans. K. Waterhouse and W. Hall (Dir. and Des. FRANCO ZEFFIRELLI; Cost. RAIMONDA GAETANO). *The Party* T. Griffiths Dir. JOHN DEXTER; Des. JOHN NAPIER). *Measure for Measure* (Dir. JONATHAN MILLER; Des. BERNARD CULSHAW) Mobile Company. *The Tempest*

(Dir. PETER HALL; Des. JOHN BURY). *Eden End* J. B. Priestley (Dir. LAURENCE OLIVIER; Des. CARMEN DILLON). *Next of Kin* J. Hopkins (Dir. HAROLD PINTER; Des. TIMOTHY O'BRIEN and TAZEENA FIRTH). *Spring Awakening* Wedekind, trans. E. Bond (Dir. BILL BRYDEN; Des. GEOFFREY SCOTT; Cost. DEIRDRE CLANCY). *The Marriage of Figaro* Beaumarchais, trans. J. Wells (Dir. JONATHAN MILLER; Des. PATRICK ROBERTSON; Cost. ROSEMARY VERCOE)

1974–5

Romeo and Juliet (Dir. BILL BRYDEN; Des. HAYDEN COFFIN) Mobile Company. *The Freeway* P. Nichols (Dir. JONATHAN MILLER; Des. JOHN BURY). *Grand Manoeuvres* A. E. Ellis (Dir. MICHAEL BLAKEMORE; Des. JOHN BURY). *John Gabriel Borkman* Ibsen, trans. I. S. Ewbank and P. Hall (Dir. PETER HALL; Des. TIMOTHY O'BRIEN and TAZEENA FIRTH). *Heartbreak House* Shaw (Dir. JOHN SCHLESINGER; Des. MICHAEL ANNALS). *Happy Days* Beckett (Dir. PETER HALL; Des. JOHN BURY). *No Man's Land* H. Pinter (Dir. PETER HALL; Des. JOHN BURY) *Engaged* W. S. Gilbert (Dir. MICHAEL BLAKEMORE; Des. MICHAEL ANNALS)

1975–6

Phaedra Britannica Racine, adapt. T. Harrison (Dir. JONATHAN MILLER; Des. TANYA MOISEIWITSCH). *The Playboy of the Western World* Synge (Dir. BILL BRYDEN; Des. GEOFFREY SCOTT). *Hamlet* (Dir. PETER HALL; Des. JOHN BURY). *Judgment* B. Collins (Dir. PETER HALL). *Plunder* B. Travers (Dir. MICHAEL BLAKEMORE; Des. MICHAEL ANNALS). *Watch It Come Down* J. Osborne (Dir. BILL BRYDEN; Des. HAYDEN GRIFFIN; Cost. DEIRDRE CLANCY). *Tribute to The Lady* edited and produced by VAL MAY. 'An Impression of the Life and Work of Lilian Baylis'

Appendix 4

Plays presented at the Old Vic Theatre by other companies 1948–1975

Sources of information as in Appendices 2 and 3.

1948   THE YOUNG VIC   *The Snow Queen* Andersen, adapt. E. Schwarz, trans. S. Magito and R. Weil Dirs. MICHEL ST DENIS and SURIA MAGITO; Des. MOTLEY)

1949   THE YOUNG VIC   *As You Like It* (Dir. GLEN BYAM SHAW; Des. MOTLEY) NATIONAL THEATRE OF BELGIUM   *Les Quatre Fils Aymon* H. Cloisson (Dir. JACQUES HUISMAN; Des. DENIS MARTIN; Cost. CLAIRE LIMBOSCH)

1950   THE YOUNG VIC   *The Black Arrow* Stevenson, adapt. J. Blatchley (Dir. MICHEL ST DENIS; Des. JOSEPH CARL)

1951   THE YOUNG VIC   *The Merchant of Venice* (Dir. GLEN BYAM SHAW; Des. GAY DANGERFIELD)

1952   BRISTOL OLD VIC   *Two Gentlemen of Verona* (Dir. DENIS CAREY; Des. HUTCHINSON SCOTT) BIRMINGHAM REPERTORY   *Henry VI: 3* (Dir. DOUGLAS SEALE; Des. FINLAY JAMES)

1953   BRISTOL OLD VIC   *Henry V* (Dir. DENIS CAREY; Des. PATRICK ROBERTSON) BIRMINGHAM REPERTORY   *Henry VI: 2 and 3* (Dir. DOUGLAS SEALE; Des. FINLAY JAMES)

1956   BRISTOL OLD VIC   *Major Barbara* Shaw (Dir. JOHN MOODY; Des. PATRICK ROBERTSON) BIRMINGHAM REPERTORY   *Caesar and Cleopatra* Shaw (Dir. DOUGLAS SEALE; Des. PAUL SHELVING)

1961   VIC–WELLS ASSOCIATION   *The White Devil* Webster (Dir. PETER ELLIS)

1962   BRISTOL OLD VIC   *War and Peace* Tolstoy, adapt. A. Neumann, E. Piscator and G. Prufer, trans. R. D. Macdonald (Dir. VAL MAY; Des. GRAHAM BARLOW; Cost. AUDREY PRICE) VIC–WELLS ASSOCIATION   *Inca* J. O'Connor (Dir. JOSEPH O'CONNOR)

1964   BRISTOL OLD VIC   *Love's Labour's Lost* (Dir. VAL MAY; Des. MICHAEL ANNALS) *Henry V* (Dir. STUART BURGE; Des. GRAHAM BARLOW) PROCLEMER–ALBERTAZZI COMPANY   *Hamlet* trans. G. Guerrieri (Dir. and Des. FRANCO ZEFFIRELLI; Cost. DANILO DONATI)

1965   BERLINER ENSEMBLE   *The Threepenny Opera* Brecht (Dir. ERICK ENGEL; Des. KARL VON APPEN)

Days of the Commune Brecht (Dirs. Manfred Wekwerth and Joachim Tenschert; Des. Karl von Appen)

Coriolanus Dirs. Manfred Wekwerth and Joachim Tenschert; Des. Karl von Appen)

Resistible Rise of Arturo Ui Brecht (Dirs. Manfred Wekwerth and Peter Pelitzsch; Des. Karl von Appen)

NATIONAL YOUTH THEATRE   *Antony and Cleopatra* (Dir. Michael Croft)

Troilus and Cressida (Dir. Paul Hill)

THEATRE DU NOUVEAU MONDE, MONTREAL *L'Ecole des Femmes* Molière (Dir. Jean Gascon; Des. Robert Prevost)

Klondyke J. Languiraud and G. Charpentier (Dir. Jean Gascon; Des. Robert Prevost)

1969   COMPAGNIE RENAUD–BARRAULT *Rabelais* J.-L. Barrault with R. Baldick (Dir. Jean-Louis Barrault; Des. Matias)

GREATER LONDON ARTS ASSOCIATION *Poems of Love and Hate* (Dir. Bernard Braden)

1970   NOTTINGHAM PLAYHOUSE COMPANY *The Alchemist* Jonson (Dir. Stuart Burge; Des. Trevor Pitt)

King Lear (Dir. Jonathan Miller; Des. Patrick Robertson; Cost. Rosemary Vercoe)

A Yard of Sun C. Fry (Dir. Stuart Burge; Des. Robin Archer)

ABBEY THEATRE, DUBLIN *The Dandy Dolls* G. Fitzmaurice and *The Well of the Saints* Synge (Dir. Hugh Hunt; Des. Alan Barlow)

1971   OCTAGON THEATRE, BOLTON *The Father* Strindberg, trans. M. Meyer (Dir. Geoffrey Ost; Des. Edward Furby)

THEATRE ROYAL, YORK   *The Last Sweet Days of Isaac* G. Cryer; Music N. Ford (Dir. Donald Bodley; Des. Richard Marks)

BELGIAN NATIONAL THEATRE *Pantagleize* M. de Ghelderode (Dir. Frank Dunlop; Des. Van Nerom)

The Seventh Commandment D. Fo (Dir. Arturo Corso; Des. Dario Fo)

1975   NOTTINGHAM PLAYHOUSE COMPANY   *Comedians* T. Griffiths (Dir. Richard Eyre; Des. John Gunter)

Notes

2 Seeking a public 1816–1834

1 John Booth, *The Old Vic 1816–1916* (Stead, London, 1917) p. 4.
2 Thomas Dibdin, *Reminiscences* 2 vols. (Colburn, London 1827) II p. 112.
3 Booth, *The Old Vic* p. 6.
4 *Theatrical Inquisitor* 20 January 1820 pp. 201–4.
5 James Winston, *Drury Lane Journal: Selections from James Winston's Diary 1819–27*, A. L. Nelson and G. B. Cross (Society for Theatre Research, London 1974) p. 48.
6 I[fan] K[yrle] F[letcher]: 'Balfe and Barrymore at Milan' in *Theatre Notebook* vol. 7 no. 3 (1953) pp. 60–2.
7 D. F. Cheshire, Sean McCarthy, Hilary Norris, *The Old Vic Refurbished* (Old Vic, London, 1983) p. 7.
8 Unidentified cutting in Theatre Museum, London.
9 Quoted from Queen Victoria's Journal in the Royal Archives, Windsor Castle, by gracious permission of Her Majesty The Queen.
10 Henry Crabb Robinson, *The London Theatre 1811–1866: Selections from the Diary of Henry Crabb Robinson*, ed. Eiluned Brown (Society for Theatre Research, London 1966) p. 89.
11 *House of Commons Select Committee on Dramatic Literature: Report* (1832) p. 79.
12 Quoted by Booth, *The Old Vic* p. 7.
13 The main collections of playbills on which this account draws are in the Theatre Museum, London; the Harvard Theatre Collection; and the Folger Shakespeare Library.
14 Winston, *Drury Lane Journal* p. 30; p. 41.
15 E. L. Blanchard, 'The Victoria Theatre' in *The Era Almanack 1873* p. 9.
16 William Hazlitt, 'The Minor Theatres' in *The London Magazine*, March 1820, reprinted in *Collected Works* eds. A. R. Waller and Arnold Glover 13 vols. (Dent, London 1903) VIII p. 409.
17 Dibdin, *Reminiscences* II pp. 211–12.
18 Conveyances and other legal documents in the Archives of the Royal Victoria Hall, now in the University of Bristol Theatre Collection (henceforward cited as RVHA).
19 Winston, *Drury Lane Journal* p. 14.
20 Cheshire *et al.*, *The Old Vic Refurbished* p. 6.
21 Original kindly made available to me by Mr Roy Waters.

22 J. R. Planché, *Recollections and Reflections* (Sampson Low, London, 1901), p. 89.

23 Winston, *Drury Lane Journal* p. 48; pp. 56–7.

24 *Survey of London* (Athlone Press, London 1953), XXIII p. 31.

25 J. W. Cole, *Life and Theatrical Times of Charles Kean* 2 vols. (Bentley, London, 1859) I pp. 162–3.

26 *Theatrical Observer*, 9 July 1831.

27 *Theatrical Inquisitor*, 1820 pp. 89–94.

28 Winston, *Drury Lane Journal* pp. 26–8.

29 Walter B. Jerrold, *Douglas Jerrold: Dramatist and Wit* 2 vols. (Hodder and Stoughton, London, 1914) I p. 98; p. 72; p. 88; p. 120.

30 Philip H. Highfill: 'Edward Simpson's Talent Raid on England, 1818' (pt 3) in *Theatre Notebook* vol. 13 no. 1 (1958) p. 12.

31 Henry Crabb Robinson, *The London Theatre 1811–1866* p. 89.

32 Booth, *The Old Vic* p. 35.

33 *House of Commons Report* p. 78.

34 Booth, *The Old Vic* p. 35.

35 Quoted from Queen Victoria's Journal in the Royal Archives, Windsor Castle, by gracious permission of Her Majesty The Queen.

36 *Diaries of William Charles Macready*, ed. William Toynbee 2 vols. (Chapman and Hall, London, 1912) I p. 28.

37 Leslie Sheppard and Herbert R. Axelrod, *Paganini* (Paganiana Press, Neptune City, N.J., 1979) pp. 407–11.

3   Seeking survival 1834–1880

1 *Figaro in London* 23 August 1834.

2 *Figaro in London* 13 September 1834.

3 *Figaro in London* 4 October 1834.

4 Blanchard, 'The Victoria Theatre' p. 9.

5 Blanchard, 'The Victoria Theatre' p. 10.

6 *Figaro in London* 22 November 1834.

7 *Figaro in London* 11 April 1835.

8 Walter Donaldson, *Fifty Years of an Actor's Life* (Lacy, London 1858), pp. 48–9.

9 Frederick Boase ed., *Modern English Biography* 2 vols. (Netherton and Worth, I p. 1345; Supplement II pp. 584–6 Truro, 1892).

10 *Era* 7 April 1839.

11 Charles Kingsley, *Alton Locke* (Macmillan, London, 1881) p. 117.

12 Kingsley, *Alton Locke* p. 23.

13 Kingsley, *Alton Locke* p. 61.

14 Henry Mayhew, *London Labour and the London Poor* 4 vols. (16 Upper Wellington St., Strand, London, 1851) I pp. 287–9.

15 Paul Schlicke, *Dickens and Popular Entertainment* (Allen and Unwin, London, 1985) p. 196.

16 *Household Words* 30 March 1850.

17 Mayhew, *London Labour* p. 18.

18 *Theatrical Times* 13 February 1847.

19 Mayhew, *London Labour* pp. 18–20.

20 *Theatrical Times* 26 September 1846.

21 Booth, *The Old Vic* pp. 52–3.

22 *Era* 5 January 1851.

23 *Era* 12 January 1851.

24 *Era* 16 November 1856.

25 John Hollingshead, *My Lifetime* 2 vols. (Sampson Low, London, 1895) II p. 152.

26 *Era* 2 January 1858.

27 Booth *The Old Vic* p. 57.

28 Joseph Cave, *A Jubilee of Dramatic Life and Incident* (Vernon, London, 1894) p. 204.

29 Arthur Sketchley, *Mrs Brown Goes to the Play* (n.p., London, 1870) pp. 12–13.

30 Sketchley, *Mrs Brown Goes to the Play* p. 14.

31 Sketchley, *Mrs Brown Goes to the Play* pp. 31–2.

32 Sketchley, *Mrs Brown Goes to the Play* p. 35.

33 Sketchley, *Mrs Brown Goes to the Play* pp. 44–5.

34 Cave, *A Jubilee* pp. 206–7.

35 Cheshire *et al.*, *The Old Vic Refurbished* pp. 12–13.

36 *Builder* 30 December 1871 pp. 1029–30.

37 Cave, *A Jubilee* p. 208.

38 *Era* 6 June 1880.

39 Lilian Baylis, 'Emma Cons: The Founder of the Vic' in Cicely Hamilton and Lilian Baylis, *The Old Vic* (Cape, London, 1926) pp. 254–68.

40 Booth, *The Old Vic* p. 59.

41 Hollingshead, *My Lifetime* II p. 152.

42 Conveyances and other legal documents now in RVHA.

43 Booth, *The Old Vic* p. 61.

44 Cheshire *et al.*, *The Old Vic Refurbished* p. 15.

45 *Era* 20 June 1880.

46 H. Barton Baker, *The London Stage: Its History and Traditions from 1576 to 1888*. (W. H. Allen, London, 1889) II p. 240. Baker assigns this to Joseph Cave's final performance on 9 September 1871, before the remodelling of the interior, but claims: 'The Victoria, then under the management of Mr Cave, ceased to exist as a theatre', suggesting the later closing date, 12 June 1880.

4 Seeking improvement 1880–1914

1 *Era* 2 January 1881.

2 Hamilton and Baylis, *The Old Vic* p. 276.

3 *ibid.* p. 277.

4 Robert Speaight, *William Poel and the Elizabethan Revival* (Heinemann, London, 1954) p. 58.

5 *Era* 20 January 1883.

6 *The Times* 21 February 1930.

7 Hamilton and Baylis, *The Old Vic* p. 251.

8 *ibid.* p. 278.

9 Edwin Hodder, *Life of Samuel Morley* (Hodder and Stoughton, London, 1887) p. 436.

10 *Era* 9 January 1886.

11 *Annual Report 1885–6*.

12 *South London Press* 6 February 1886.

13 Raymond Mander and Joe Mitchenson Collection.

14 Beatrice Webb, *My Apprenticeship* (Longman, Green, London, 1926) p. 263; p. 258.

15 Bill in Minet Library, Borough of Lambeth.

16 Richard Findlater, *Lilian Baylis: The Lady of the Old Vic* (Allen Lane, London, 1975) pp. 38–9.

17 Theatre Museum, London: Old Vic holdings, published on microfiche by Chadwyck-Healey (Cambridge, 1987) cited below as Theatre Museum.

18 Edward J. Dent, *A Theatre for Everybody: The Story of the Old Vic and Sadler's Wells* (Boardman, London, 1945) p. 30.

19 Theatre Museum.

20 Theatre Museum.

21 Denis Richards, *Offspring of the Vic: The History of Morley College* (Routledge, London, 1958) p. 69.

22 C. A. Martineau, 'Our College – How It Works and What It Is Now' in *Morley College Magazine* October 1894.

23 City Parochial Foundation, London, Archives.

24 *ibid.*

25 *ibid.*

26 Conveyances and other legal documents in RVHA.

27 Original in City Parochial Foundation Archives.

28 *ibid.*

29 City Parochial Foundation Archives.

30 *ibid.*

31 My account of Lilian Baylis's early life and career is drawn wholly and gratefully from Findlater, *Lilian Baylis*.

32 RVHA.

33 *Annual Report 1884–5.*

34 Morley College, London, Archives.

35 Richards, *Offspring of the Vic* pp. 136–7.

36 Theatre Museum.

37 *ibid.*

38 *Annual Report 1904–5.*

39 *Annual Report 1909–10.*

40 All minutes of Governors' Meetings are cited from RVHA.

41 W. R. Titterton, *From Theatre to Music Hall* (Swift, London, 1912) *passim.*

42 RVHA Governors' Minutes 15 May 1908.

43 Harcourt Williams, *Four Years at the Old Vic* (Putnam, London, 1935) p. 50.

44 RVHA Governors' Minutes 16 November 1906.

45 RVHA Governors' Minutes 14 February 1912.

46 Hamilton and Baylis, *The Old Vic* p. 278.

47 RVHA Governors' Minutes 11 September 1912.

48 Findlater, *Lilian Baylis* p. 103.

49 Now in RVHA.

50 RVHA Governors' Minutes 16 July 1913.

51 RVHA Governors' Minutes 13 November 1913.

52 RVHA Governors' Minutes 22 April 1914.

53 Findlater, *Lilian Baylis* p. 105.
54 Findlater, *Lilian Baylis* p. 106.
55 RVHA Governors' Minutes 10 June 1914.
56 Findlater, *Lilian Baylis* p. 107.

5 Seeking Shakespeare 1914–1933

1 Hamilton and Baylis, *The Old Vic* p. 197.
2 RVHA Governors' Minutes 14 December 1917.
3 Margaret Webster, *The Same Only Different* (Gollancz, London, 1969) p. 322.
4 Quoted by Winifred Isaac, *Ben Greet and the Old Vic* (privately published, London, 1964) pp. 130–1.
5 Findlater, *Lilian Baylis* p. 132.
6 Harcourt Williams ed., *Vic–Wells: The Work of Lilian Baylis* (Cobden-Sanderson, London, 1938) p. 9.
7 Findlater, *Lilian Baylis* p. 123.
8 Sybil and Russell Thorndike, *Lilian Baylis* (Chapman and Hall, London, 1938) pp. 144–5.
9 Findlater, *Lilian Baylis* pp. 139–40.
10 Findlater, *Lilian Baylis* p. 160.
11 Thorndike, *Lilian Baylis* pp. 162–4.
12 RVHA Governors' Minutes 8 December 1922.
13 RVHA Governors' Minutes 14 December 1923.
14 Findlater, *Lilian Baylis* p. 167–8.
15 RVHA Governors' Minutes 11 April 1924.
16 Dent, *A Theatre for Everybody* p. 42.
17 Doris Westwood, *These Players* (Heath Cranton, London, 1926) p. 222.
18 *ibid.* pp. 27–8.
19 *ibid.* p. 153.
20 Richards, *Offspring of the Vic* p. 200.
21 *ibid.* p. 204.
22 RVHA.
23 Hamilton and Baylis, *The Old Vic* p. 221.
24 Westwood, *These Players* p. 8.
25 RVHA Governors' Minutes 10 July 1925.
26 RVHA Governors' Minutes 19 June 1925.
27 RVHA Governors' Minutes 11 June 1926.
28 RVHA Governors' Minutes 12 September 1925.
29 RVHA Governors' Minutes 3 June 1927.
30 RVHA Governors' Minutes 2 September 1927.
31 RVHA Governors' Minutes 26 June 1929.
32 RVHA Governors' Minutes 14 January 1929.
33 RVHA Governors' Minutes 27 February 1929.
34 Harcourt Williams, *Four Years at the Old Vic* (Putnam, London, 1935) p. 43.
35 RVHA Governors' Minutes 7 January 1927.
36 Denis Arundell, *The Story of Sadler's Wells* (Hamish Hamilton, London, 1965) p. 188.
37 John Gielgud, *Early Stages* (Macmillan, London, 1939) p. 140.

38 Dent, *A Theatre for Everybody* p. 98.
39 RVHA Governors' Minutes 28 October 1931.
40 RVHA Governors' Minutes 23 March 1932.
41 Anthony Quayle, *A Time To Speak* (Barrie and Jenkins, London, 1990) p. 164.
42 *ibid.* p. 166.
43 *ibid.* p. 166.

6 Seeking the stars 1933–1940

1 Tyrone Guthrie, *A Life in the Theatre* (Hamish Hamilton, London, 1960) p. 114.
2 *ibid.* p. 115.
3 *ibid.* p. 113.
4 *ibid.* p. 113.
5 RVHA Governors' Minutes 12 April 1934.
6 Findlater, *Lilian Baylis* p. 273.
7 RVHA Governors' Minutes 24 February 1939.
8 RVHA Governors' Minutes 11 June 1938.
9 *Annual Report 1937–8*.
10 *Annual Report 1938–9*.
11 RVHA Governors' Minutes 3 October 1938.
12 James Forsyth, *Tyrone Guthrie* (Hamish Hamilton, London, 1976) p. 168.
13 *ibid.* p. 169.
14 Guthrie, *A Life in the Theatre* p. 173.

7 Seeking shelter 1940–1944

1 RVHA Governors' Minutes 9 February 1940.
2 RVHA Governors' Minutes 9 February 1940.
3 Ronald Hayman, *John Gielgud* (Heinemann, London, 1971) pp. 123–8.
4 Christopher Hassall, *The Timeless Quest: Stephen Haggard* (Arthur Barker, London, 1948) pp. 141–2.
5 Diana Devlin, *A Speaking Part: Lewis Casson and the Theatre* (Hodder and Stoughton, London, 1982) p. 20.
6 RVHA Governors' Minutes 11 July 1941.
7 RVHA Governors' Minutes 12 December 1941.
8 Laurence Olivier, *Confessions of an Actor* (Weidenfeld and Nicolson, London, 1982) p. 143.
9 RVHA Governors' Minutes 6 March 1944.

8 Seeking supremacy 1944–1976

1 RVHA.
2 Guthrie, *A Life in the Theatre* p. 203.
3 James Forsyth, *Tyrone Guthrie* p. 193.
4 RVHA.
5 RVHA Governors' Minutes 12 July 1946.

6 Quoted by Irving Wardle, *The Theatres of George Devine* (Cape, London, 1978) pp. 105–6.

7 RVHA Governors' Minutes 1 July 1948.

8 RVHA Governors' Minutes 10 March 1949.

9 RVHA Governors' Minutes 2 November 1949 and 9 March 1950.

10 RVHA Governors' Minutes 16 March 1952.

11 Wardle, *The Theatres of George Devine* p. 133.

12 John Elsom and Nicholas Tomalin, *The History of the National Theatre* (Cape, London, 1978) p. 100.

13 RVHA Governors' Minutes 30 May 1951.

14 RVHA Governors' Minutes 7 June 1951 and 20 June 1951.

15 Frank Dunlop quoted in Wardle, *The Theatres of George Devine* p. 141.

16 RVHA Governors' Minutes 27 March 1952.

17 Ronald Harwood, *Sir Donald Wolfit* (Secker and Warburg, London, 1971) p. 217.

18 RVHA Governors' Minutes 26 June 1952.

19 RVHA Governors' Minutes 12 February 1953.

20 RVHA Governors' Minutes 16 April 1959.

21 Elsom and Tomalin, *The History of the National Theatre* pp. 121–2.

22 Sally Beauman, *The Royal Shakespeare Company* (Oxford University Press, Oxford, 1982) p. 253.

23 RVHA Governors' Minutes 27 January 1961.

24 Beauman, *The Royal Shakespeare Company* p. 258.

25 *ibid.* p. 253.

26 RVHA Governors' Minutes 25 April 1962.

27 Elsom and Tomalin, *The History of the National Theatre* p. 131.

28 RVHA Governors' Minutes 15 November 1972.

29 RVHA Governors' Minutes 15 January 1974.

30 RVHA Letter from Angus Sterling, Deputy Secretary-General, Arts Council, dated 4 July 1975.

31 RVHA Governors' Minutes 26 July 1976.

9   Seeking an identity 1976–1983

1 RVHA Governors' Minutes 18 October 1976.

2 RVHA Governors' Minutes 14 December 1976.

3 RVHA Governors' Minutes 7 April 1977.

4 RVHA Governors' Minutes 29 June 1977.

5 RVHA Governors' Minutes 1 August 1977.

6 RVHA Governors' Minutes 5 October 1977.

7 *ibid.*

8 Prospect Productions' Submission to Arts Council (March 1981) in RVHA.

9 RVHA Governors' Minutes 6 September 1978.

10 RVHA Governors' Minutes 20 December 1978.

11 RVHA Governors' Minutes 30 May 1979.

12 RVHA Governors' Minutes 21 September 1979.

13 Prospect Productions' Submission p. 6.

14 Prospect Productions' Submission p. 7.
15 Prospect Productions' Submission pp. 7–8.
16 Prospect Productions' Submission: Statistical Tables.
17 Prospect Productions' Submission p. 9.
18 Prospect Productions' Submission p. 10.
19 Prospect Productions' Submission p. 11.
20 Letter to Chairman RVH dated 24 September 1982 in RVHA.
21 Cheshire *et al.*, *The Old Vic Refurbished* p. 28.
22 *ibid.* pp. 31–48.

Bibliography

Primary Sources

The Archives of the Royal Victoria Hall Foundation, now in the University of Bristol Theatre Collection.

Annual Reports of the Royal Victoria Hall Foundation, 1882–1940; 1951–64.

Playbills relating to the Coburg / Royal Victoria Theatres; Royal Victoria Temperance Music Hall / Old Vic Theatre in
Folger Shakespeare Library
Harvard University Theatre Collection
Minet Library, London Borough of Lambeth
Theatre Museum, London

Secondary Sources

Arundell, Denis, *The Story of Sadler's Wells* (Hamish Hamilton, London, 1965)

Baker, H. Barton, *The London Stage: Its History and Traditions from 1576 to 1888* 2 vols. (W. H. Allen, London, 1889)

Beauman, Sally, *The Royal Shakespeare Company* (Oxford University Press, Oxford, 1982)

Booth, John, *The Old Vic 1816–1916* (Stead, London, 1917)

Cave, Joseph, *A Jubilee of Dramatic Life and Incident* (Vernon, London, 1894)

Cheshire, D. F., McCarthy, Sean, Norris, Hilary, *The Old Vic Refurbished* (Old Vic, London, 1983)

Clarke, Mary, *Shakespeare at the Old Vic* 5 vols. (vols. I, II, III A. and C. Black, London, 1954–6, vols. IV and V Hamish Hamilton, London, 1957–8)

Dent, Edward J. *A Theatre for Everybody: The Story of the Old Vic and Sadler's Wells* (Boardman, London, 1945)

Devlin, Diana, *A Speaking Part: Lewis Casson and the Theatre* (Hodder and Stoughton, London, 1982)

Dibdin, Thomas, *Reminiscences* 2 vols. (Colburn, London, 1927)

Donaldson, Walter, *Fifty Years of an Actor's Life* (Lacy, London, 1858)

Elsom, John and Tomalin, Nicholas, *The History of the National Theatre* (Cape, London 1978)

Fagg, Edwin, *The Old 'Old Vic'* (Vic–Wells Association, London, 1936)

Findlater, Richard, *Lilian Baylis: The Lady of the Old Vic* (Allen Lane, London, 1975)

Gielgud, John, *Early Stages* (Macmillan, London, 1939)

Guthrie, Tyrone, *A Life in the Theatre* (Hamish Hamilton, London, 1940)

Hamilton, Cicely and Baylis, Lillian, *The Old Vic* (Cape, London, 1926)

Harwood, Ronald, *Sir Donald Wolfit* (Secker and Warburg, London 1971)

Hassall, Christopher, *The Timeless Quest: Stephen Haggard* (Arthur Barker, London, 1948)

Hayman, Ronald, *John Gielgud* (Heinemann, London, 1971)

Hazlitt, William, 'The Minor Theatres' (*London Magazine*, March 1820) in *Collected Works*
     eds. A. R. Waller and Arnold Glover 13 vols. (Dent, London, 1903) VIII

Hodder, Edwin, *Life of Samuel Morley* (Hodder and Stoughton, London, 1887)

Hollingshead, John, *My Lifetime* 2 vols. (Sampson Low, London, 1895)
     Ragged London in 1861 (London, 1861)

House of Commons Select Committee on Dramatic Literature, *Report* (1832)

Howard, Diana, *London Theatres and Music Halls 1850–1950* (Library Association,
     London, 1970)

Hunt, Hugh, *Autobiography* (Microfiche: Emmet Publishing, London, 1991)
     Old Vic Prefaces (Routledge and Kegan Paul, London, 1954)

Isaac, Winifred, *Ben Greet and the Old Vic* (London, 1964)

Jerrold, Walter B., *Douglas Jerrold: Dramatist and Wit* 2 vols. (Hodder and Stoughton,
     London, 1914)

Kingsley, Charles, *Alton Locke* (Macmillan, London, 1881)

Macready, William Charles, *Diaries* ed. William Toynbee 2 vols. (Chapman and Hall,
     London, 1912)

Mayhew, Henry, *London Labour and the London Poor* 4 vols. (London, 1851)

Newton, H. Chance, *The Old Vic and Its Associations* (Fleetway Press, London, 1923)

Nicoll, Allardyce, *A History of English Drama 1660–1900* 6 vols. (Cambridge University
     Press, Cambridge) esp. vol. IV *Early Nineteenth Century Drama 1800–1850* (1955)
     and vol. V *Late Nineteenth Century Drama 1850–1900* (1959)
     English Drama 1900–1930. The Beginnings of the Modern Period (Cambridge University
     Press, Cambridge, 1973)

Olivier, Laurence, *Confessions of an Actor* (Weidenfeld and Nicolson, London, 1982)

Quayle, Anthony, *A Time To Speak* (Barrie and Jenkins, London, 1990)

Richards, Denis, *Offspring of the Vic: The History of Morley College* (Routledge, London,
     1958)

Roberts, Peter, *The Old Vic Story* (W. H. Allen, London, 1976)

Robinson, Henry Crabb, *The London Theatre 1811–1866: Selections from the Diary of Henry
     Crabb Robinson*, ed. Eiluned Brown (Society for Theatre Research, London, 1966)

Royal Coburg/Victoria/Old Vic Theatre, *Playbills in Theatre Museum, London* (Micro-
     fiche, Chadwick-Healey, Cambridge, 1987)

Schlicke, Paul, *Dickens and Popular Entertainment* (Allen and Unwin, London, 1985)

Sheppard, Leslie and Axelrod, Herbert R., *Paganini* (Paganiana Press, Neptune City,
     N.J., 1979)

Sketchley, Arthur, *Mrs Brown Goes To The Play* (n.p., London, 1870)

Thorndike, Sybil and Russell, *Lilian Baylis* (Chapman and Hall, London, 1938)

Titterton, W. B., *From Theatre to Music Hall* (Swift, London, 1912)

de Valois, Ninette, *Come Dance With Me* (Hamish Hamilton, London, 1957)

Wardle, Irving, *The Theatres of George Devine* (Cape, London, 1978)

Webster, Margaret, *The Same Only Different* (Gollancz, London, 1969)

Westwood, Doris, *These Players* (Heath Crampton, London, 1926)

Williams, Harcourt, *Four Years At The Old Vic* (Putnam, London, 1935)

   Old Vic Saga (Winchester Publications, London 1949)

Williams, Harcourt (ed.), *Vic–Wells: The Work of Lilian Baylis* (Cobden-Sanderson, London, 1938)

Williamson, Audrey, *Old Vic Drama 1934–1947* (1948); *1947–1957* (1957) (Rockliff, London)

Winston, James, *Drury Lane Journal: Selections from James Winston's Diary 1819–27*, eds. A. L. Nelson and G. B. Cross (Society for Theatre Research, London, 1974)

Periodicals

Actors by Daylight

All the Year Round especially
  16 June 1866
  23 June 1866: 'Mr Whelks at the Play'
  30 June 1866: 'Mr Whelks over the Water'
  7 July 1866

The Builder

The Era

The Era Almanack

Figaro in London

Household Words especially
  30 March 1850: 'Amusements of the People'
  13 April 1850

Morley College Magazine

The Old Vic Magazine
  October 1919–December 1930

becoming *The Old Vic and Sadler's Wells Magazine* January 1931–September 1939

becoming *The Vic–Wells Association Bulletin* 1946–

South London Press

Theatre Notebook

Theatrephile

Theatrical Inquisitor

Theatrical Times

The Times

Index

London theatres are entered under their names; other theatres under their location.

194